Counseling
Christian
Workers

RESOURCES FOR
CHRISTIAN COUNSELING

RESOURCES FOR CHRISTIAN COUNSELING

Volume One
Innovative Approaches to Counseling   *Gary R. Collins*

Volume Two
Counseling Christian Workers   *Louis McBurney*

Volume Three
Self-Talk, Imagery, and Prayer in Counseling   *H. Norman Wright*

Volume Four
Counseling Those With Eating Disorders   *Raymond E. Vath*

(Other volumes forthcoming)

Counseling Christian Workers

LOUIS McBURNEY, M.D.

RESOURCES FOR CHRISTIAN COUNSELING

General Editor

Gary R. Collins, Ph.D.

WORD BOOKS
PUBLISHER
WACO, TEXAS
A DIVISION OF
WORD, INCORPORATED

COUNSELING CHRISTIAN WORKERS, Volume 2 of the Resources for Christian Counseling series. Copyright © 1986 by Word, Incorporated. All rights reserved. No portion of this book may be reproduced in any form, except for brief quotations in reviews, without written permission from the publisher.

Unless otherwise identified, all Scripture quotations in this volume are from the Holy Bible, New International Version. Copyright © 1983 International Bible Society. Used by permission of Zondervan Bible Publishers.

Library of Congress Cataloging-in-Publication Data

McBurney, Louis.
   Counseling Christian workers.

   (Resources for Christian counseling; v. 2)
   Includes index.
   1. Counseling for clergy.   2. Pastoral counseling.
I. Title.   II. Series.
BV4398.5.M33   1986   253.5   86–13249
ISBN 0–8499–0586–9

6 7 8 9 8 FG 9 8 7 6 5 4 3 2 1
Printed in the United States of America

To Melissa

Who has patiently, faithfully,
and lovingly taught me
what becoming *one* is all about.

She is
remarkably gifted by God
and
a cherished gift to me from Him.

ACKNOWLEDGMENTS

I NEVER USED TO PAY much attention to the acknowledgments authors made in their books until my own book, *Every Pastor Needs a Pastor,* was published. Then I realized how much of a cooperative effort a book is. Now I read acknowledgments.

It may not be quite accurate to list the following as co-authors, but in that spirit I gratefully salute:

My family—Melissa, Brent, Andrea, and Bruce—for their cooperation and sacrifice.

Gary Collins, who edits the Resources for Christian Counseling series and graciously invited me to participate.

ACKNOWLEDGMENTS

Evelyn Bence, who was very helpful in her editing of the final manuscript.

Doug Self, friend, pastor, and editor of the *Pastoral Care Newsletter,* for his encouragement, insights, and suggestions.

Ed Bratcher, who can almost "walk on water" and has been my mentor for ten years. His understanding of ministers and ministry problems is second to none.

Scott Middleton and Bryan Williamson, Jr., who serve with Ed on the Marble Retreat board of directors and are friends far beyond that duty.

Carol Fortune, Joani Lubrant, and Mary Finger, my secretaries, who *struggled* through the manuscript.

And especially to the hundreds of Christian workers at Marble Retreat and elsewhere who have become vulnerable in sharing their hurts. Their stories which appear in these pages have been altered to protect their identities, but are truly symbolic of the real-life tension of the ministry.

CONTENTS

EDITOR'S PREFACE

WHERE DOES A COUNSELOR GO for help? When psychologists or psychiatrists have personal problems, where do they get therapy? When a pastor is depressed, anxious, or burned out, who is available to give sensitive, confidential counseling?

For many years these questions were ignored. Perhaps we assumed that counselors were strong enough to handle their own problems. Maybe we forgot that even burden-bearers at times need help with their pressures. Even when they admit the need for help, many counselors wonder where to turn. When you know most of the pastors and other counselors in the community, it can be humbling and risky to tell one of these friends that you are having trouble coping.

When he was a psychiatric resident at Mayo Clinic, Louis McBurney first became aware of the needs of ministers and other Christian workers. "I saw clergy patients who faced unique pressures because of their vocations," he says. "Yet, many were resistant to getting help." Dr. McBurney and his wife started praying about a ministry to needy pastors. A retreat center in the Colorado mountains was the result.

In the pages that follow, Louis McBurney shares many of the insights that have come from his work as a counselor of Christian workers.

As every counselor is well aware, we currently are living in the midst of a "counseling boom." Surely there has never been a time in history when so many people were aware of psychological issues, concerned about personal problems, interested in psychological writings, and willing to talk about their insecurities, inadequacies, and intimate concerns. Within only a few decades we have seen the birth of a great host of theories, degree programs, books, seminars, articles, new journals, radio programs, films, and tape presentations that deal with counseling-related issues. Numerous counselors have appeared, some with good training and great competence, but others with little sensitivity and not much awareness of what they are trying to accomplish.

Perhaps it is not surprising that the counseling field is confusing to many people, threatening to some, and often criticized both within the church and without. Nevertheless, people still struggle with psychological and spiritual problems, stress is both a personal and social issue, and many seek help from counselors.

And how does the counselor keep abreast of the latest developments? Many turn to books, but it is difficult to know which of the many volumes on the market are of good quality and which are not. The Resources for Christian Counseling series is an attempt to provide books that give clearly written, practical, up-to-date overviews of the issues faced by contemporary Christian counselors. Written by counseling experts, each of whom has a strong Christian commitment, the books are intended to be examples of accurate psychology and careful use of Scripture. Each will have a clear evangelical perspective, careful documentation, a strong practical orientation, and freedom from the sweeping statements and undocumented rhetoric that sometimes characterize books in the counseling field. All of the Resources for Christian Counseling books will have similar bindings and together they will comprise a complete encyclopedia of Christian counseling.

As one of the first books in this series, it is appropriate to have a volume by Louis McBurney on the counseling of Christian workers. In a cover story, *Partnership* magazine called Louis and Melissa McBurney "Pastors to the Clergy." Nestled in the heart of the Rockies, their Marble Retreat is a crisis intervention and counseling center for Christian leaders and their spouses. It is from that place of healing that the author has written a book that is almost certain to serve two purposes. It will bring insights and help into your own life and it will help you to counsel other Christian workers.

Gary R. Collins, Ph.D.
Kildeer, Illinois

INTRODUCTION

YOU'D PROBABLY LIKE Henry Watson—if you could ever get to know him. Henry is a pastor who has been in the ministry twenty-one years. He is married and has three children. He has worked hard at his job, not for money, but because he feels he was called by God into the pastoral ministry. At times he has felt successful, seeing his church grow in membership and in spiritual maturity. At other times he has been in the depths of despair, the congregation apathetic and stagnant.

When we met Henry a few years ago he was in a serious crisis—one which almost ended his ministry. He had been in a difficult church situation for almost three years. When he had taken the church, it had seemed to offer great promise.

There had been some problems, of course, but the search committee had assured him they weren't serious. But the committee had been either naive or dishonest. There was a group of dissentious and wealthy individuals who felt their power was slipping away. They wanted Henry to restore their dynasty. He was really caught in the middle of a smoldering, bitter battle.

Henry, a peace-loving man, hated conflict. In the face of disagreement he felt fearful and powerless. His sense of control and adequacy quickly eroded. The long hours he spent trying to avoid confrontation yet bring harmony were fruitless, and he began to feel depressed. It would have been a relief to just disappear—even death would have been welcomed. He withdrew more and more into himself.

For a while his wife, Joan, was able to bring him some encouragement and solace. A steady, no-nonsense person, she helped put things in perspective. She was also more competitive than Henry, perhaps even more powerful in relationships. She urged him to confront the troublemakers head-on. Have it out with them. Run them off if necessary. That was her style. But Henry just didn't have the confidence that it would do any good. He even began to avoid Joan so he wouldn't have to feel the pressure she was putting on him.

All the while Joan became more and more angry. She was mad at the church members who were creating such turmoil. She was mad at the other members who were remaining silent. She was distrustful of just about everyone since confidences seemed so easily betrayed. She was angry at God for allowing them to step so innocently into this mess. Most of all, she became increasingly angry at Henry. His passivity and withdrawal left her feeling vulnerable and insecure. At times, she was tempted to take the children and leave. She didn't like that feeling. They had had a good marriage and she just wanted to wake up tomorrow and find things back to normal. She became irritable and critical toward Henry and the children and started hating herself for being that way. Nothing seemed to be able to stop the terrible downward spiral.

The crowning blow came in July of their second year. Henry had been able to continue to be effectively involved in some aspects of the ministry. One of these was counseling. He was a natural—warm, sensitive, caring, a good listener, and a wise adviser. It was probably his counseling skill that was holding his ministry together and accounting for some growth in the church. Troubled people in the community heard about Pastor Watson and sought him out. Among the seekers was Carolyn, an attractive woman in her late twenties who had a bad marriage and a lot of unmet dependency. It certainly wasn't "love at first sight." Neither Henry nor Carolyn were looking for a romance to complicate their already confusing lives. There developed between them the kind of deep, caring relationship that often happens in counseling. Over a three-month period that began to change; they were falling in love.

It's not hard to see what attracted them to each other. Each was lonely, loving, and emotionally alive. It was only natural that their relationship began to be more and more important to them both. The professional nature of the relationship was broken one day after Henry had caught a full blast of Joan's frustration and criticism. He was really hurting when Carolyn came for her session. Instead of maintaining his usual objective position he broke down in tears during his time with Carolyn. He couldn't seem to stop the flood of emotion that swept over him. His own pain and need seemed to overwhelm his judgment. Carolyn's response was just what he so desperately wanted. She came to his side and held him. She comforted him. She reassured him. She accepted him. She said soft and soothing words. She told him she loved him.

Neither of them had much energy to fight off the intense force that drew them together. The tremendous exhilaration of finding understanding and warmth was overpowering. Their relationship quickly progressed from comforting embraces to passionate kisses and from there to sexual intimacy.

It didn't really last long. It couldn't have. Henry's guilt was too intense. Not only had he violated his vow of marital fidelity, but he began to lie to cover the hours of unaccountable absence. His weakened faith was utterly destroyed. His very identity, seriously shaken. Who was he? Where was God? What was happening to his world? He was completely broken. His tearful confession was hardly a surprise to Joan, who had intuitively suspected what was going on.

Now they were plunged into a new crisis—what to do next? Could Henry's ministry possibly survive? Could their marriage? Would they have to leave town? What would they tell the children? Their parents? Their friends? How could Joan forgive his infidelity? How could he forget Carolyn? Could they possibly find the answers alone?

The last question was the first to be answered. They found themselves incapable of working through the hurt and confusion on their own. They had to have help.

That realization was hardly comforting. What would happen to them if they went to a counselor? They both had the feeling that it was unsafe to see anyone in their denomination. Henry also felt an inner need to protect the reputation of Christianity from criticism by any nonbeliever. Besides that, they had heard stories of counselors attacking a person's faith. Underlying all those fears and questions was the conviction that anyone in Christian service should be able to handle life without the help of a counselor.

Henry and Joan's story is painfully common. Since 1974, troubled Christian workers have been coming to Marble Retreat—over six hundred now. They have poured out their pain, their fear, their anger, their guilt, and their doubts. Many of their problems are those common to mankind, but it has become equally obvious that many of their pressures are unique to their calling. Serving in Christian ministry carries some peculiar difficulties and many barriers to finding help. For a counselor to provide the maximum help to those in ministry it is important to understand these unique issues. That's what this volume in the Resources for Christian Counseling series is all about. We will look behind the masks, take off the clerical collars, and see the wounded, desperate, lonely, lovely people who have given their lives to minister to their world in the name of Jesus. It was Jesus who said, "Take my yoke upon you and learn of me. . . . For my yoke is easy and my burden is light" (Matt. 11:29–30). It is my prayer that we who counsel can help the helpers find that easy yoke.

We'll begin by examining some of the unique problems that face today's Christian workers. Then we'll look at role-related pressures and we'll describe specific areas of resistance that must be overcome. Part II deals with symptom complexes as they are present in the life of a minister. Finally, we'll consider therapeutic approaches and principles as they relate to counseling Christian workers.

PART ONE

UNDERSTANDING THE HURTING CHRISTIAN WORKER

CHAPTER ONE

PROBLEMS AND PRESSURES OF THE MINISTRY

WHEN I TELL PEOPLE I operate a counseling center for ministers, I often get a puzzled look. The more sympathetic may say, "Well, I guess ministers do take on lots of burdens from others." At the other end of the spectrum are those who simply can't comprehend the notion that a person called by God could possibly need a counselor. They assume we are teaching counseling techniques. Some even say, "I'm sure anyone who'd need to see a psychiatrist has no business in the ministry in the first place." Recognizing the humanity of those in Christian work is the first step in being able to help them deal more effectively with their stress.

THE SCOPE OF THE PROBLEM

There have been a number of interesting surveys confirming that those in ministry often suffer from conflict and crises as much as everyone else. In 1970 the Baptist General Convention of Texas conducted a survey of all its pastors. The results were surprising at the time. Of the two-thirds who responded to the survey, two-thirds said they had felt the need for professional counseling at least once during their ministry. That means at least 50 percent of Texas Baptist pastors at that time were willing to admit to needing help.[1] I'm sure many of the others were too threatened or defensive to respond.

David and Vera Mace surveyed 321 clergy and wives in 1976–79 and identified many areas of pressures. Those checked most frequently—handling negative emotions and couples' communication—are issues that often require help by a trained counselor. They also found that many denominations were doing very little to provide specific help for their clergy families. It is encouraging however that they identified a growing awareness of the problems.[2]

Our experience at Marble Retreat and at pastoral conferences across the country confirms these investigations. The pressures of ministry are felt universally in all areas and at all levels of ministry. We have talked with ministers from all ranks—large urban churches and very small rural parishes. The specific pressures may vary slightly, but none seem exempted or protected from the problems of ministry. This is also true of different kinds of ministers—pastors, musicians, educators, youth ministers, administrators, evangelists, and missionaries. All are affected.

INTENSITY OF THE PROBLEMS

Pressures in the ministry aren't new. Paul was obviously aware of the difficulties when he recommended a life of celibacy because of the demands of ministry. It may be that the intensity of the problems has not changed since. The loss of privacy, the poor pay, the unrealistic expectations, and the frustrations inherent in church work have long been identified. In ways, there have been improvements in some of these areas. For instance:

1. More ministers own their own homes now than ever before.
2. The salary base has risen steadily.
3. Congregations are more likely to have written job descriptions.
4. There is a growing awareness on the part of laymen that the minister cannot carry on the work of the church single-handedly.

However, there are other indications that life in the ministry may be increasingly difficult. The community respect that clergy once commanded has been eroded. Movies most often depict clergy either as scoundrels who are out to con the unsuspecting or as incompetent fools who have little to offer of serious consequence. I had an interesting experience about eight years ago which confirmed that to me. Our local junior high school was beginning a community volunteer program. Anyone and everyone was invited to come and share a skill or area of knowledge with the students. I volunteered to teach a course. The principal began to find reasons to deny my proposal, then asked me what church I pastored. When I told him I wasn't a minister, but a psychiatrist, his attitude changed immediately to acceptance.

Another changing statistic is the number of clergy divorces. There has been a marked rise in the number of clergy marriages ending in divorce in the last ten to fifteen years. Needless to say, this is a reflection of many factors—attitudes about marriage, acceptance of divorce, self-actualization philosophy, the women's movement, affluence, and so forth. There is no simple cause or universal conclusion. One effect has been an increasing sense of insecurity and anxiety among clergy. Though more accepted by the church, divorce is still quite disruptive to any family and perhaps more so to the clergy family. People still hold the hope that Christianity offers the promise of answers to the difficulties of interpersonal conflict. The minister is looked to as a model for that hope. More than anywhere else he is expected to demonstrate the benefits of commitment and redemption in his marriage.

One other statistic seems to indicate an increase in the pressures on ministers. The number of individuals who leave Christian vocations for "secular" work has shown an increase in recent years. One major denomination has experienced a loss of about 2 percent of its ministers per year in the 1980s.[3]

Similarly, there has been a dramatic increase in firing of ministers. In 1983–84 approximately 1500 churches of one denomination alone asked for their ministers' resignations.[4] Since job security has been a serious problem traditionally, this sudden rash of dismissals has intensified the anxiety of clergy in many denominations. In our experience at Marble Retreat, we've sensed that even those denominations that promise job security have been easing out those it sees as incompetent or out of step with the predominant viewpoints.

Finally, a glance at seminar topics currently in vogue substantiates the awareness of increasing pressures. The issues presented are much more likely to be in the area of interpersonal relations than in theology. Some common themes are: avoiding burnout in ministry, coping with stress in ministry, marriage survival for clergy, conflict resolution in the church, time management for pastors, finding fulfillment in the ministry, and where to go for help.[5] These are vital concerns for clergy these days. There is increasing awareness that effective ministry depends on the ability of the minister to deal with the reality of emotional stress. With this realization has also come an increased openness among clergy to seek professional counseling.

To meet the increasing demands for counseling Christian workers it is important to understand the unique crises present in the lives of ministers. I will discuss five general areas of conflict: 1. the crisis of authority; 2. the crisis of identity; 3. the crisis of priority; 4. the crisis of integrity; 5. the crisis of dependency. Those in Christian work face these aspects of life from positions that create unique burdens.

THE CRISIS OF AUTHORITY

The church is a strange phenomenon. It is the "body of Christ," the "called out," the agent of God's love in a fallen world. Her mission is dictated—to "make disciples" (Matt.28:19). Her character, defined—they'll "know that you are My disciples if you love" (John 13:35). Her source of power, determined—"you will receive power when the Holy Spirit comes on you" (Acts 1:8). Her spiritual authority, delineated—"Christ is the head of the church" (Eph. 5:23). The flaw comes in the humanity of the church. As we who are being redeemed try to live out the character and mission of the church, our self-centeredness thrusts its way into her structure and foundation. It's easier to look piously to Jesus at the "head of the Church" than to submit ourselves to another person exercising power over us. There's no hesitation to point to God's Word as our authoritative document, but it's not so simple to agree on its interpretation. We sanctimoniously declare the buildings we erect to be "God's house," but react viciously if our own territorial rights are ignored. In the middle of the confusion are the clergy. Men and women attempting to give leadership to the unwieldy army of volunteers trying to be the "called out ones." The clergy are the ones who feel the most distress when the battles for control are fought out. We see three common battlefields in this ongoing warfare: the contest of control (who's running this show?), the question of direction (God's Word versus man's ideas), and the issue of ownership, (protecting the sacred shrines).

The Contest for Control

John was called to Saint Stephen's to get the church moving again. The parish had been living in the fading splendor of yesteryear, a time of vitality, excitement, growth, influence, and spiritual power. They were now beginning to realize that they couldn't continue to live in that past, and they wanted to find renewal (a popular word in the church these days). John seemed just the man for the job. He had a solid seminary education and ten years of successful ministry under his belt. He had served in two small churches. Each had grown under

27

his ministry. The last had even successfully completed a building program for which John had given strong leadership. Saint Stephen's felt he could give them the new direction they needed.

Everyone was excited about this new beginning. John was as enthusiastic as he was personable. He was urged to bring whatever changes he deemed necessary to revitalize the church. His initial innovations in the worship and liturgy were well received. There was a willingness, even an eagerness, for this fresh approach to worship. New faces began to appear on Sundays. New faces also began to appear on the various decision-making committees. Fresh ideas seemed to abound on every issue.

The first mumblings of discontent were hard to identify and, for the most part, went unnoticed. John recalled later having been invited to lunch by Mr. Ravensbrook, one of the most prominent members of the old guard. He had been one of the most involved members during those exciting first years three decades ago. The lunch went well. There were no angry words or harsh rebukes. John realized afterwards that there seemed to be a tone of concern expressed about the way things were going. Not clear opposition, just cautious optimism that John would be sensible about whom to trust. John agreed wholeheartedly. He also felt confident about those being given responsibility and power.

The next messages of dissatisfaction were not so subtle. A group of fairly agitated individuals were very vocal in a business meeting about a proposed curriculum change. The new plan had been carefully studied and was highly recommended by several of the newer members. They had been unaware of the strong negative feelings of the only dissenting member of the committee. As you might guess she was one of the older members. Her points of objection seemed vague, but she began to miss their work sessions. No one really suspected her mounting anger. The curriculum was approved.

The next event was a visit to John by a delegation of irate members who presented him with a long list of their complaints. Most had to do with recent decisions and with supposed disregard for the opinions of the long time stalwarts of Saint Stephen's. John felt defensive but listened patiently. He conceded some points and offered his apologies. He didn't recognize the power struggle that was taking shape. Nor did he identify the real source of the tension.

It was John's wife, Susan, who first realized what was going on. She had been at a women's luncheon and sensed the hostility in Mrs. Ravensbrook. As the luncheon was breaking up, Susan seized the opportunity to linger behind and talk with her. She was astounded at the intensity of feelings that came her way in a stream of angry accusations. What right did John have to come prancing into their church and take over? Who did he think he was? Mr. Ravensbrook was the one who had always made the important decisions at Saint Stephen's. He was always consulted by their former pastors. Where did they think their salary was coming from in the first place? That was the problem with this new generation—no respect for authority. Well they might as well get it straight then and there—the Ravensbrooks were not going to put up with this any longer. They had tried their best to make sensible, calm suggestions, but had been totally ignored.

Only then did it become apparent that the Ravensbrooks had been behind all of the divisive criticism. Their power was silently at work manipulating those under their influence to undermine the upstarts who refused to acknowledge the old authority.

John's story is very common. Middle-aged ministers are particularly vulnerable to being caught in such power disputes. Young ministers tend to unconsciously submit to the power structure while older men have learned how to deal with it diplomatically. The middle-aged minister who has begun to feel confident of his leadership abilities and his ministry strengths is more likely to take command. Developmentally he is at the age of establishing himself as a competent adult. He needs to feel a sense of control. The problem is not with a lack of respect for his elders but with a life phase that involves relinquishing mentors and becoming mentor to those under his care.

An exception to this general rule is the minister with a very low self-esteem who may be threatened at every age and unable to give power to anyone else. These persons find themselves in conflict over authority very early and throughout their ministry. The combatants in the church are likely to be the charter members, a prominent family in the community, or a wealthy supporter of the church. In some cases it's a Ravensbrook who is all three. For ministers the inner conflicts involve sorting out their own developmental needs, their expectations of being empowered by ordination, and their desire to be a servant to their people.

The Authority of the Word

A second common conflict over authority has to do with the place of the Bible in the beliefs and practices of the church. Even when the minister and the congregation agree in theory about the role of Scripture there can develop significant disputes over its proper interpretation. The minister may feel he has the proper background as a theologian to make the final pronouncement regarding any theological dispute. Not everyone is willing to submit quietly to an interpretation that disagrees with his own. The clergyperson involved is faced with a difficult dilemma. On the one hand, he or she may stand strongly on the position learned at seminary even though it alienates those who disagree. On the other hand, he or she may accept another interpretation and feel compromised in a basic faith position and in his leadership.*

Often the very basis of belief seems to hang in the balance. Is the written Word the authoritative revelation of God or not? Is there any place for human ideas or truth from nonbiblical sources? *Leadership* recently featured an article discussing when it is and is not appropriate to fight for one's beliefs. In his article, John Cionca urges patience and gentleness even when we are convinced of our doctrinal stance. Our attitude can increase the likelihood of our position being heard and considered. He also points out the importance of carefully assessing one's own point of view to see whether or not it is

---

* Because most of my work has been with male pastors, and for the sake of ease of style, I generally use the pronoun "he" when referring to ministers. By this practice, I don't mean to imply that all clergy are men.

an issue worth fighting for. If it is, it may be worth resigning for, or, it may be important enough to stay put and work for one's viewpoint.[6]

In such instances, it is also important for the minister to separate his own need for authority from issues of doctrine. It is easy to use some question of biblical interpretation as a battleground to establish personal power. Such struggles become marked by arrogance, pride, and judgmentalism. Fred Smith has penned an incisive poem, "Inerrant Love," that begins: "I was beating on him constructively, Lord, when he turned vicious on me." [7]

Faced with the tension of disagreement, many ministers find themselves taking just such an unloving position. Their defensive posture often arises from fear and insecurity. A counselor must be able to help the minister identify his underlying feelings as he faces conflicts over biblical authority.

Territorial Disputes

The third common area of conflict in authority has to do with territorial disputes. There is probably no issue that creates more intense immediate reaction than for a minister to trespass on someone's territory. In the book and movie *Never Cry Wolf* the author, Farley Mowat, who was studying the behavior of wolves, observed a pair of wolves marking their territory by urination. He met their societal pattern by marking his in the same way. Unfortunately, there is not so obvious a system among human church goers. It is extremely easy to invade someone's sacred space without knowing the boundaries.

Bob came to one of the oldest, most respected churches in his conference. He was excited about being called there and considered it a great honor. His coming was equally exciting to the congregation which felt fortunate to have him accept its call. But the enthusiasm began to die the first Sunday. From the pulpit he commented that one of the first things he wanted to do in renovating the sanctuary was to tear out "those hideous old organ pipes." They were indeed unsightly and had not been in use for years. Bob's idea of replacing them with a large wooden cross had definite aesthetic appeal.

But they were a loving (and expensive) memorial gift from the most prominent family in the church.

If that weren't enough, Bob then cancelled plans for an elevator which he saw as a foolish waste of money. That sacred cow was the pet project of one of the influential board members whose elderly mother could no longer use stairs.

Trespassing on two critical territories in the first month proved to be his undoing. Bob was never able to repair the damage. His basic error was in not "sniffing out" the boundary lines before barging ahead. When his decisions were questioned, he felt his authority being challenged and he became rigidly entrenched. He finally had to take his "authority" to another church and start over, a sad outcome to the hopeful beginning.

Ministers frequently find themselves in these crises over authority. There remains confusion over who is in control. Often the pastor is left with most of the responsibility for the "success" of the church without the power to make it move. This naturally leads to frustration and anger or despair. The problem may be significantly reduced by effective negotiation and honest communication between the minister and the congregation.

Similar conflicts occur in multiple-staff churches between the senior pastor and the associates. Unless clear lines of authority are delineated each staff member may be busily building a personal empire with little concern for the overall program. Such competitive attitudes create a climate of distrust and uncooperation.

Since the senior pastor is often held responsible for every aspect of the ministry, it is helpful for him to have the power, which can readily be buttressed by a mutual accountability and team spirit. When these are lacking, an analysis of personality factors and leadership styles may help reduce tension. Some of the more common elements will be considered in the next chapter, concerning specific ministry conflicts.

THE CRISIS OF IDENTITY

One of the earliest psychological tasks and one that continues for years is finding identity. The infant first begins to individuate, discovering the boundaries between self and the universe. Throughout childhood aspects of that self are further differentiated as autonomy, initiative, and skill development progress. The adolescent separates from his parents and nuclear family as identification with peers takes ascendancy. In early adulthood an increasing sense of identity is derived from career and proving oneself as a competent member of the social order.

Thus by the midtwenties most people have a fairly well defined sense of identity. A significant part of this self-concept is related to work. After introductions of who you are and where you live, the most common information exchanged is what you do. That question is fairly easy for a machinist, a housewife, an engineer, or a school teacher. It may also be easy for a minister to say, "I'm pastor of the Community Church." Identifying what that means is another question. This is the second area of ministry crisis a counselor needs to consider. The vocational and social identity of the minister is often complex and poorly defined. There may be confusion as to professional roles, social relationships, sexuality, and belonging.

Vocational Identity

The most obvious point of tension comes in attempting to fulfill all the role expectations faced in ministry. Pastors (and other ministers) are usually expected to be adept at all aspects of church life: preaching, teaching, administration, counseling, engineering, public relations, fund raising, maintenance, accounting, law, and computer technology. Ed Bratcher includes this phenomenon in what he calls *The Walk-on-Water Syndrome.*[8] Frequently the minister accepts this impossible job description and tries time and again to keep on top of the water. As one minister told me, "I can almost make it for five or six feet if I get a good running start, but then I sink every time."

Dr. Gerald Caplan has shown that one of the three important factors in coping with stress is knowing what to expect.[9] The element of role confusion keeps a minister off balance. He never knows what to expect.

33

I can vividly recall the stress I felt as an intern when the emergency room would call. I didn't know what would be there waiting. I was more comfortable if it was an adult with a medical problem, less confident about evaluating a pediatric medical symptom, and quite anxious when a surgical or trauma patient was presented. Later, as a psychiatric resident, I felt far less stress. I knew it was unlikely I would be facing a trauma case. The E.R. wouldn't call a psychiatrist for medical or surgical cases. Psychiatric problems I could handle.

A minister never knows what the next call may be, so his stress level stays high. Most ministers confess that they hate to hear the phone ring. It might be a person threatening suicide or a request to come repair the church furnace. For some, either of those tasks would be preferable to meeting with the church finance committee to hash out a budget problem.

This aspect of the identity crisis decreases with positions in larger churches where specialization can occur. Even there the requirements in teaching, preaching, performing the sacraments, counseling, and administration may remain. The minister in a small church (which includes the vast majority of America's four hundred thousand clergy) is still a general practitioner who may be expected to do it all.

Social Identity

Another aspect of the identity crisis is the minister's sense of who he is socially. It is sometimes difficult for a clergyman to be "himself" anywhere. He may not know what that means in the first place. Many ministers have no sense of personhood apart from their identity as pastor. At Marble Retreat we sometimes forbid "shop talk" among the clergy, and it often becomes very quiet. Denied that aspect of their identity, they frequently feel invisible or at least a bit uncertain. Some clergy seem to have a poorly defined identity structure apart from the vocational mask.

It is difficult at times to sort out whether this keeping up the mask is mostly a defense against internal fears or is somehow thrust upon ministers from their environment. In most cases it seems to be a combination of the two. For the minister, staying behind the mask may protect him from self-disclosure and vulnerability. For those in his world it maintains distance from a person endowed with priestly (and perhaps mystical) powers. The laity may feel a need to keep their minister in a superhuman status. This gives a sense of security when sins must be absolved or sacred rites conducted or death faced. The layperson may feel the priest who intercedes with the Holy must be held aloof from the profane.

Where does that leave the minister? Isolated and confused about who in heaven or who on earth he is. He enjoys the safety of the pretense of holiness, but must somehow reconcile that with what he knows inside about his own humanity.

This problem also extends to the minister's family. Most pastors' wives have echoed what Virginia said recently: "I don't think anyone knows or cares who I am as a person. I'm just the 'pastor's wife.' I'm sure most of them don't even know my first name. When I approach a group in church the whole conversation changes. There is this instant phoniness and pseudo-spiritual sweetness that makes me sick at my stomach. I want to be me. I want to find out if I really exist or if I'm just some sort of shadow of my husband, the pastor."

Even the children share the confusion. They feel pressure to be something special, to be models of good behavior for all the other kids who can just be "kids." They are caught in a no man's land. We've often heard them tell of church members saying, "I'm surprised that you'd do that! What would pastor think?" Out of the church environment their friends exclude them with, "Well, I know you can't go with us since you're the preacher's kid."

The entire family ends up feeling like lepers. It's lonely when there's not even a leper's colony for them to go to.

Sexual Identity

Less known is the strange attitude about the minister and sexuality. There is a common saying among clergy that there are three sexes: male, female, and clergy—presumably neuter. The phenomenon has two roots—historical ecclesiology and cultural stereotyping.

From the standpoint of church history, the priests from the fifth century to the Reformation were celibate and some still are. That image persists as the world considers the "man of God." Sex seems to be the most powerful symbol of the flesh, our fallen, carnal nature. It feels sinful to imagine the minister (Catholic or Protestant) having sexual drives like everyone else. Thus laymen symbolically control a priest's lust of the flesh by vesting in him sexual neutrality. To adequately represent us before God we need our clergy to be pure, i.e., asexual, not of the flesh.

The second of the two factors, cultural stereotyping, is the more prominent in our day. The media image of a real man is a muscular, hard fightin', tough talkin', hard drinkin', fast drivin' woman chaser. That hardly fits the man of the cloth. When did you last see a real strong character portraying a minister in a movie or on television? It just doesn't fit. Consequently a minister often feels excluded by the "real men" of the community.

How does a minister feel inside when some guy apologizes to him for cussing in his presence? What does he think about his own masculinity when the boys in the locker room change their conversation about the sexy blonde by the pool? He may have no desire or inclination to cuss or talk about the blonde's anatomical configuration, but he may still feel excluded from the world of men.

On the other hand, some ministers feel more comfortable with women anyway. Frequently these have grown up in a predominantly female family or environment and have inner doubts about their strength as men. They have been taught how to relate to women, but feel ill at ease around men. The church world may perpetuate that tendency. This doesn't mean they do not have normal male sexual drive and heterosexual orientation, but their feelings may serve to create inner tension and discomfort about their own sexual identity.

Rootedness

A final area of identity that is sometimes disrupted for ministers is the feeling of having roots, belonging to a place. With frequent moves and "borrowed" houses it is hard to feel "settled in." Many fear sinking roots when a move is likely to come. The words of the old spiritual fit: "This world is not my home. I'm just a-passin' through." That sounds romantically wistful sung in four-part harmony around a campfire, but, in reality, the minister and his family may feel as displaced as the black slaves who first sang it.

The effects of not having a place to call home are varied. They include a sense of cultural displacement, a lack of ownership, and the perception of being excluded, all contributing to a gradually increasing level of hostility or grief.

The sense of cultural displacement relates to the loss of extended family and generational continuity, a lack of shared communal history, and the loss of special anchors. In our highly mobile society these experiences are common, but nonetheless disruptive. To some degree they may be more noticeable to a minister who functions in a subculture that is more stable and tradition-bound than the broader community. There is likely to be a core group within the church that remains intact. The minister, who is less likely to establish permanence, gets frequent reminders of his impermanence. One of the most poignant is the loss of his extended family. The church celebrates family in many ways, and worship events are frequently occasions for family. Many family groups attend church together every week and follow worship with Sunday dinner at Grandmother's. Communion, confirmation, baptism, weddings, anniversaries, funerals, Christmas, Easter, and Thanksgiving are church-centered family events. The minister serves the gathered clans as an outsider, directing the participants but not sharing the common bonds.

One minister's wife told us recently of a particularly difficult Thanksgiving in their home. As usual, they were serving in a church a long way from their extended family, and they were unable to be together for this holiday. Their congregation seemed insensitive to the pastor's family's personal needs and were wrapped up in their own groups and traditions. For some reason the pastor's family was also displaced from its usual house that week. They had no place to go to celebrate. Thanksgiving seemed especially lonely. She recalled the empty feeling she had as they were watching families leaving the church service on their way to cozy homes and traditional feasts. One matronly member sensed her sadness and said, "Well, how could you act so ungrateful on a day for being thankful to God? You'd better get straightened up." The minister's wife watched her leave with several laughing grandchildren in tow. The emptiness changed to bitterness. The loneliness was compounded by rage. It was difficult to feel thankful as she, her husband, and their two small children drove to a restaurant for a lonely, impersonal plate of turkey. She kept thinking of those other families and her own miles away enjoying the warmth of the holiday.

Another area of displacement is the lack of shared history. The minister is a stranger to the town traditions. He and his family didn't survive the terrible tornado or flood. They weren't in on the grand and glorious centennial celebration. They don't even know the local heroes of the state championship team of '52. Their own memories of landmark events of childhood are meaningless to these strangers surrounding them. No one's homecoming court is very important unless you're within a twenty-mile radius of the school.

We have now lived in our area of the Rockies for twelve years. Only in the past two or three have we begun to feel a part of the local history. We are almost "old timers" now in an area with very few natives. In most communities ministers are long gone within ten years, never gaining that sense of partnership.

A similar component of belonging is the anchoring of identity to places and things. The house we grew up in, the lake where we spent lazy summer days, that private stretch of beach, the secret glade in the woods, the towering oak tree, the city park and corner store—all are important to our sense of who we are. Going back to those familiar spots often brings a feeling of well-being that transcends attempts at logical explanation. Part of the experience is certainly retrieving the positive emotions associated with earlier events. Part must be the comfort of touching the unchanging in a world of rapid change, and the feeling of being in unity with that dependably steadfast scene. A part seems to be a spiritual experience that goes beyond memory.

Douglas is a typical minister who has served in six different towns in his twenty-seven years since seminary. He's been through many of the crises, the hurts, and the victories of church life. As we talked about his life, one thing stuck with me. Every year he goes on a personal retreat. His family has a secluded lake house where they spent summer vacations throughout his childhood. I could feel the sense of peace and nostalgia, of comfort and belonging in his spirit as he told me of those annual pilgrimages. He said when he made the last turn down that wooded lane, it was as though the weight of the world lifted and he was flooded by a feeling of well-being. For the next four or five days he renewed his inner strength sitting by the water, strolling among the trees, listening to the rhythmic calls of the birds, feeling the power in a thunderstorm, watching a doe and her fawn in the fading evening light, and falling asleep to the night sounds that were always there year after year as they had always been from his earliest memories. No matter where he worked, a part of him lived there and rejoined him every year. That is an experience of anchoring that many ministers miss by their displacement. They don't have a place they belong.

Another aspect of rootlessness for many pastors is their lack of home ownership. This contributes to feelings of financial insecurity, but also to a lack of personal control. The parsonage, even when very nice, is someone else's property. It is decorated by a church committee according to its taste—not necessarily in accord with the residents' desires. There is often the spoken or implied rule that nothing can be changed in the house without approval. This feeling of not having control is a daily reminder of not really belonging. Often tenants have more freedom to personalize their living quarters than most parsonage families.

This problem is alleviated for ministers who are allowed to buy their own houses. Their difficulty may relate to the frequent moves that seem to come with the profession. A lack of choice in the matter of when to move and where may create tremendous financial hardship. If they move away from a depressed real estate market, they are likely to get stuck with a house that doesn't sell or that they have to sell at a loss. When they move into an inflated market their previous equity may be woefully inadequate. Under these conditions the minister may suffer not only the financial stress, but also feelings of resentment toward the church (or God) for forcing him into the situation.

One other aspect of not having a place to call home is the frequently reported perception of being excluded. Several ministers and their wives have told us, "We have never felt that we ever really became a part of the community." One said, "It was not that the people weren't nice to us. At times we were uncomfortable with their kindness. They gave us gifts. They always showed respect. They were sensitive to our physical needs and generous in providing for us. The thing that was lacking was feeling included in their lives. It may be like royalty must feel—never being at one with the common folk. When we were invited, we still would feel like some special guests instead of just one of the gang."

It seems that many of the laity maintain a we–they attitude toward their clergy. I see this in part as a defense against the pain of separation. The minister is seen as a transient who will be leaving soon. The separation can be more easily dealt with if there never was a close relationship. Many lay people, feeling the church is "ours," not "theirs," resist allowing the minister to put down roots: He's not seen as "one of us." He doesn't really belong.

There are other attitudes that contribute to the exclusion. Many lay people believe that ministers shouldn't have close friends, and they consciously avoid even appearing to be close. Others feel intimidated by the professional position or educational background of the pastor; they think they have nothing in common with him and handle the discomfort with distance. Some exclude the minister because of feelings of sinfulness; they are afraid that if they allowed the minister to know them they would have to clean up their act. The hunters or golfers may think it wouldn't be much fun having to leave the booze at home or changing their language just to invite the pastor to join them. The wives may think their bridge parties or gossip sessions would have to give way to Bible studies and prayer meetings, if they included the pastor's wife.

The minister probably hasn't considered these elements. He only knows he feels rejected. He doesn't belong "here" and begins to wonder if he belongs anywhere. He's left with the slave's lament, "This world is not my home. . . . If heaven's not my home then Lord what will I do?" The final effect is a combination of identity confusion, grief, and anger.

THE CRISIS OF PRIORITY

Perhaps the most common complaint from a minister's family is his being "married to the church." They become accustomed to being stood up and let down. Special family celebrations are suddenly preempted by someone else's emergency, vacations are routinely interrupted by funerals, and mealtime is usually spent listening to one side of a telephone conversation. The family feels left out and second (or fifth) best. That hurts. It creates anger in them. Consequently it is one of the principal sources of tension and guilt for the minister. He feels caught in a no-win situation. The elements of this crisis area are relatively simple: the expectations of the church, the expectations of the minister, the minister's personal and family needs, and his time management skills.

The most obvious one of these is the expectations of the congregation. The demands are expressed on various levels. On the surface are the clearly defined requirements that are written in a job description or contract: The minister is to participate in or direct worship services on Sunday. He is to keep certain office hours for counseling and administrative functions. The sick are to be visited. The church finances are to be promoted, building expansion supervised, and Christian education directed. Conducting weddings and funerals may be optional. *Any two of these are easily forty-hour weeks.* On paper they are coupled with optimistic perks: One-and-a-half days off each week, two to four weeks of vacation time, two weeks of continuing education allotment, and lots of staff and volunteer support. That's one level of expectation.

Just below the surface are the unwritten traditional requirements. These may vary from one church to another. They usually include participation on most of the church committees which means at least one evening meeting a week.

Availability for counseling in crises which ordinarily occur between midnight and 3 A.M. Conducting weddings and funerals which are not always scheduled according to the minister's calendar. Participating in various community affairs, which include the ministerial association, scouting, service organizations, school parent-teacher groups, and perhaps even political office. There may also be social activities begun by a previous minister who liked to host parties such as a traditional Christmas open house, Thanksgiving buffet, or Labor Day picnic. None of these expectations may appear on the written job description, but parishoners may still feel serious disappointment if they aren't fulfilled.

As if those weren't enough, each parishioner may bring his or her own special expectation into the equation. The Joneses have always expected the pastor to have Sunday dinner with them. Mrs. Smith has become accustomed to a weekly visit from the pastor (on Friday mornings). Tom and Hank expect the pastor to go on their annual fishing trip to the lake. The previous minister's wife always made a decorated birthday cake for each member of her Sunday school class. The individuals may each know rationally that these desires can't be pushed off on the new pastor, but what happens emotionally is another issue.

A second complication to setting priorities (just below the expectations of the congregation) is the expectations of the minister. We frequently talk with clergy who have more unrealistic expectations for themselves than their congregations have. Individuals who enter Christian work often find their sense of value in being a servant. That is certainly in keeping with Jesus' teaching about leadership. He said, "The greatest among you will be your servant" (Matt. 23:11). However, that ideal may become distorted when a person's sense of worth becomes inexorably linked with being needed. When that has happened, setting any limits on the demands of others becomes impossible. Saying no produces not only guilt of not being a worthy servant but also fear of rejection. Because of this many Christian workers are manipulated by their own expectations: They must be available to everyone at all times. That inner drive is intensified by their guilt and fear. In that vulnerable position, they unconsciously misread environmental signals as cries for help or demands for service. A parishioner simply mentions a problem he's having, and the minister feels compelled to come to the rescue. His sense of usefulness depends on it.

Common expectations we see in Christian workers are: 1. to be tireless; 2. to be above being hurt; 3. to be excellent at every task; 4. to be emotionally self-sufficient; 5. to be free from material needs; 6. to be spiritually perfect. These may or may not have been verbalized. They may need to be identified and interpreted *for* the minister on the evidence of his lifestyle and the conflicts in his daily existence.

The third ingredient in the priority crisis is the personal and family needs of the minister. The minister's personal needs may not enter the picture until relatively late in his career. When he is young and still in the process of proving himself, a minister may be able to deny personal needs and have enough energy to maintain the drive toward "success" as defined by his and others' expectations. As the midlife transition comes into the picture, he may no longer be able to avoid his own needs for reevaluation, renewal, intimacy, and facing his own mortality. These physical and emotional tasks become harder and harder to ignore as energy wanes.

Family needs, on the other hand, may continue to be ignored if that has been the established pattern. More typically, the family has not been so willing to allow the ignorance and it demands some attention. This conflict is one of the most common among the clergy. In *What's Happening to Clergy Marriages?*, David and Vera Mace identify this as the number-one problem in clergy marriages.[10] Most of the couples who spend two weeks in a session at Marble Retreat admit it's the first time they've been away alone together since their honeymoon (which may have been twenty to thirty years ago). They have been busy denying that need while they have served others. All the while they've realized the distance and hostility that have been building up between them.

The same thing is likely to be happening with their children. So many children of Christian workers finally just give up after seeing their need for attention subrogated to those of "the church" time and time again. In their desperation for attention, some demand it through misbehavior. This can be destructive of their parent's ministry, but is often even more destructive to their own lives. That's a sad price to be paid because priorities aren't handled effectively.

Obviously finding solutions to these conflicts is not simple, especially since a fourth factor—the time management skills of the individual minister—can further complicate the task. We frequently find ministers woefully untrained and unskilled in this area. I've often wondered if the ill-defined end points and hazy signs of success that characterize the ministry dissuade organized, goal-oriented individuals from making ministry a career. It seems more common to find people in ministry whose time is scheduled by whoever makes the loudest demand. Such a person seems totally unable to make goals, establish schedules, and set limits on activities. Driven by the expectations of a church, the expectations from within, and the needs of self and family, these individuals are perpetually caught in a crisis of priorities.

THE CRISIS OF INTEGRITY

Our local church has been studying how to more effectively reach the unchurched people in our community. Many of these have moved to the mountains to escape traditional suburban life and to find freedom to be themselves. One of our goals has been to learn to listen to where they are in their spiritual attitudes and beliefs. Interestingly, one of their more common statements about the church is that there is "too much hypocrisy" in Christianity. They point out the sinfulness of church members, the emphasis placed on money, and the inability of Christians to love each other, much less love unbelievers.

Sometimes their complaints are based mostly on those general impressions of our culture, but at times they are based on some personal incident in their lives. One man said he could never trust Christians because a local "Bible-thumping" businessman had cheated him on a deal. Many give the financial appeals of the TV ministries as their excuse for seeing the church as hypocritical. One middle-aged woman said she'd never go back to a church because when her mother was terminally ill, twenty years ago, no one from the church had come to offer help. These events are serious in the lives of our neighbors and contribute significantly to their negative attitudes.

The person who is most likely targeted for these accusations is the Christian minister. Like it or not, he's the one who is most scrutinized. It is his behavior that is passed through their filters of negative bias. His life is being perpetually judged and his words distorted and reinterpreted to fit with the preconceptions of each individual. Herein is the crisis of integrity. How can any person live up to the high calling of Christianity? Of course no one can. Within the church we know that it is only by God's grace that we ever attain righteousness, but even within the church that is sometimes forgotten. The minister often feels the daily stress of trying to live up to the demands for perfection. The discrepancies between the teachings of Christ and the minister's working those out in his own life can become overwhelming. If he somehow forgets that for a moment, there is some eager critic who will gladly remind him of his hypocrisy.

One of the most common areas of struggle for Christian workers is that of finances and materialism. On the one hand stand the principles of Jesus who said to seek God's kingdom first; if you see your neighbor in need you should provide; do not store up treasure on earth where moths corrupt. On the other, the minister feels the pressure of his world to provide for his family, to live on the level with those he serves, and to regard his level of financial compensation as a measure of his worth as a person. Finding the balance between those sometimes opposing forces is tricky.

These true-life illustrations will show you how tricky walking that tight rope can be.

John is forty-five. He has three teenage children. The oldest is just starting college. His church has no retirement plan, and he took a salary cut to come to his present position because of the ministry outreach possibility. Now the church powers are resistant to the growth his ministry is producing, and he's being forced to leave with no system for reappointment. He's scared. John doesn't want money to be the primary motivation in his life. In fact, he disregarded it in his last job selection. Now he's worried about how he'll sell their house in a depressed market, how he'll educate his children, and whether or not this "failure" in ministry will affect his ability to relocate.

Bill was in his midthirties when he came to a small, newly organized church. He had one child at the time. He and his wife had few demands and were comfortable with the small salary he was given. They lived modestly in an ancient relic of a rental house which was hard to heat and crowded even for their family. Some of the church members complained about his not having a very decent place to live. Finally a gift was given that allowed the church to furnish the down payment on a house. Bill and his wife and child gratefully moved into a spacious, lovely home. When two more children arrived there was plenty of room for them, and they were also much better able to entertain church members frequently. But recently there has been grumbling from a few people in the church about the preacher living in such a "big house."

Margaret is a single woman who does Christian conference ministry. She happened to be heir to a significant inheritance. In her family it was common to have luxury items such as jewelry, nice clothes, and new cars. She does her ministry for a very small fee, yet is frequently under criticism for her "life-style." Her critics have no idea how much she gives to Christian causes and how little she asks from anyone. They only see her diamonds and cars.

Fleming is quite opposite. He is a brilliant young man from a modest background. He did outstanding scholastic work through a doctoral level education and was consequently highly sought as a pastor. He stepped from the church he served as a seminary student into an affluent suburban church of nearly one thousand members. One of his priorities was to retain his lifestyle, in keeping with his modest roots and his theological convictions. When he was being considered by the church, his stand was affirmed and applauded, but the church members became increasingly uncomfortable with his old car sitting in the pastor's parking place and with his inexpensive wardrobe. Now he has to decide whether or not to accept the new car and clothing allowance they want him to have.

Even on the mission field, the battle goes on. Tim and Nancy, committed to missionary work in a Third World country, raised their support, learned the language, and moved to the field. They had wanted to live on the level with the people as much as possible. Although they found this more difficult than they had anticipated, they were determined to succeed. Then they were approached by some of the local believers who wondered why they would not hire household servants like other westerners since jobs and money were so hard to come by in their country.

By contrast, Sam and Joan are missionaries with a denomination that provides central support for all its missionaries. The Board policy is to see that the missionaries' needs are comfortably met to free them from financial concerns and allow them to give themselves wholeheartedly to their ministry. But Sam and Joan find themselves under criticism on the field for having "too much" and not living an exemplary lifestyle.

"You're damned if you do and damned if you don't." I think you can begin to understand how difficult it is for the Christian worker to walk the financial tight wire. He not only has his inner struggle to do what is right, but must also try to answer critics from all sides. A frequent result is a loss of integrity where materialism is concerned.

A second common pressure area regarding integrity is the minister's own spiritual discipline. The Christian worker knows and teaches that maintaining an active life of prayer, meditation, and Scripture study is an essential ingredient to a growing spiritual life. Yet most get into dry periods in their own lives where those practices become drudgery and may even be abandoned. That doesn't change the truth of their usefulness or the need to encourage them in others, but the minister is left in a very uncomfortable position. Can he avoid the subject which he honestly believes is vital? Can he maintain any sense of integrity while teaching the importance of prayer when his own prayer life is completely shut down? This crisis seems inevitable as long as we wear our humanity.

Similarly, feeling the absence of the fruit of the Spirit in one's life is a common experience for us mortals. Who has not been unloving, unkind, impatient, or selfish from time to time? For the minister, these times of falling short may create tremendous guilt or even serious doubts about what he professes to be truth. Probably nowhere in his life is this more true than in his family. There he is seen without a mask. His wife feels the selfishness or hears the unkind remarks. The children live with the impatience and try to avoid the temper outburst.

Not long ago a pastor called. He was almost in tears as he confessed his sin to me. He had a problem with his anger. If he expressed anger at all, it tended to be completely out of control. He found himself swearing and at times being physically abusive to his wife or children.

He had had an eruption again just a few minutes before he called me. He was under tremendous pressure in his church and felt totally isolated. He carried the weight of the world on his shoulders. It seemed that not even his wife understood. That day she had made a cutting, critical remark—just one, quietly delivered, deftly on target. He exploded. She received the full force of his frustrations. He called her unspeakable names and slapped her several times before he regained control.

As he wept, he kept asking how he could ever call himself a minister of God. He felt like a phony. He wanted to die or disappear.

Finally, there can be an integrity crisis as a minister struggles to integrate his principal roles of prophet and priest. In many ways this is analogous to our need to integrate our opposite personality characteristics, the need to embrace our maleness and femaleness. It is expressed in aggression and passivity, in law and grace, in stern rebuke and gentle nurturance. How does the Christian minister achieve a comfortable balance between prophet and priest?

Some evangelicals see these qualities as separate spiritual gifts (as in Romans 12, 1 Corinthians 12, Ephesians 4) and would see no need for a person to exercise any blending of these in ministry. Those who would be prophet simply speak forcefully their "thus saith the Lord." Those who have gifts of "mercy" or "helps" can carry out more priestly functions. But in most settings a minister must struggle with both aspects of his call and administer exhortation and love. He must point out sin and offer acceptance to the sinner. He must rebuke and give consolation.

Craig was the prophet type. He was highly intellectual and carefully assessed each situation with a keenly incisive mind. When he arrived at a conclusion, he knew he was "right." Furthermore, he could convincingly argue down all opponents. The only problem was that the feelings of other people were not an important piece of information in his logical processes. He was rather consistently winning the battles, but was steadily losing the war.

As we talked about this relational problem, Craig realized the nature of his trouble in getting along. He also became increasingly uncomfortable. As we explored his anxiety, he finally realized that he felt he would have to give up his sense of integrity to let anything other than pure "right" motivate his behavior. He could not allow the congregation's need for a priest erode the strength of his position as prophet.

Ken was as gentle, kind, and loving as anyone you could ever hope to meet. His church loved his sensitive, caring spirit. His ministry flourished under his tender loving care. Then conflict came between two groups in the fellowship. As with most church conflicts, the problems were with personalities as well as with issues. Ken tried to bring about resolution but refused to take a firm stand against anything or anybody. He was so afraid of conflict that he retreated totally into passivity. He felt he was called to teach love but could not see that confrontation was a part of love. His inability to serve as prophet almost allowed the disagreement to become a disaster.

In so many ways a Christian worker is caught in a crossfire of values and needs. A common outcome is a feeling of crisis in personal integrity. The apostle Paul expressed it: "Oh, what a terrible predicament I'm in! Who will free me from my slavery to this deadly lower nature? Thank God! It has been done by Jesus Christ our Lord. He has set me free" (Rom. 7:24–25, LB).

THE CRISIS OF DEPENDENCY

As a counselor to Christian workers, you are in a particularly advantageous position to help deal with this crisis area in ministers' lives. In fact, you may be the only person in his or her life who can say, "It's okay for you to hurt, to be dependent" and be heard by them.

Ed Bratcher has an excellent discussion of the humanness of the minister in his book, *The Walk-on-Water Syndrome.* He points out the combination of attitudes that serve to reinforce within ministers a need to be superhuman: 1. the expectations of the laymen; 2. pride; 3. conscientiousness; 4. sensitivity in the minister. He also delineates the tragic consequences of falling into this trap.[11]

Very few of the nearly four hundred ministers (or their spouses) who have come to Marble Retreat have comfortably accepted their own dependency. In one recent group, a pastor in his fifties said, "I have never been anywhere that I could let anyone see what I'm really like. I guess I felt comfortable about doing it here because I knew all of us were here because we have problems. I must admit though, as I looked around that first night I wondered what on earth could possibly be a problem for Joe and Ann. They seemed to really have it all together. Now I realize I've been looking at everyone else pretty much the same way and feeling I'm the only one who doesn't have it altogether. I'm not sure I'll be able to be much more open when I go back home, but at least I know it's okay not to be perfect."

Having to be strong and not need anybody is not a characteristic exclusive to clergy. Probably most individuals are taught that self-sufficiency has a high survival value, and it does. But it is also true that life can be far more enjoyable and effective when people admit their need of others and allow a comfortable mutuality. Some professions reinforce the tendency toward denial of dependency. Being a helper of others allows a person to maintain a relational advantage. From their perspective of being "taller" than others, they can avoid the discomfort of having to reach up for a helping hand.

I just had an interesting interruption from writing—a call from my good friend Doug Self, who is also my pastor. Doug was asking me and Melissa to join a group for dinner out this weekend. I was about to say no since we had planned a big anniversary dinner in a few days and our budget wouldn't allow it. But he said, "Now don't worry about the expense because your anniversary celebration next week is already paid for." That was hard to take. I like to have great celebrations and enjoy being the magnanimous host who arranges it all and treats his friends. In fact, I had made all the reservations and plans this time. Now, these so-called buddies of mine are taking away the pleasure of my being the total host! I had to realize again that I'm uncomfortable with dependency. Doug said, "Sorry, you're just going to have to learn to receive."

Besides the discomfort of needing help, ministers also want to avoid the vulnerability involved in realizing one's own weakness. There is a risk in exposing your soft parts. Sadly, that is true even within the Christian community, and the Christian worker has often learned from experience that it is sometimes unwise to reveal problems or needs.

I learned that lesson in a painful way several years ago. I had naively assumed that the church was a fellowship of forgiving, loving people who were busy about the business of being redemptive. A young pastor had confessed to me an adulterous relationship he was having with a church member. His wife knew and had forgiven him. I advised him to break the relationship and to confess to his elders, asking for forgiveness and restoration. He did both. Breaking up was hard for him emotionally, but was helped by the understanding and warmth of his wife. The confession was a mistake. There was not a redemptive word spoken. He was immediately fired with a loud and public display of anger and unforgiveness. Fortunately, he was forgiving toward me, and we both learned an important lesson. Now I advise openness, but cautiously, with one or two trusted supporters.

Unfortunately, as a person spends more time in ministry

and advances in responsibility the degree of isolation increases. The Buford Foundation and the staff of *Leadership* have been convening seminars for pastors of large churches and their experience is similar to ours. These highly visible men have felt alone and fearful of expressing their own dependency. In each of their sessions, the participants have unburdened themselves of tremendous feelings of pressure and tension after coming to realize they weren't the only ones with pain. A useful outgrowth has been that many have continued the supportive relationship with one or two colleagues with whom they don't have to be strong.

You may wonder why I may call this a crisis of dependency. It is my perception that the resistance to accepting one's dependency is greater among ministers than other groups and that this gap comes at a time when the stress of ministry is escalating. The clergy are hurting, but for the most part they suffer in silence until they reach some crisis point.

About the only exception to this rule is the reliance on a spouse to help carry the load. In his book *Ex-Pastors,* Gerald Jud reported that wives were the most usual confidant of pastors.[12] Time and again we have confirmed that a mate is the only one in whom the Christian minister confides. Of course this puts the spouse under considerable pressure to deal with his or her own stress plus that of the minister mate. This may in fact create the crisis that brings the minister to your office.

Betty was thirty-five and married to a pastor. They had three small children and were in a growing, busy suburban church. She called the Retreat because of anxiety. She felt she was "losing it" and might completely flip out. Her husband indicated his concern for her and his willingness to cooperate in treatment for her nervous tension. He acknowledged that the pressure of the children and her struggle to find her place in the church was wearing on her. As for himself, everything was fine.

As we explored her symptoms, we discovered that a significant (if not major) component was her concern for her husband's well-being. He was doing okay in his pastorate, but was struggling with some adjustments and facing some complaints. She was the only person who heard about these problems. She got a continual dose of his worry about his survival in ministry, his anger toward his critics, and his growing gloominess. Only after she broached the subject did he begin to share these negative feelings. It was a great relief for her not to be the only one aware of his pain, and he saw that her nervous tension was increased greatly by his own. The redistribution of his dependency enabled her to cope more successfully with her other life stress.

Just by giving permission to Christian workers to admit their problems to another person you can help alleviate the dependency crisis. As Carlyle Marney phrased it, we can be "priests to each other." [13] Your recognizing the pressures in ministry and hearing them with compassion will ordain you to your priesthood as a pastor *pastorum*.

CHAPTER TWO

ROLE-SPECIFIC PRESSURES

IF YOU ARE a psychiatrist who uses psychopharmacology you face a different set of difficulties than if you are a marriage counselor—and vice versa. I'm not sure either has it easier than the other. We all simply become familiar with the territory and learn ways to minimize the risks. So it is in "the ministry." There are peculiar problems that pastors face that a missionary may be protected from. I'm pretty certain the stresses on a youth minister must stand toward the top of the ecclesiastical pressure gauge. It is important for you as a counselor to differentiate these various aspects of the clients' experience rather than lumping them all together as "ministers." Naturally each person must be evaluated as an individual, but there are some generalizations that may help you. We'll consider these different positions: 1. pastorate, 2. foreign missions, 3. youth ministry, 4. music ministry, 5. evangelism, and 6. para-church ministry.

PASTORATE

The pastor is the preacher-teacher and administrator of most local churches. There are about 289,000 * pastors in the United States. They serve churches with an average membership of about 250 for an average salary of $13,127.* Many pastors make far less and have to work at other jobs. Pastors' average length of stay in a particular parish is about eighteen months. For this, many pastors have trained in seminary requiring three years after an undergraduate degree. The pastorate holds some other distinguishing features.

Impossible Tasks

The most easily identified mark of the pastorate is that it is an impossible job. The expectations are vastly unreasonable, the markers of goal achievement are ill defined, and the preparation often inadequate. Fred Smith, a corporate executive for many years, said in an article in *Leadership,*

> One time I became interested in trying to find a job in the Bible like our preacher has. You can't find one like the modern preacher to save your life. There's no job in there like that! We don't have a scriptural set-up. We have one that's grown up out of tradition. And I'm not too sure but that ministers haven't developed it themselves. Like everyone else, they reached for more and more authority, more and more prestige, more and more power, and created for themselves a job which nobody else can do. It takes an absolute genius to adequately do the pastor's job. One morning I thought, "What if today I were a pastor instead of a corporation president?" That

---

* Bureau of Census 1979 figures. Other data from Southern Baptist Convention.

idea scared me to death. I am totally inadequate to really fulfill the job that most pastors have. I'm afraid many of them are inadequate, also.[1]

I think I would say "most" are inadequate rather than "many." That leaves most pastors in a position of scrambling to try to avoid feeling inadequate. That sense of insecurity motivates much of their behavior: needing to control every aspect of the church life, working to increase membership, trying to please everybody, and being under the tyranny of the urgent.

Another result of a feeling of inadequacy is the image a pastor projects. I see many pastors who come across as being so phony you could pick them out of a crowd. They are squeaky clean, have a perpetual pasted-on smile, and talk with a ministerial tone that is syrupy sweet. It's refreshing to get behind that mask and discover a real live person. Those more secure in themselves can begin to reveal the real self more and more comfortably. While still behind the mask a pastor often feels isolated and lonely. Yet the fearful prospect of being "found out" reinforces the charade.

Even among other pastors—or perhaps especially among other pastors—the masks are kept in place. All the while many pastors detest the phoniness and avoid meeting with colleagues. One pastor was telling me about a typical ministerial alliance get-together. There were the brethren smiling, shaking hands, patting backs, and lying to each other. As he looked around the room he thought about each person. Tom was in serious conflict with his church board and would probably be forced to resign. Martha was not being accepted as the first woman pastor in her church. Joe was having an affair which was widely suspected in the community. Bill and his wife were also near divorce. Don's son had been causing him terrible grief with his rebellious behavior, and my friend was in serious financial difficulty because of some bad investments. Here they were with a few others my friend didn't know much about. All were hurting desperately, yet none was willing to be honest. What a sad, common story about the pastorate.

Mandate to Succeed

One aspect of ministry that sets it apart from other jobs is the sense of "calling" that clergy feel. Most pastors (and other ministers) have chosen their profession primarily on the basis of their call by God. A common problem we frequently work through with pastors is the serious question, "If God called me to be a pastor why aren't things going better in my life?" As this question is pursued, many separate issues emerge. One is whether or not the "call" was from the Lord. Another is what God promises to his called-out ones. A third is whether or not God in his sovereignty brings on the disasters that sometimes come into life. A fourth issue is how a pastor can be true to his call and belief system and admit or express his anger toward God. Another is how one can know what God is calling him to do or be.

As I work with pastors, I frequently ask them about their call. It is understandable that their initial response is usually a strong affirmation of that event. After all they have staked their life on it—often at great cost. Some will share a spiritual experience in which they sensed a divine presence. There may have been a vision or the voice of God or Jesus telling them to enter the ministry. More commonly I hear of a strong inner feeling, an awareness of need, a strong positive attraction, or an empowered passage of Scripture which was inescapable. When yielded to, this force seems to provide an unforgettable sense of well-being and peace. If resisted, there is an unexplained restlessness or fear.

At times, however, the "call" is not so clearly a spiritual experience. It is not uncommon for individuals who grew up in a religious environment to be told by some important adult that "God has something special for your life." Parents may pray that if God will grant them some desire (a healthy baby or relief from some distress or financial blessing or a son or a daughter) they will dedicate this child to his service. When those kinds of declarations are made to a child, it becomes difficult to know whether his compelling commitment is a response to God or a desire to please a significant person. It is a fearful choice to ignore the potent voice of authority when ignoring that word may also call down the disfavor of God!

Answering this kind of call also holds out an unspoken promise of acceptance by the one who "called." I remember one broken-hearted pastor, who at age forty-five realized that he had entered the ministry expecting to finally get his father's blessing. When it never came, he believed he just needed to be more "successful" in ministry. No matter how hard he worked or what positions of prestige he acquired, the approval was still withheld. It was painful for him to finally realize that he had answered a false call in an attempt to achieve a futile goal.

What does God promise to his "called"? This question, too, needs an answer. I try to help each minister identify what his early expectations of ministry were. That's often a difficult question for a pastor to answer honestly. The "right" spiritual response is to be able to serve the Lord faithfully regardless of where ministry leads, or perhaps to be able to share love with fellow human beings. A few might say, "Well, I expected to be at peace or be blessed by God." Not many would admit they expected to have success, to see their churches grow, their reputation spread, and their salary steadily increase as they would move to ever larger, more prestigious assignments. Even though unspoken, that expectation is frequently lurking somewhere under the surface.

Since only a small percentage realize those dreams, there are a lot of pastors who are left with disappointment or resentment.

It can be helpful to the pastor to identify the expectations and put them in perspective with what Scripture teaches (to be fishers of men and to receive spiritual blessings as well as some persecution). It can also help to identify some of the intangible rewards that make pastoring worth the costs (the effects of the pastor's efforts on an individual life, the opportunity to bring light into darkness, the joy of faithfulness to eternally significant ideas).

When life is caving in, those rewards may be overshadowed by the question of God's sovereignty. How can God do this to me, or does he bring disasters into life for some undisclosed purpose? The doubt and anger associated with this question need to be talked about. A pastor desperately needs a nonjudgmental, empathic listener whose faith is not shattered because a pastor is struggling in the pain of doubt. It's critical to hear that those feelings are okay and understandable when life's events and God's role in them aren't understandable at all. John Claypool's book *Tracks of a Fellow Struggler* presents one pastor's painful pilgrimage through the valley. It presents no pat answers but a strong testimony to faith.[2]

Finally the question of interpreting one's call may be important. What is God calling the individual to do or be? I'll never forget one seminary student who came with his wife for counseling. Their marriage and his career were falling apart even before he finished school. He had experienced a moving conversion as a young adult. He and his wife came to be deeply involved in religious life and activities. He was a committed believer and secondarily an electrician. Then one day, as he was discussing his sense of calling to follow the Lord as closely as possible, his pastor interpreted that "call." God must want you to enter "the ministry." The problem was that he was already in "the ministry." The pastor's narrow notion of sacred and secular failed to affirm the important ministry he had as a Christian tradesman. His wife had a clearer view of the Christian call than their pastor, but her voice wasn't heard. He quit his job, sold their house, and uprooted the family to enter seminary. His wife never adjusted and the crisis ultimately stopped them short.

Not long ago I had a visit with a former pastor who thought his world had come to an end when he was forced to resign his pastorate. He felt so convinced that being a pastor was God's call on his life that any other job looked like total failure. Quite unexpectedly he was given a chance to serve as a prison chaplain. Now he is happier than he had ever been as a pastor. In retrospect, he agreed with his wife who saw that he had always been ill-equipped for the pastorate. Many pastors end up in highly stressful positions because their interpretation of God's call was too narrow. Career evaluation with interest/aptitude testing may give an individual the opportunity to find a "ministry" better suited to personality and giftedness (see Appendix 2).

One result of the confusion about being called is the guilt generated by failure. A pastor has trouble seeing a vocational change as a simple lateral move. It carries with it a strong sense of unfaithfulness to God. Such guilt must be dealt with directly. If the pastor has committed some personal sin that contributed to the failure, he can be helped to confess the sin, repent, and ask God's forgiveness. In some instances, you may take on the role of priest. A pastor's confession may need to be extended to people that have been hurt—perhaps a whole congregation. If the guilt is neurotic and not based on real sin, the pastor can be assisted in developing insight and released from the false guilt. A simple "You shouldn't feel that way" is inadequate in either case.

Another aspect of working through the guilt of unsuccess in a pastorate is the need for receiving a blessing—approval from a strong parent-figure for what the person is. Giving your personal word of blessing serves to absolve the guilt. This adds an important interpersonal dimension to the spiritual forgiveness promised by God and the release received from others. As counselor/confessor, you are in a position of authority that gives you the power to bring closure to the sin event. Acceptance as a person is again experienced.

We recently had a pastor at Marble Retreat who was bound up in guilt over having to resign his church. He had in fact done some things that were primary in his dismissal. He had accepted God's forgiveness, but still struggled with a deep sense of guilt at having destroyed the position he had worked so hard to achieve. He felt totally worthless. Only as he sensed the love and acceptance of the group and of me as the leader did he begin to be released from his guilt. We finalized the process by having an "ordination" service giving him a blessing to pursue a new ministry as a Christian layman.

Job Insecurity

A recent phenomenon in the pastoral ministry is the growing number of forced resignations. Churches are firing their pastors. Only a few years ago congregations tended quietly to ask pastors to consider leaving and then they happily provided letters of recommendation. Although the ordeal was uncomfortable and inconvenient, most pastors could find another position and slip away. Now the "musical church" game seems to have stopped. Often the pastor is forced to resign, given a token severance pay, and moved out.

This new trend has contributed significantly to the anxiety a pastor carries. When you realize that pleasing everyone as a pastor is impossible and that the nature of church politics often gives remarkable power to one or two people, serving in pastoral ministry takes on the flavor of a game of Russian roulette instead of "musical church." Even in the denominations with appointive systems, being fired can seriously jeopardize a pastor's well-being.

Bob was forced out of his last church unceremoniously. The district superintendent was called in to remove him immediately. That was the first serious problem he had experienced during his eleven years as a pastor and it dramatically altered the upwardly mobile trend he had enjoyed. What seemed to Bob to be a very small, vocal group had conferred on him the aura of a *persona non grata*. The district superintendent didn't want to risk his own position, so he assigned Bob to a less prestigious position. Now Bob wonders whether or not he can ever regain a positive reputation. His anxiety about that will certainly affect his ability to minister effectively.

I've rarely seen a church fire some disgruntled member who may have set out to fire the pastor. Such people often stay to demolish several pastors in a row, and facing that danger is one of the challenges of being a pastor. One pastor said, "There's nothing wrong with my church that wouldn't be solved by a few well-placed funerals."

Unexpressed Anger

Pastors are often intensely angry individuals. Their feeling of being in a no-win situation is magnified by the taboo of their expressing any anger. At times this restriction is dictated by their environment. More often it is mandated by their own conscience. They are genuinely convinced that to have anger is wrong or un-Christian—at least for a pastor. Holding that super-Christian viewpoint that forbids anger leads to denial of negative emotions.

As you know, denial or suppression is not highly effective, and the anger is eventually expressed. You can find it in many places, sometimes in the highly competitive quality of the pastor's life. It is easy to see a need to exert control and power—to win—in his leadership style, his recreation (if he has any), in his driving habits, even in his sermons. It may be expressed in somatic complaints. Ulcers, colitis, low back pain, and headaches are common. As you evaluate a pastor you may pick up nonverbal clues in muscle tone—especially the masseters (jaw muscles) and hands. You may read the hostility in facial expression and eyes. You may hear the anger in his voice tone.

Yet as you ask about anger you may hear a blanket denial. It may be helpful to ask about his attitude and theology of anger. Some permission and gentle interpretation of the signs you see can help him begin to develop awareness of the volcano boiling within. It may also be helpful to point out that unspoken anger is frequently expressed through depression. The effects of a depressive illness have become so commonly known that most individuals definitely want to avoid a clinical depression. Though he is unable to see his hostility, the pastor may recognize that the depression he finds recurring in life relates to the level of "frustration" he experiences in his job.

A joint interview with a spouse can also help identify the anger. The spouse may in fact be relieved to have a safe place to confront the issue, as the pastor may let down the mask and allow feelings to be expressed honestly only at home.

Financial Pressure

Pastors frequently suffer from heavy financial stress. They find themselves caught in a Catch-22. They are underpaid and yet expected to live up to the lifestyle of their congregations. This bind is made worse by their attitudes about money.

A prominent attitude among pastors is that they are not supposed to have any desire for money, and because of this they conceal their legitimate financial needs. They fear doing so would make them look unspiritual. We began attending a small church several years ago and were amazed to discover that the pastor's salary was four hundred dollars a month.

Needless to say, he couldn't get by on that, so he spent many hours each week moonlighting to try to make ends meet. Although the congregation was quite able to give much more to his support, he had never even hinted about getting a raise. Unfortunately, it's rare to find a church layman who is aware of or sensitive to the pastor's needs. In my experience, when a pastor is comfortable in honestly stating his financial needs, the congregation usually meets those requests.

A second attitude that is equally destructive is a sullen, resentful spirit. This pastor feels persecuted and mistreated and responds passive-aggressively. He may not pay his bills. He may hint for handouts and use guilt to manipulate others into doing him favors. He is the type minister who gives pastors a bad reputation as crooks or dead beats. This attitude creates hostility in the congregation which responds by withholding support which serves to perpetuate the problem.

A third attitude is one of self-deprecation. This individual feels so unworthy and inadequate that he feels guilty about receiving any money at all. He may be unconsciously setting up a poor pay scale to confirm that he really isn't worth much. Such a pastor may gradually convince others of his ineffectiveness as he drops down the economic ladder to lower and lower rungs, each reduction proving what he has always believed about himself—"I'm worthless."

Pastors may be helped to accept their realistic financial needs and encouraged to negotiate better salaries. When this is successfully done (as it usually is) they begin to feel better about themselves and do a better job in ministry. This also alleviates the pressure of trying to live up to a standard that's just too high. Churches can learn to talk about money and to adequately provide for their pastor. You may serve the church and the pastor by mediating their negotiations.

FOREIGN MISSIONARIES

In our ten years at Marble Retreat we have seen a remarkable change in the attitude mission boards have regarding counseling for their personnel. One board's medical director recently told me that he had to go to battle with the board's administration to send the first couple to us about eight years ago. Last year those same board members asked what he thought about requiring counseling for every furloughing missionary. They have even hired a full-time psychologist for their personnel department. In a decade the attitude has changed from the belief that missionaries are too spiritual to need help to a realization that missionaries are under tremendous stress and can use all the help available. That's progress.

As we have worked with missionaries, we have seen a number of unique problems repeated many times. Among these are: cross-cultural adjustment, conflicts with colleagues, fatigue, pressure to maintain the "super-Christian" image, and family problems.

Cross-Cultural Adjustment

Most foreign missionaries are faced with the challenge of learning to live successfully in another culture. Some make the adjustment easily; others, not at all. Those who struggle with this problem are usually in their first term. Those we have counseled have shared two common responses. One is the surprise they felt at the severity of the problem. The other has been their extreme sense of failure and guilt.

Mission volunteers expect that their deep concern for the people they are going to serve will empower them to cope with any adversity. Unfortunately they have little recognition of the totality of change awaiting them.

Walter and Cindy are a delightful young couple who recently came home on medical leave after two years in a Third World country. After feeling a definite "call" to foreign mission church planting, they had prepared for years. They knew the living conditions were going to be primitive. They realized the climate and food would be different, and of course they were taking time for language study to help bridge the communication gap. Having no indoor plumbing, hauling and boiling water, and food preparation taking much of the day were just a few of the challenges they expected. But they didn't realize how much energy the tropical climate would take out of them each hour, and that made all of the other problems much harder to face. They found themselves wishing for just one meal of their favorite food. They both learned the language fairly easily, but what surprised them was the completely different way of looking at life. For instance, they were accustomed to basic honesty and integrity in relationships. Instead, they found that lying, stealing, and cheating were standard qualities in that culture.

Another totally unexpected stress was the complete loss of privacy. As foreigners, they were so different in their remote village that they were constantly surrounded by curious children (and adults). They not only looked at them, followed them, and asked questions, but also wanted to touch their skin and hair. The villagers would even look into their house to see how they lived. The house was little refuge because it was connected to the neighbor's by a common wall so thin that even after dark they felt as if they had other people living in their space. They were unprepared for the totality of change confronting them. The stress was creating tension between them and ultimately became unbearable.

One effect of their collapse was an overwhelming sense of failure and guilt. They had invested much of their identity in being missionaries. Their total commitment to that goal set them apart as special people. Now they weren't so special. They had failed themselves and God. They had also failed their supporters. What could they say to the many individuals who were giving sacrificially to enable them to go? They now faced major reorientation of self-concept as well as direction in life. They were angry, depressed, confused, and fearful. Before they began to feel some wholeness return they had to sort out and work through many issues.

Another aspect of the cross-cultural adjustment will be discussed with family issues since it seems to affect children more than their parents: Children seem to have a hard time readjusting to life in the United States after living abroad. Of course the longer a missionary family serves abroad, the more difficult this transition becomes.

Conflicts with Colleagues

The number one problem we have dealt with in missionaries has been their difficulty in getting along with other missionaries. One explanation for this statistic is doubtless our patient selection process. Missionaries are often referred to us by their boards which are trying to ease relational conflicts. In investigating these missionaries' problems, however, we have come to believe that their problems are typical of others'. Several factors contribute to this pattern.

In the first place, those who go into mission work are usually highly individualistic. They are adventurous and loner-type people who do not function best as part of a staff taking directions from someone else. They want to be independent and do things their own way. That is the core of a lot of problems. They're all chiefs and there are no Indians. They tend to be much more comfortable working with the local people who look to them as leaders. Having to make reports and submit themselves to a field council is anathema. Perhaps related to their individualism is the tendency of missionaries to be persons who never fit in well in the crowd. We've discovered that they frequently felt different and didn't do well in developing social skills. They seem to communicate better and make relationships more effectively among the local people to whom they were ministering. With their missionary peer group they sometimes feel more out of place and awkward. They seem particularly inept at resolving conflicts. One particular mission group was having so much interpersonal conflict that the board considered sending us out to the field rather than bringing all the missionaries back to us. We didn't do it, but it's not a bad idea. Missionaries on the field can be helped by workshops on communication, dealing with feelings, and learning conflict resolution skills.

Another factor in colleague disputes is variation in mission strategy. This seems to occur especially between missionaries of different generations. Philosophy of missions has changed through the years and continues to change. As new missionaries arrive they are enthusiastic about making their impact on the world. Fresh from training, they eagerly set out to correct all the mistakes of the old approaches. Needless to say the "old approachers" are the veteran missionaries in their midst. They don't appreciate these "kids" bouncing into their territory and enumerating their mistakes. The tension creates relational problems for both generations and often leads to feelings of isolation and nonsupport. Enthusiasm melts into frustration which builds into bitterness.

Needless to say, conflict is also generated or at least intensified because of the overall stress pressuring everyone on the field. The cross-cultural adjustment, financial pressures, political tension, and overwhelming needs of the people all serve to diminish each person's ability to cope with stress. It is hard for us to imagine the intimidating stress of living in a politically chaotic country. One missionary couple shared the terror of the hour-by-hour uncertainty they experienced living in a country during a revolution. They had little energy to deal with interpersonal problems within the mission organization. Everyone was anxious and edgy and tempers flared easily. That situation was only an escalation of the usual stress level which erodes coping abilities.

Finally, colleague conflicts are frequently related to the structure of a mission. The use and distribution of power, the provision of materials, the control and accounting of money, the type of support systems established are frequent sources of disputes. Missionaries in the midst of conflict often feel that their home office has little interest in helping. Their perception is that getting the "job" done is the only thing that matters to the mission board. Interpersonal problems are ignored or simply treated as sin that needs to be repented so the ministry can continue.

Fatigue

Furlough is a great concept designed to provide rest, recuperation, and retraining for missionaries. Missionaries really need it and deserve it. When it finally rolls around, most are suffering from significant degrees of fatigue. Unfortunately furlough is often more hectic than life on the field. Most missionaries have to raise their own support; during furlough they must visit their financial backers to report on the work, to secure their continued giving, and often to raise more money to combat tremendous inflationary increases in their costs. Consequently deputation uses up most of the furlough—that means hundreds or thousands of miles of travel, staying in different homes every few days, being separated from family, and meeting a hectic schedule of speaking engagements. Sandwiched with deputation are physical evaluations, reports to the mission, continued education, and visits with extended family who haven't been seen for three or four years. Does that sound like rest and relaxation to you? The missionary remains chronically fatigued as crates are packed for moving back to the field.

"Super-Christian" Image

I suppose most Christians see foreign missionaries as super saints who are giving themselves more completely to the Lord's service than anyone else. How often have you heard someone say, "I'm willing to do anything the Lord wants me to, but I hope he doesn't call me to darkest Africa"? We really see missions as the ultimate in self-denial, and it may be. One result of that is the deification of the missionary, and that creates some unique pressures.

Perhaps the most destructive effect on missionaries is their need to deny the struggles they face. They feel pressure to present themselves as happy regardless of the circumstances. Even though they are fatigued and may be struggling with hurt, the smile must be in place. They are afraid to tell about the turmoil on the field. People want to hear about success. If they admit to the struggles the donations might drop off. They can share the spiritual victories, maybe the challenges, but certainly not the personal failures. If a missionary were to reveal his humanity, it might shatter the image of missions held by supporters at home. Of course that has serious implications if counseling is necessary. The mask must be gently removed and the underlying wounds exposed.

Another effect of the super-Christian label is not being able to escape the demand for ministry. Missionaries are such heroes of the faith that people naturally expect them to be able to solve all their problems. Anyone who faces pagan witch doctors and wrestles crocodiles can easily provide the answers for our mundane problems. Besides their special gifts and closeness to God, they are safe to talk to because they are leaving in a day or two. Often stateside Christians feel they can unload on them without having to worry about facing any consequences.

One especially difficult aspect of this phenomenon is that the extended family also puts "their missionary" in a savior role and lays all the family burdens on him, too. There's no safe place. The missionary has to be the one to counsel all the relatives who are having marriage crises and all the rebellious teenagers. He has to decide what to do with the senile parent. He gets to minister to the family sick, bury the dead, baptize the believers, and probably is the one to say grace over every meal served. Rarely does a missionary have someone who treats him like a fellow human being who hurts and gets tired.

Family Problems

Missionaries face complicated problems with their children. I continue to be amazed at how well integrated most M.K.s (missionary kids) turn out to be. Their childhood is marked by growing up in a foreign country, sometimes requiring a second language. They are often sent away to boarding school at a very early age (as young as six). When they are home for holidays their parents may have very little time to be with them. They come back home every three or four years where they must try to adapt to a completely "foreign" culture of affluent and pleasure-seeking peers. They have a year in a new school trying to fit in with their North American classmates and then are moved back to the mission field and boarding school. They experience feelings of not really belonging anywhere. They usually think of their mission country as "home," but they don't have citizenship there and aren't completely accepted. On the other hand, they don't feel comfortable with the lifestyle and value system they find in the U.S. and Canada. So they are displaced persons confused about who they are and where they can find a future.

The missionary parents often struggle with ambivalence toward their children. On one hand, they feel guilty for the pain and disruption in their offsprings' lives. On the other, they may resent the interruption that the children create in their ministry. This ambivalence erodes their parenting skills and further adds to the confusion. The M.K. frequently struggles with the same mixed feelings—guilt at causing problems for his or her overworked parents and anger that life is so complex.

We've known many missionaries who survived mission life well until their children reached adolescence. Those years sometimes demand a leave of absence from the mission to help guide a rebellious child into adulthood. Those who make it through their teenage development without serious rebellion may, nonetheless, carry resentment for the tension, confusion, and loneliness they felt. I have one M.K. friend who still gets quite worked up over the sense of abandonment he felt in his adolescent years. His parents were on the field and the mission board provided only token support as he went to school in the States.

Simply giving a missionary family a protected place to talk to each other helps them get acquainted and begin to resolve conflicts. The M.K. particularly needs to feel that his parents really care about him or her as a person. Your office and presence may be the only safe spot they can find.

YOUTH WORKERS

Consider the minister of youth. These fearless men and women have my total admiration. They have one of the most difficult jobs in the church, Christendom, and the cosmos. It takes more than running shoes, a T-shirt, and a McDonald's charge card to survive. Often these unsung heroes have the most critical influence on a person's spiritual life. I know that was true for me. Our youth minister challenged me to commitment while making the Christian life exciting and fun. But that's not all . . .

Surrogate Parent Role

Adolescents need nonparent adults. The youth ministers often meet this important need. They become role models who blend Christian value systems with zany, nontraditional behavior. This allows the necessary differentiation from parents to occur within "safe" boundaries. They are trusted confidants who can hear the secrets and the sins while maintaining an accepting stance sometimes difficult for a parent. They understand the pressures kids are facing and at the same time give a mature perspective to their charges.

This position between parent and peer can be a tight spot to be in. Parents sometimes feel threatened by the special influence the minister of youth has with the son or daughter. Fearfulness of losing control or jealousy over losing affection may produce antagonistic attitudes or actions. Such attacks are hard for the youth worker to understand and even more difficult to defend against. These situations may be intensified by the adolescent. One minister told me recently of a conflict he had with a dad who threatened to beat him up physically for "giving his son drugs." The boy had been using drugs and was caught red-handed by his father. When confronted by his furious dad the boy figured if he could deflect his dad's anger from himself to the youth minister he could escape the wrath. It almost worked. The youth minister barely escaped with his job intact and his nose unbroken.

High Energy Output

Life expectancy of the species *ministerius youthii* is shorter than a snail darter. Definitely an endangered species, most youth ministers move on to some other ministry in their late twenties or early thirties. That's primarily because of the tremendous energy requirement in the job. Adolescents relate through physical activity: competing, touching, pushing, shoving, hugging, hitting, running, bouncing, swinging, rocking, and rolling. Youth ministry seems to succeed in direct proportion to the activities it provides.

Consequently one of the limiting factors in the life of *ministerius youthii* is its ability to withstand fatigue. One youth minister who came to Marble Retreat needed rest as much as counseling. She had almost been killed a few years earlier when she had gone to sleep at the wheel of her car while hauling a truck load of canoes to summer camp. She had been going full speed for weeks and finally ran out of gas. Fortunately, she survived.

The effects of fatigue are not only seen in falling asleep

while driving. They can also be manifested in poor decision making, irritability, depression, anxiety, insomnia, and physical illness. Often church members see the minister of youth as a grown up kid who just plays around or goofs off with the young people. The stress of the job may be unrecognized.

Loss of Privacy, Dignity, and Sanity

Nothing is sacred to the adolescent—least of all the space, time, emotions, or mental balance of the minister of youth. One youth minister I know had to develop a signal to the kids to keep them from coming into his house all through the night. He would leave his porch light on when they were welcome. When his light was out, they were not supposed to disturb him. It usually worked. Before he set some limits, his marriage and family life was being completely destroyed. As you know, adolescents are egocentric and rarely stop to consider how their immediate needs or demands may affect others. A quick pizza at 2 A.M. sounds like great fun and any good friend should be eager to join in—especially the youth minister.

The youth minister who is unwilling to set limits may face serious conflicts at home. Spouses and children may not be quite as understanding of 2 A.M. pizza or 4 A.M. counseling sessions.

Poor Pay, Power, and Prestige

On top of everything else the youth minister is often on the bottom of the totem pole, the bottom of the pay scale. He or she may have little power in staff decisions and at times is treated more like one of the church youth than a professional minister.

In some ways the position of a youth minister is like that of medical interns who are expected to be grateful for the opportunity to work eighteen hour days, live at the hospital, and receive less than minimum wage after twenty years of school. The new seminary graduate may serve a similar initiation into "the ministry."

Since youth ministers are serving their apprenticeships and

their futures depends on the recommendations they get, they may be reluctant to talk about their pressures or needs.

Sexual Seduction

An adolescent is struggling to incorporate adult sexuality into his or her identity. Especially in our culture, this is often achieved by sexual activity. The minister of youth is particularly vulnerable to the seductive behavior of the older adolescents who see themselves as more sophisticated than the peer group. In their minds, older men or women can really understand them and relate as mature companions. That often means sexual interaction. This is, of course, one of the most dangerous aspects of youth ministry. The single minister must be alert to the potential for disaster that lurks in this area. What may begin as a meaningful involvement in the life of one of the kids can easily end in sexual involvement causing hurt and pain to the young person, his or her parents, the church, and the youth minister. Even an innocent friendship may be misinterpreted or prompt false accusations by an angry adolescent.

We have counseled several ministers whose careers and marriages were almost destroyed by improper sexual conduct during their youth ministry. Joe was typical. He was just out of seminary, newly married with a small child. He was energetic and enthusiastic, eager to be a success in his first job. He was frantically involved with the young people in all sorts of events. Over several months time he began to find himself repeatedly involved with one of the girls. She was a beautiful seventeen-year-old who was more mature than her peers. They began to play tennis together, and she was frequently the last to leave group activities. Joe couldn't remember who made the first move toward sexual intimacy, but once that happened it snowballed remarkably fast. He couldn't believe he had allowed himself to get so entangled. Somehow he escaped almost certain ruin. They broke off the relationship and he moved. His own guilt followed him, but his marriage and ministry survived.

Youth ministry is not all ski trips, summer camp, and songs by an open fire.

MUSIC MINISTERS

David said, "I will sing a new song to you, O God; on the ten-stringed lyre I will make music to you" (Ps. 144:9).

Mankind has been responding to God through music for thousands of years. From Handel to Amy Grant, our worship is enhanced through melody. Often the unsung inspiration of our celebration is the minister of music. These men and women are expected to prepare us emotionally to worship God, yet may receive little affirmation. There are several aspects of their position and personality to keep in mind as you counsel them.

The Creative Personality

We mustn't forget that church musicians are creative artists. As such they are right-brain dominant and likely to be intuitive, feeling, expressive, and spontaneous. Creative individuals often see life differently from those around them. They tend to be more sensitive emotionally, more critical professionally, and more attention-seeking personally. These traits frequently create relational conflicts.

The emotional sensitivity of musicians is legendary. The "temperamental artist" is often excused for outbursts of rage or attacks of melancholy that would be unacceptable in someone else. This quality is in part biological and in part sociological.

Biologically, the nervous system of musically creative people is highly receptive. They have increased perceptive abilities for tactile and auditory stimuli. They also have a heightened awareness of emotions. This sensitivity to human feelings contributes significantly to their ability to use music to create a mood in their audience. That giftedness enhances worship. Unfortunately it makes them more vulnerable to being emotionally hurt by others. A negative remark or facial expression that would be unnoticed by most people registers strongly on their acute receptors. Their nervous system is like a highly developed radar system picking up signals imperceptive to less finely tuned instruments.

Sociologically, the rigorous life of specialized training and

75

practice necessary for developing the musical talent isolates many musicians. While their peers are learning relational skills in the give and take of neighborhood play, musicians are practicing flute or singing scales. Their whole world becomes more and more restricted to music, and their value, identified with their musical performance. Consequently, they may feel socially insecure apart from their musical ability. A friend of mine who is a trained vocalist has said that as she was growing up her singing became a ticket for acceptance. She felt insecure and inadequate as a person and related almost exclusively through her musical talent. She avoided involvement with peers and was overly sensitive to any perceived rejection. She was seen as a "temperamental musician."

Another characteristic that musicians usually demonstrate is a critical attitude toward technique and style. They are more keenly aware of the technical quality of musical performance and focus on imperfections they hear. One music minister said he seldom enjoys musical productions because of his hyperacute ear. Musicians' critical interpretive ability is applied to themselves as well as to others and increases their feelings of insecurity. If they verbally critique everyone else's talent, they will drive others away. I can imagine that directing church choirs of mostly untrained (and at times untalented) voices must be painful to the minister of music.

Since musical tastes vary so drastically within a congregation, the minister of music may find it impossible to please everybody. If he has developed a disdain for certain styles of music, he may unintentionally insult its aficionados. At the same time, he may be hearing frequent criticism for his musical choices. A less critically trained person might be able to select Bach, Gaither, or Petra with equal enjoyment.

A third characteristic of musicians is their need for attention and applause. They become accustomed to being the center of attention. The spotlight feels warm and the applause delightful. When performance of any skill has been a person's main pathway to acceptance it may seem essential to seek the praise for reassurance of worth. Applause can be addicting and the need for attention critical. When present, this quality gives a musician a self-centeredness that is distasteful. Everybody may enjoy hearing the music but resent the musician's craving for their applause.

This combination of qualities (emotional sensitivity, critical attitude, and need for attention) sets the musician up for frequent conflicts. For the musician, life may seem confusing. His or her talent is in demand, but he or she may feel unwanted as a person. Learning to live with this contradiction is stressful.

Subordinate Role

Besides their own temperament, a church musician must also adapt to a difficult role. The minister of music is placed in a position secondary to the pastor and expected to perform in a supportive role. At times there is very little freedom of individual expression allowed. The pastor or a "worship committee" may dictate what, when, and how music is to be a part of the church.

One music minister recently in counseling with us was in an acute anxiety crisis. She was a highly creative person, a composer, instrumentalist, and vocalist who delighted in innovative worship. Her folk masses with guitars and some of her delightful praise songs had given her widespread popularity in her denominational conference. That reputation brought her a job offer in one of the largest churches of the area. She was honored to be given the opportunity to minister there. She was a little scared, but excitedly optimistic. Her first Sunday she was almost overwhelmed by the size and the splendor of the sanctuary. With her heart filling with joy and praise, she opened the service, not with the usual choral anthem, but with a praise song she had composed for the occasion. With a guitar and flute as accompaniment, she sang her heart out.

It was too much, too fast for the stuffy vestrymen. She received a stinging criticism and rebuke followed by a directive that the senior pastor must approve all of her musical plans from then on. She wanted to be a submissive servant to her church, but felt she was being asked to deny her own giftedness. For a creative person there's no more frustration than being in a position that doesn't allow the freedom of creative expression.

As a staff member who must serve the program needs of the entire church, the music minister may also feel denied the right to determine priorities for his own use of time. Other pastors and their desires often have control over the music ministry. Consequently, time demands and staff conflicts regarding control affect the musician's feeling of autonomy.

Pressure to Entertain

Not many years ago the choir's anthem or a vocal solo in church was about the only musical performance many people ever heard. That's definitely not true anymore. Daily, people have living-room access to the world's best musicians. The music minister may fall into the trap of trying to provide entertainment for the community rather than a worship experience directed to God. When that happens the stress mounts. Can you imagine trying to compete with the media spectaculars that are at our fingertips? Many churches have fallen into the trap. Each televised service becomes a musical extravaganza. Meanwhile, the music minister of an average church— two hundred people, a choir of twenty, one piano and a reasonably talented trio—has a real problem.

I was just talking to a music minister friend of mine who said he had to fight constantly against the pressure to produce some supercalifragilistic dog and pony show at least once a year. He has chosen not to do a big annual musical just so the "Can you top this?" mentality doesn't develop. He is an individual who is quite secure in himself and doesn't have to have the praise and accolades to feel okay about himself. That's not true for all church musicians.

Generally, the church music program is designed around the use of volunteers. This puts the director in a precarious position. Think of trying to run an effective counseling program if you never knew whether your cotherapists, secretaries, testing psychologists, social workers, or clients would show up for work or not. That's about the way it is for the average minister of music. Yet the scheduled performance, whether Sunday morning's service or the Christmas cantata, is scheduled and will go on, ready or not. The more perfectionistic or insecure or entertainment oriented the church musician is, the more threatening the volunteer system becomes.

Financial Insecurity

Music ministers and assistant football coaches have a lot in common. Their position depends on the success or failure of the boss. In many church systems the pastor determines the other members of the staff. If Pastor Smith gets depressed or commits adultery or absconds with the building fund, the minister of music may be suddenly unemployed. He or she may be asked to serve while a new pastor is found, but then will likely be asked to leave. Finding another position is often difficult.

There is not much hope for employment outside of the church. Most ministers of music have training in "church music" and aren't qualified even to apply their skills through schools. At age forty or fifty they may face the need to find nonmusical employment for which they have no training. Try advertising: "Position wanted: choir director and soloist with twenty-seven years experience in graded music program, fifty-plus performances yearly." Theiss Jones, a music minister in Texas, told me of a former music minister who was unemployed for almost two years after a pastoral change forced his resignation.

Even when the church job continues, the pay may not be enough to adequately support a family. That can be said of many ministry positions, however, so at least the minister of music has the understanding of colleagues. They may not come to his defense at church budget time though—for fear of jeopardizing their own salaries.

Survival as a church musician really depends on having a firm conviction that one is singing a new song unto the Lord who hears and responds with love. Any other expectation will only lead to insecurity and despair.

79

EVANGELIST

The first image that comes to my mind when I think of an evangelist is a sawdust-strewn tent meeting on a sultry summer night. There, in white shoes and a loud tie and waving a red Bible in the heavy air, is an Elmer Gantry. Pounding the pulpit and shouting a fire and brimstone sermon, he coerces his hearers into repentance and donations.

The second image is Billy Graham speaking year after year to crusades the world over, packed with thousands of seekers. Gazing with his penetrating eyes and punctuating his simple message with, "the Bible says," he shares the good news of Jesus Christ.

But not all evangelists are Elmer Gantrys or Billy Grahams. Who are these unusual ministers and what problems do they face on the sawdust trail or in the shadowy background of the T.V. lights?

Evangelists tend to be high-energy extroverts. Whether their gregariousness is a defense against insecurity or an expression of confidence, it gives them the appearance of being all-sufficient. They often feel pressure to live up to that image. Consequently, facing problems can be difficult, and denial of need maintained tenaciously. Furthermore, the tendency toward isolation and independence is enforced by their ministry demands. Their travel makes it hard for them to sustain close supportive relationships, so it's easy for them to hide behind the superman facade and remain a loner.

The evangelist is frequently forced into counseling by his family or board of directors. The most difficult task is overcoming his defensiveness or outright hostility about having to subject himself to a counselor. The event that precipitates the crisis is usually directly related to the ministry and personality of the evangelist.

There are four distinct problems I commonly hear from evangelists: 1. lack of intimate marriage and family life; 2. living under constant pressure to perform miracles; 3. bearing the personal burdens of host pastors; 4. facing frequent sexual temptations. A fifth factor may complicate each of the other four: the absence of accountability to a supportive community.

Lack of Intimacy

Marriage and family problems are the most common precipitating crisis that brings the evangelist to counseling. Like many career-oriented men, the evangelist may invest himself wholeheartedly in his vocation, letting his wife raise the children. He either maintains distance entirely or falls into the Santa Claus routine of being the gift-bearing visitor who pops in and out of the home. Neither pattern contributes positively to the family structure.

Levinson's study of the adult male life cycle would indicate this orientation is common among young adult men. Their primary ego need is to establish themselves in their work world. The need for intimacy is set aside until midlife, when more urgent tasks are settled one way or another.[3] The young evangelist may feel hostile if he has to take time away from his crusades to deal with the emotional demands of wife or family. Taking time to understand the stages of adult development and to have instruction in parenting and marriage skills can reduce this hostility.

Bill is a dynamic, aggressive man who just turned forty. He looks back now on his early evangelistic ministry with some humor. "I was Larry Lightning. I thought the louder I screamed, the more souls I'd save. I didn't know what to do at home. The screaming didn't seem to work so well there. I finally just avoided Ann and the kids completely. I was having too good a time blowing and going to face the negative input from them. I'm amazed they stayed with me."

Someone finally began to teach Bill about being a husband and father. Then he wasn't as threatened by feelings of inadequacy at home. His maturity also helped him stop screaming and start listening. The hostility dissolved as well. He and Ann are experiencing real intimacy and "Larry Lightning" is long gone.

The Miracle Worker

Evangelists are gifted speakers who are sought for their ability to motivate people to commitment. In many churches the spring and fall "revivals" are firmly set as the semiannual spiritual fix. Those few nights of preaching are expected to win the lost, add members to the church, increase the tithing, solve relational conflicts, recruit the Sunday school teachers, get the adolescents off drugs and sex, slide back the back sliders, eliminate apathy, and cure cancer.

Week after week these ministers face the unrealistic expectations that somehow the Lord is going to do through them what the church has been unwilling to do the rest of the year. If the miracle happens, the emotional high for the evangelist is unparalleled. If it doesn't, the despair is devastating. The pressure to perform, to stay on the high, is keenly felt. When the "failures" come, serious questions about God's empowering or existence invade. Whatever the facts are about the unrealistic expectations, the involvement of the people, or the leadership of the Spirit, the evangelist usually gets the credit or the blame. His life is lived on an emotional and spiritual roller-coaster.

What's worse is that his financial well-being depends on his "success" as a miracle worker. If he's not riding high, his invitations to speak begin to decline and the pressure to produce mounts up with wings as eagles.

Pastor Pastorum

Since beginning our counseling for clergy, we've become aware that evangelists are the most trusted confessors to many clergy. Here is a "safe" person. He has no power over the clergyperson he serves. He has no close ties with the denominational offices. He is spiritually committed. He understands the problems in the local church. And, most important, he'll be gone in a week!

Although many evangelists see this as an important (though unexpected) part of their ministry, they often feel it is a heavy burden. The sense of desperation that many clergy carry is dumped onto this safe listener. Staggering under that load can be overwhelming when the evangelist has no one to share the pain with and no easy answers.

As his counselor you can relieve much of his burden by sharing the hurts, giving an alternative source of help for those who are dumping on the evangelist, and, at times, helping him develop his counseling skills. Since he will continue to be the first (or only) person the pastors will open up with, he needs to be able to cope effectively with this unnatural aspect of his ministry.

Sexual Object

One of the serious vocational hazards of evangelism is the sexual temptations involved. His personality is powerful and winsome, his communication skills are persuasive, his dress and appearance are attractive, and the environment of emotional responsiveness in his meetings are conducive to openness and trust. There are many women who find this combination of factors irresistible. Impressionable adolescents discovering their sexuality are swept off their slightly unsteady feet. Hysteroid women who repeatedly seek meaning and identity genitally are neurotically motivated toward this powerful male figure. Lonely wives who are craving intimacy and romantic excitement allow their fantasies to overcome reality as they strive to fill a void in their lives.

Mix these available women with the loneliness, pressures, and testosterone levels of the evangelist and you have an explosive mixture. Titrate into the chemistry the freedom from restraints of a motel room and the reaction heats up. The final ingredient is a strangely ironic one. The super spirituality of the setting somehow gives a pseudo-righteous rationalization for the sexual encounter. "God must have brought us into each other's arms. How can we resist?"

Without the usual restraints of wife, family, and friends, the evangelist is free to abandon his inner moral values. His unresolved sexual conflicts may be expressed in promiscuity, homosexual encounters, pursuit of pornographic stimulation, or any of the perversions.

Unaccountable Agent

For most Christians, clergy and laity alike, being a part of a fellowship of believers is critical to spiritual health and growth. Within the fellowship of a church community are support, teaching, and at times confrontation. The evangelist has to work to establish and maintain this for himself outside the usual church context, and it's far easier for him to simply "go it alone."

The relational elements that contribute the most to closeness and growth are time investment and self-disclosure. For a powerful, broadly involved individual, both of these are difficult. The time necessary to establish a trusting relationship not only must be of adequate duration but also of sufficient frequency. Getting together for an hour or two every three weeks won't do it. Those requirements are tough for someone who travels three weeks each month. Self-disclosure may be even harder for a person who is seen by himself and others as a self-sufficient miracle worker. What a threat to the image to become vulnerable by letting someone else hear your doubts or fears. Without such a group to hold him to accountability the evangelist is susceptible to self-deception. Thus his awareness of dangers is blunted into oblivion and his growing tension denied. All other problems intensify in their destructive potential.

A Professional Postscript

Two important considerations relate to the common personality and behavioral characteristics of an evangelist. One is the degree of sociopathy that may be present. The evangelist and/or his board of directors may need to be confronted by dysocial patterns. The second is the possibility of manic-depressive illness. I have been consulted on a number of cases with high-energy, aggressive evangelists who turned out to have rather classic bipolar affective disorder and responded well to Lithium treatment. Sometimes it's necessary to educate several people involved in the situation to the biological substrate of this disease.

Parachurch Minister

There is a growing army of ministers who work outside of the boundaries of "the church." These include such ministries as Fellowship of Christian Athletes, InterVarsity, Campus Crusade, Young Life, Prison Fellowship International, Youth for Christ, Christian Women's Clubs, and hundreds of relief organizations and foreign mission societies. Although these various organizations each have definite distinctions, they share some common features that affect their people. I want to discuss three—the pressure of fund raising, the lack of emotional support, and the high turnover rate.

Fund Raising

Most Christian workers in parachurch ministry must raise their support. Some have no problem with that. Others have constant discomfort with having to ask for support and with the uncertainty as to whether or not the money will continue in adequate amounts. Needless to say, there is tremendous competition for support dollars among Christian ministries and charitable groups. That means each person has to present his or her ministry in a convincing, compelling way. Then the task is to keep the supporters by maintaining contact and giving feedback regarding the effectiveness of the work.

Some organizations provide administrative help in this process, mailing out donation receipts, short reports, and envelopes for future gifts. They will collect, disburse, and do accounting as well. In some ministries the worker is responsible for all of these functions. One way or another, the minister must "sell" him or herself to attract continued giving.

A significant pressure in the past several years has been the difficulty of increasing the support to meet rising costs of ministry. Most of these ministers spend considerable energy each year raising the required monthly support only to find their funds woefully inadequate within a year's time. For the individual who finds it hard to ask for money anyway, that creates lots of anxiety.

Loneliness

The parachurch minister is usually a lone ranger in the work. The contact with his organization is minimal. There may be meetings or conferences every one to six months, but the day-to-day stress is faced alone. I was recently at a regional staff conference for one group. The main concern I heard was this feeling of isolation and the toll it was taking on their lives. As job demands increased they had no one to go to for advice or sympathy. Because they are ministers, they don't feel free to share their tensions in a local church. The nearest colleagues or supervisors are hundreds of miles away, and their next retreat is six months down the road.

Lone rangers don't always have a faithful Indian companion, Tonto. The parachurch minister suffers not only from physical isolation, but also from the loneliness of facing overwhelming odds. The story is told of a serious disturbance in a small Texas town. The mayor sent a cry for help to the Texas Rangers. The tensions erupted into riot proportions and the mayor desperately watched for the help to come. At the height of the shooting, the train arrived and a single Texas Ranger stepped off the coach. The mayor stared in disappointment and disbelief. "Did they only send one Ranger?" he stammered. The tall Texan drawled, "Well, there's only one riot!" At times the parachurch minister wishes there were only one riot to be handled. Many find themselves unable to continue to cope with the onslaught of human needs they face. No one else seems to care.

High Turnover of Personnel

Contributing to the feeling of loneliness and isolation is the rapid turnover rate in many parachurch groups. I was talking to one of the staffers at the conference I mentioned. I have known him for eleven years and have talked with him at several of their staff conferences. He was telling me that he was the only person still on staff from a group I had met five years before. That seems to be true for many of the parachurch groups.

It's not surprising from the pressures involved in the work that many look for other ways to minister. That serves to further increase the pressure. Losing colleagues when the support is minimal already creates grief and uncertainty.

This phenomenon is even being seen in foreign mission associations. Traditionally, foreign missionaries were life volunteers returning to their assigned field term after term for thirty to forty years. Now individuals train for their ministry, go to language school, begin their work and last two terms. I don't know if this is indicative of more pressure on the missionary (which is true financially and politically) or of less commitment to a life-time work. Whichever is true, the older missionaries feel resentment toward the new appointees who don't seem willing to stick it out.

At times the high turnover creates confusion and disruption in the ministry. One person builds the ministry, making friends in the community, becoming familiar with the group being served, and organizing programs to meet the needs. When that person leaves the progress may be completely lost and the replacement may have to start from scratch. No foundational structure sustains the work, as in the local church.

Speaking of the local church, let me close with a story not unfamiliar to those in parachurch ministry. Wayne is an enthusiastic young man who was just beginning his ministry in a youth-oriented group. He moved to a small town to work with the high-school kids. He thought he should start by introducing himself to the local pastors. He was confident that they would warmly receive him and encourage his work. He already knew the youngsters in the town were not being effectively reached. To his surprise, he kept hearing excuses from the pastors why they couldn't see him. From a couple he received rude rejection and others cold indifference. He finally cornered the pastor of the church he and his wife had decided to attend and told him of the lack of spiritual and emotional support from the pastors in town. He wondered if he had offended anyone. The pastor finally admitted that they were all worried that he would succeed and, in doing so, would take away the few young people in their churches. They saw him as competition rather than a complement to their ministries.

Often the church adds to the pressure of those in parachurch organizations because of the perception that they are out to attract people away from the church rather than to the Lord.

As you can see there are common pressures among Christian workers, but many significant differences that need to be understood. Take the time to investigate the specific stresses of the individual coming to you. I'm sure you can see that serving as a Christian minister is not a summer Sunday's stroll down a flower-strewn path. It's often an uphill climb through a briar patch.

CHAPTER THREE

RESISTANCE TO COUNSELING

I'M PRETTY KLUTSY as an auto mechanic. No, that's not true, I'm supremely klutsy as an auto mechanic. When there's a noise under the hood I shudder, knowing that what looks like a simple task is really a clock-eating, knuckle-busting gremlin waiting to ambush me. This morning our son Brent started off to basketball practice in his VW Rabbit. A few minutes later, he was back stomping off the snow and his frustration. The fan belt had come off. So I got the snow plow out and went down the hill to tow him back to our garage. Now you'll probably say to yourself, *That's no problem. Putting on a fan belt is easy.* Ah-ha! You forgot about the gremlin. We got the alternator loosened and the belt back on. Simple. No problem. But trying to get the belt tightened up and the alternator bolted back in place was as difficult as I had feared.

First, we couldn't get to the bolts. Then one of the nuts became stripped. So we had to find a bolt that would fit, etc., etc. Meanwhile I was late and later for a scheduled task. At least this time I wasn't alone; I let Brent get the busted knuckles.

You get the picture. Maybe you even have a similar area in your life where fierce gremlins wait to waste you. I've found that there are some of those hidden gremlins in counseling Christian workers. In fact, one thing that first awakened my interest in working with clergy was their resistance to getting help. Since then we've identified several factors that block a successful counseling experience. They can all be knuckle busters! Sensitivity to these special resistances can assist you and the client in working through to a positive outcome.

If Brent and I had had the right tools and equipment we could have outsmarted the gremlin. Here's your anti-gremlin kit.

BELIEF IN THE INFALLIBILITY OF MINISTERS

When I first began to investigate the needs of clergy for psychological help, I was surprised at two discoveries. The first was how widespread the needs were. The second was hard to understand in light of the first. There was a prevalent sentiment that ministers should never need to have counseling from a therapist—Christian or not.

Part of the reason for this attitude is that the laity would like to keep its leaders safely enshrined on a pedestal. This is basically a neurotic transference problem. The child within is still hoping for a perfect parent, and the minister is a likely object for the fantasy. Part of the fantasy is that this daddy or mommy is perfect. This will be the parent who will meet all the infantile needs. Such a parent can't have problems or trouble coping with life.

On the minister's part, the pedestal can look enticing. It's nice to be adored. As a counselor you know how tempting the trap can be. "Oh, doctor, you're the only person who can help me. You're just wonderful." Such words sound sweet to the ego. So the minister accepts the worship, climbs up on the pedestal, and tries to live up there. It soon becomes obvious that he doesn't deserve a throne, but it is hard to admit that and descend to the ranks of mortal man.

That can be especially hard if the system resists granting humanity to the minister. We've had several ministers who have met with significant resistance from their church when they indicated a desire to go for counseling. Many others come without telling anyone because they know the prevalent attitude in the congregation or the denomination.

Several years ago I was invited to speak at chapel in a large seminary. I talked about the pressure of ministry, the pain and loneliness, and encouraged the seminarians to seek help when necessary rather than trying to cope alone. Some of those men and women already knew the truth of what I was saying. They felt the tension in their marriages. They had found themselves in conflict with church layleaders. They realized their need for someone to understand and comfort them. They applauded as I sat down. Then the seminary president strode to the microphone for the benediction. Without a word to me he prayed a simple prayer: "Dear God, we're grateful we have the power of Thy Spirit within us and need nothing more. Amen." He made his point.

The belief in the infallibility of the minister is sometimes based on a Christian worker's theological position regarding sanctification. One interpretation of this doctrine is that believers are "being" sanctified or perfected. This view sees sanctification as a process that is begun when one becomes a Christian and continues throughout one's life in Jesus. Another interpretation is that once we are indwelled by God's Spirit at conversion or in the baptism of the Holy Spirit we are instantly sanctified. We are perfect, complete, holy, and can no longer sin. According to this viewpoint, anyone in ministry is definitely sanctified and infallible. There are no problems in his life. Of course it becomes difficult to appropriate enough denial to maintain that position.

Joseph was having that inner struggle when he came to Marble Retreat. He was in his late twenties and had been out of Bible college six years. He was pastoring a small church from the holiness tradition. He believed he was supposed to be sanctified, but knew he wasn't perfect. His problems plagued him daily. As he began to question his theology he realized he had been fighting feelings of anger and confusion for years in response to his father who claimed to be sanctified. The truth was that his dad was a very rigid, self-centered man who was hard to live with. Joseph finally decided if that was what being sinless was like, he didn't want it.

In admitting his own humanity he was able to begin to work on several conflicts in his life including his unresolved hostile dependent relationship with his dad.

Occasionally, you'll find it helpful to discuss the theology of sanctification with your client. Such discussion is not meant to attack someone's beliefs, but it may help break down some resistance to openness and promote growth.

FEAR OF EXPOSURE AS A FAILURE

Bill had a recurring dream. In the dream, he is on the platform of the church where he is on the pastoral staff. The place is packed with people and he has the feeling it is for a special service of some kind. The choir is just finishing a majestic anthem. His fellow pastors are on the platform with him and turn to him to lead the next part of the worship. The sounds of the organ and choir die away and there is quiet in the sanctuary. All eyes are on him. He stands and begins to address the congregation, then suddenly realizes he's naked. He is overcome by shame and runs from the auditorium.

This is not an uncommon type of dream, being totally exposed for everyone to see. I've had that kind of dream and hear them frequently. In exploring the dream there is usually the association of being found out—exposed as a fake or failure. For Christian workers, the fear of exposure touches on two levels: failure as a representative of God and failure as a person.

Most Christian workers have a deep sense of calling to ministry and a commitment to serve God faithfully. Trying to live up to that high calling creates an impossible situation. One pastor said it was like trying to keep a dozen Ping-Pong balls submerged in a bath tub. Just when you think you've got them all under water, a couple pop up to the top. Although most ministers don't realize it, it's a no-win situation. They continue to try harder. They think to fail at their "high calling" will bring dishonor to God. Accepting the expectation of being able to walk on water, they feel that the whole community is basing its faith on their ability to do it. That's a heavy responsibility. You'd be surprised how many ministers try to operate from that position.

Bill, the minister with the exposure dream, fit that picture. He was the oldest of three children in a church-going family. He was an obedient, highly successful achiever. His mandate from his parents and his church was to be a perfect example as a Christian. He was. He was an honor student in high school and college. He was popular and won many honors. He was friendly and caring for everyone, often going out of his way to quietly do a favor for someone in need. He was a sparkling, lovely witness for Christ.

He did so at growing emotional cost. He knew that inside he wasn't perfect. He was morally pure, but had normal aggressive and sexual impulses which were totally forbidden to himself. So he lived with the burden of knowing his inner imperfection but hearing over and over again that the Lord was depending on him as an example of Christianity. To fail was not just being exposed for what (he thought) he really was. It was to show the world that Christianity was false. It didn't work if he couldn't be perfect.

There is another expectation that enters into the picture. When a person answers a call to serve God, it seems only right that God should give some sort of special favor. This hope is often held inside on an emotional level even when a minister intellectually and theologically rejects it. This fantasy is hard to let go of because it fits so well with our reward system of behavioral training. If you are good, you'll get a cookie.

What happens if there are no cookies? There seem to be two options: either there is no Cookie Giver or you haven't been good enough. The first option is hard for a Christian to take, especially for one who has invested years of time in preparation and service. Saying God doesn't give rewards to the faithful is difficult. Choosing the second is more comfortable, even though it means more work and more denial. Admitting that things aren't okay and that it is hard to cope threatens the denial system and creates anxiety. Going to a counselor and admitting the problems raises questions about God's love. The minister needs to be able to express those doubts without fear of criticism.

On a personal level, getting counseling may seem like being exposed as a worthless person. There is a lot of nervous joking in our groups about being at the "funny farm" or "loony bin." A few come right out and confess that they've been really reluctant to see a psychiatrist because they thought only "really sick" people need a head-shrinker.

I always ask our clients how they felt about coming for counseling. Although the attitudes have changed some over the last ten years, there is still a lot of anxiety about being inadequate to cope and having to seek help. One of the positive effects of using group therapy is that individuals are able to see that these other people in pain are not terrible failures or "crazy." The jokes go on as a working through of that anxiety. On my desk I have a cartoon sent to me by a pastor. A smiling person is saying, "I don't think I've gone crazy, but if I have, it isn't as bad as I thought it would be."

Like it or not, for many people seeing a pyschologist, psychiatrist, or any mental health counselor (including a pastor) still makes them feel as if they're being exposed as a "really sick" person.

Finally, seeking counseling reveals that a person isn't self-sufficient. Facing the truth of one's dependency can be very threatening. People in helping professions seem to have invested a lot in being the helper rather than having needs. I know because I am one.

As I write this I'm having a flood of association about dependency: the fear of dependency for those whose needs were ignored in childhood, the "big boys don't cry" message for the developing male, the encouragement to be able to "do it yourself," the great American ideal of fierce individualism, the risk of hurt in becoming emotionally close and vulnerable. There seems to be a preponderance of signals in our world that teach us to deny dependency.

Scott Peck, in *The Road Less Traveled,* identifies dependency as immature if it remains the predominant position a person occupies. He differentiates "dependency" from "dependency feelings" or needs that are a healthy part of an adult being.[1] Arriving at a safe balance between dependence and autonomy is critical for maturity—and especially for intimacy.

For many ministers, particularly men, exposing their dependency feels scary. In *Intimate Strangers,* Lillian Rubin discusses the emotional issues and conflicts that form the foundation for that fear. Because a boy must differentiate from his mother more than a girl does, he resists closeness and dependency on her. Yet the emotional need for closeness remains. Men often have a hard time allowing themselves to develop intimacy because of this earlier need to separate from mother. Women do not have that same problem and are usually more emotionally open in relationships.

The counseling relationship repeats the early feelings of helplessness and vulnerability. It's important that these be discussed as part of the work. The Christian worker must be able to admit weakness and inadequacy without feeling exposed as a failure or allowed to become totally passive and dependent.

Walter is a minister from the Southwest, a ruggedly handsome pastor who looks like he stepped out of a Marlboro commercial instead of the pulpit. He is an exprofessional athlete and has been doggedly independent. He came to Marble Retreat because of growing loneliness and depression. They were distinctly related. He consciously held himself apart from others, even his wife, but was aware of more and more sadness in his life. He had considered suicide recently and that really frightened him.

It seemed to Walt that he should be able to just start getting close to people. He tried to become more intimate with his wife. Nothing seemed to work. He was not only awkward in making friends, but also felt afraid when conversations left superficial subjects or highly intellectual discussions. He was mystified about what was happening to him.

As we explored Walt's childhood, we began to see the roots of his anxiety. He had been a weak, sickly boy with overprotective parents. At every turn he was encouraged to be careful and not push himself. That relationship became smothering and intolerable to him as he entered puberty. With a phenomenal growth spurt and some athletic successes, he decided to break away. He cut the apron strings and sought to be his own man.

He succeeded tremendously in every aspect but one. In becoming independent he had to deny any needs or hurts or he was "babied" back into dependency. His only option was to show no vulnerability. He had many admirers and acquaintances, but no one was allowed to get close. Closeness continued to hold the danger of his feeling like a helpless child again. That's why he became anxious when a relationship moved toward emotional self-disclosure. He was surprised to find that he could express his dependency needs without losing his manhood. He is still learning the skills of openness and still fights with the anxiety at times, but his successes have served to give him hope and relieve the depression. For the first time, his wife feels she has a husband.

On the opposite extreme was Dan. He was not smothered by overprotective parents, but abandoned. His parents were alcoholic and were unavailable to him and his sister. He learned very early in life that he had to take care of himself and his little sister. No one else was going to do it.

Growing up in the city, he became street-wise before he was in school. As an adolescent, he fought in gangs, stole to support himself, was arrested several times, tried drugs, alcohol, and sex, and dropped out of school.

His life was changed by a church youth minister who reached out to him. He gave his life to the Lord and everything turned around. He got his G.E.D., then finished college and seminary. He met a nice Christian girl in school and his life was wonderful except for his isolation.

He felt distant from his wife and children. He knew that

deep inside he had a longing to be held and loved, yet he managed to hold everyone at arm's length. He soon began to understand that being dependent had been so painful to him as a child that he had unconsciously determined not to need anybody. He wept as he began to relive the pain of those early years of his parents' drunken oblivion. He began to see that everyone else wouldn't respond like they had. He could risk saying "I need you."

I mentioned earlier that I, a "helper," could identify with the need to be self-sufficient. That need gets expressed in my life in countless ways—from the serious to the frivolous. In 1977 I had a slowly developing flu-like sickness which I kept ignoring. My symptoms finally became so severe, especially the headache, that I reluctantly asked Melissa to drive me to the doctor's office. I'm surprised I didn't try to drive myself. When I got there, they took my blood pressure: 230/180. My need to be strong and self-reliant had almost stroked me out.

You'd think I would have learned from that to be willing to admit my desire for help, but I'm still not much better. The other day I was up on a ladder getting some things out of storage. Melissa was twenty feet away in the next room. I was stacking things up for a perilous descent when I heard her soft voice below me, "Would you like some help?"

My first impulse was to say, "No, I can get it," when I realized how stupid that was. It didn't hurt a bit to hand some things down to her. She even seemed to enjoy being helpful.

FEAR OF REJECTION

It's really not surprising that Christian workers resist getting help in view of the way the church has responded to weakness in its leaders. There's too much painful truth in the saying, "the Christian army is the only one that shoots its wounded." There may be actual rejection if the church discovers that its minister had to get psychological help. The fear of rejection has some basis in reality.

I refused to believe that when I first began the Retreat. Surely, I thought, churches will be loving, supportive, and even forgiving toward a pastor who has emotional or spiritual hurts. Then the appalling truth began to dawn. I'll never forget the first instance. Kathy had been well accepted by her conference and had served effectively. She came because of depression and alcohol abuse. She began the painful road to recovery and I strongly urged her to let her church know—at least the leadership. I felt they would give her important support at a time when she needed it desperately. Unfortunately I persuaded her. Their response was devastating to her and created significant guilt in me. They called the appropriate board meetings and promptly asked for her immediate resignation. She was more forgiving toward me than they were toward her. She's still in touch and is still recovering. The rejection she has felt from her church conference has continued in spite of her good recovery and continued sobriety.

I'm glad to say I've known of times when the church acted as the body of Christ should and was totally accepting. Unfortunately the risk is still a significant one.

Even when the church is accepting, the minister may have an unfounded fear of rejection. That fear stems from basic insecurity and feelings of inadequacy. In our experience, low self-esteem is the most common problem in Christian workers. They are enslaved by chains of self-doubt and inferiority. Every time they move, the shackles rattle, reminding them that they can't expect to be freely loved. Rejection is just around the corner in every relationship. That includes the counseling experience. Whether in group or individual therapy, their inner scripts call for them to be disliked or abandoned. The most healing part of your ministry to them will be to keep them in counseling long enough to work through that negative pattern, not allowing them to sabotage the process. They must see their patterns of defense as destructive.

We're fortunate to be out at the edge of the quiet wilderness, and nature gives some vivid pictures of defense systems at work. The little creatures in the mountains have to fight for survival. It's not hard for the ministers who come to see themselves reacting to fear of rejection in those same ways.

One of my favorite assistants is a big, fat porcupine, Heathcliff, who lives just up the road. He is a frequent visitor to the Retreat. He likes the flavor of our wood decks, the pine trees out back, and the cracked corn Sandy puts out for the chipmunks. He's become pretty bold about coming around, but he still won't eat out of your hand. In fact, when approached, his old defense comes into play immediately. He turns his back and displays about a million sharp quills. Nobody wants to risk getting close. That's the way lots of ministers defend against rejection. Their words or actions say, "You're not going to get close to me. I don't want anybody to get close to me and my barbs will stick you if you try." Lots of our clients have seen themselves in old Heathcliff.

There's another interesting pattern we see particularly during hunting season. Our elk were once plains animals, but they have been driven into the mountains by the invasion of man. They have retained one strong feature of their life on the open plains. When they are startled, they run. I mean really run. The mule deer also run, but only a few yards, to the cover of the forest. Then they stop and look back curiously. Not the elk. They run for miles, as though the cover isn't there at all.

You've probably seen people like that who are easily frightened. Like the elk they take off emotionally or physically to avoid the risk of being hurt. They may not be aware of what scares them, but getting too close to their emotional pain in counseling can be one signal for them to run.

Another interesting thing about all the creatures is that if the food supply in the forest is low, as it is during the heavy snows, they'll overcome their natural fears and risk being fed by humans. Ministers in crises get pretty hungry for love. You may have them eating out of your hand if they sense acceptance and comfort.

DISTRUST OF PSYCHOLOGY

The elk of the Rocky Mountains have good reason for running at the sight or sound of humans. Usually they're carrying a 30.06 with their minds set on a big elk steak. Rarely are they bringing food. Ministers have come to see psychiatrists and psychologists in the same way. At worst, they have the impression that we are godless manipulators who are out to destroy one's faith. At best, they feel we simply don't have any answers for their problems. That general viewpoint is elaborated in Jay Adams' book *Competent to Counsel.* The arguments are certainly not without support. The problem, as I see it, is that it generalizes from the specific errors of psychiatry through the 1960s to all of psychiatry. Just as humanism overreacts to the evils and hypocrisy of religion by disavowing God, Jesus, and the Bible, many Christians throw the baby out with the bath water in the area of psychology and psychiatry. The good is discarded along with the abuses and all "non-Christian" counselors are suspect. In fact, for some, even "Christian counselors" aren't trusted.

I hear lots of horror stories about the terrible things some psychiatrist did. I try to listen objectively and nondefensively and hear the underlying fearfulness being expressed. Sometimes it's tempting to say, "Oh, wait a minute. I'm sure you're mistaken!" But that's not especially helpful. Some common stories I hear include the atheistic counselor who ridiculed the client's faith; the immoral counselor who advised unacceptable or sinful behavior; the pill pusher who never really listened, but just refilled a prescription for tranquilizers; or some "weirdo" who sat silently behind a desk, never responding at all.

I trained in a department that was not only "eclectic" in its theoretical approach to psychiatry, but was a mixed bag theologically. There were highly committed Roman Catholics heavily into mysticism, agnostics who were not active spiritually, atheists who accepted the notion of God being the creation of man's anxiety and superstitions, a number of mainline Protestants who were active in their churches, and a token Evangelical, me. In my three years there I never heard of any of these men attacking a person's faith position. In spite of their own religious belief systems, they were supportive of a person's faith. Church involvement, Bible study, prayer, and meditation were recognized as positive, healing factors. It was certainly common for an individual's beliefs to be explored regarding guilt, sin, forgiveness, love, fear, commitment, and active involvement in spiritual growth.

I think Scott Peck's viewpoints expressed in *The Road Less Traveled* are good examples of a non-Christian's interest in spirituality and encouragement toward faith. Many competent counselors would share that approach. It is interesting to know that Dr. Peck later became a Christian recognizing the truth of who Jesus is.[3]

You can allay the fears of Christian workers by stating your own faith position or by reassuring them that you're not out to destroy theirs. After all, they have a lot invested in the commitment to God's service.

Perhaps more frequent than an out-and-out attack on a Christian's beliefs are the suggestions by counselors of some action that the Christian worker sees as wrong. One pastor told me he was advised to have more sexual partners to help him feel better about his masculinity. One woman minister was enticed into bed by her "Christian counselor" because her sexual relationship with her husband wasn't good. Many are encouraged to get a divorce if they aren't "in love" anymore.

Such advice creates more problems for the minister when it leads to disobedience to God's Word. The Christian worker does not live by the world's standards of relativity and ego gratification. He or she will have to deal with real guilt in addition to whatever original conflicts there were if God's law is ignored.

Many people see psychiatrists as unsympathetic pill pushers. These individuals don't expect to be listened to, understood, or, least of all, to be given mature, sensible advice about their problems. They think a psychiatrist will just give them tranquilizers and see them briefly to refill the prescription once a month.

The papers are full of stories about abuse of prescription drugs. Lots of people are scared to death they'll become addicted to some mind-altering drug and lose control of their lives. Tranquilizers are abused. The greatest temptation in the world for a busy physician, whatever his or her specialty, is to give some medication that will relieve the patient's distress. I've heard many busy doctors say, "I knew he really needed to talk about his problems, but I always have a waiting room full of people. I can't take time to listen for an hour to someone's hurt, but I hate to see him in pain. He probably wouldn't go to a psychiatrist if I referred him. So I gave him some Valium." Unfortunately the psychiatrist may be just as busy and see the medical approach as the most promising therapy.

I can't lay all the blame on the doctors though. Some patients don't want to do the hard work of psychotherapy. In our instant society they want instant relief of the pain or conflict. They'll go from one doctor to another until they find one who'll give them a prescription for the magic pill that's going to make them feel good again. In fact, they may get three or four magic pills from three or four different doctors. That's a lot easier than looking at themselves and learning to deal with life in more effective ways. Even when spiritual help is sought, it's more likely to be some instant healing instead of commitment to growth through obedience to God.

Not all psychiatrists are seen as pill pushers though; some look worse. The stereotype of a weird, spaced out character who sits behind his tablet responding with an occasional "Um!" or "Oh?" is still with us.

I've had many clients who say, "I went to a psychiatrist for a month. It cost me $75 an hour to talk to him and he never said anything. I was desperate. My life was falling apart and he never offered any advice. He just sat there!" With experiences like that and media images of "shrinks" like Bob Newhart, it's no wonder many people distrust psychology. Trusting your secrets to anybody is hard, much less to someone who is feared or the object of ridicule.

For a Christian worker this may be even harder because of the way confidentiality has been treated in the church. There seems to be an attitude that any problem in the church family should be openly shared. I know the Bible teaches confession to each other and sharing one another's burdens, but I don't think those Scriptures were meant to give license for unauthorized telling of another person's secrets. All too often, something told in confidence to someone at church becomes a hot item of gossip. Christian workers are more conditioned by that than by the positive experience of having confidentiality maintained by professional counselors. In its effort to be a loving family, the church has been building mistrust and distance—especially for the minister.

In the first session of each new group at Marble Retreat I talk about the anxiety people feel regarding confidentiality. I then tell them that we are pledged to protect their confidentiality and anonymity and ask them to make that pledge to each other. In my individual conferences I reiterate that position and also invite each person to talk about any fears or concerns regarding secrets. Their fear often has to do with whether or not I'm going to send some report to their local church or denominational office. Sometimes that is necessary because of the circumstances. If so, we discuss that issue fully and before the two weeks are up I tell the minister exactly what I'll be saying. Being open and up front about the whole issue is critical.

If the "church" is paying the bill and wants a report, but the minister feels otherwise, some serious negotiation is needed. If you want to be helpful to the Christian worker in dealing with some crisis, you may have to pledge confidentiality. If your loyalty is more to the church office that "sent" the minister, you must make that clear and perhaps sacrifice part of the trust and openness in the relationship. At times, you can negotiate with the denomination to make a recommendation about competence for ministry or need for therapy without divulging confidential material. In my experience the recommendation of competency is really what is wanted. The details I based it on are not.

Finally, it's helpful to keep in focus the person coming to see you. The minister who steps into your office is in a terrible trust crisis. Here is an individual who believes in God and has been teaching others to share that belief. Now for whatever reasons there are serious conflicts and distress. God seems suddenly absent. Prayers are bouncing off the ceiling or have stopped altogether. What used to feel like unshakable assurance of help and strength has turned to Jell-O. If he can't trust God, how can he trust some counselor?

Dealings with this vulnerability is as vital as it is delicate. The minister wants reassurance from a person of faith, but doesn't need platitudes or sermons about "simply trusting in the Lord." Ministers know what the Bible teaches. They have probably given hundreds of people the principles of confession, repentance, forgiveness, and obedience. What's more, they've probably genuinely tried to apply them in their own conflict. It's not unusual for them to have talked with some Christian friend before they come to a counselor. They may be overwhelmed with guilt for having failed to find victory in the situation. It's amazing that they have summoned up enough courage to risk seeing you at all. You can imagine something of the desperation they must be feeling to be in your office. That person's painful submission to a fearful situation deserves all the gentle love you can give. See her or him through the eyes of Jesus and touch them with His Spirit.

LACK OF FUNDS FOR THERAPY

A very practical barrier to successful counseling with Christian workers is their lack of funds. You'll want to keep this in mind and explore payment alternatives with them. There are many options, of course, including payment by their local church and their denomination. More and more funds are being made available by the church for counseling ministers. Most denominations now have some sort of regional or national office that makes help possible for its clergy. The minister you see may not be aware of that help or may not want to admit that counseling is necessary. Most of these offices are separate from the rest of the denomination's system and confidentiality is maintained (see Appendix 2).

Dr. James Cooper's ministry is typical. Dr. Cooper's "Ministers' Counseling" office is funded by the Baptist General Convention of Texas. It is in Dallas, but across town from the convention headquarters. His records are completely confidential and he does not have to report the name of those seeking his services. At times he personally counsels a minister. Sometimes he refers them to someone on his statewide list of counselors. If financial help is needed, his office can at times provide some money or help interpret denominational group insurance policies. That sort of assistance is common, but frequently unknown to the minister.

If the minister can risk letting some of the lay leaders in the local congregation know of the need, money is often readily available. There are many generous, loving church laypeople who are eager to provide whatever help the minister needs.

About two-thirds of our clients have denominational group health insurance policies with some coverage for counseling. The minister may not even think about that possibility.

Overcoming the financial barrier may mean overcoming the Christian worker's barriers to spending money for "selfish needs." This may be the most difficult road block of all. We currently have a missionary couple in therapy. Their total life orientation is to give up self. They frequently do without necessities in order to give to someone in need. In fact, one of the sources of conflict in their marriage is his generosity to the local people who are always at their gate begging for help. Those needs seem so critical and so outweigh their own that allowing mission support money to be spent for them to get counseling is creating a heavy sense of guilt. Ministers may make a quick "flight into health" to avoid that guilt. It is important for you to convince them that they are worth it and that this is a critical investment in their future effectiveness as a minister. That's the truth!

Attitudes about having to pay for counseling may become a problem. Ministers do their counseling without receiving a specific fee and can sometimes resent being charged. Furthermore, lots of people resent having to pay for therapy for any illness. They didn't choose (consciously) to be "sick," haven't gotten much pleasure from it, and don't like the idea of having to pay for it. They feel that they've had to pay already. It's a whole lot like paying taxes. As a counselor, you're probably well aware that those attitudes exist in the general population, and Christian workers can have them too.

Some counselors feel clients will not value their services unless some payment is made. But some pastoral counselors generally do not charge a fee. I'm not convinced one way or the other. I've had lots of ministers who deeply appreciated our counsel and who made significant changes as a result, but didn't pay a dime. I'm comfortable for that to happen and we frequently provide our services at no cost to the client. I'm sure there have been times when the financial barrier could not have been overcome otherwise. We have one minister who is paying us five dollars a month (for twenty years). There are many options.

COUNSELING THE "COUNSELOR"

He would plop himself into my office chair, prop his feet up, and sit puffed up like a toad daring me to help him. What could I have to offer? He was a pastor whose "giftedness" and interest lay in counseling. He had a graduate degree and CPE under his belt. He had as much experience as I and made sure I knew it. It was hard to get below the surface of his highly intellectualized jargon-studded discussions of his "complexes." I found myself feeling more and more exasperated, wondering why he came for help. Every time I tried to break through his wall of psychologizing he would agree that he was using the denial and intellectualization as a resistance. In group therapy he maintained the pose of therapist, graciously making interpretations for the rest of the group. The group began to challenge his professional facade. I finally asked "Sigmund" if he was as lonely as he seemed. That seemed to be the key to unlocking his inner hurt. Slowly but surely the mask came down.

"Sigmund" is not uncommon. Many ministers have training in counseling and enter therapy with their fists up, ready for a fight. They may sit smugly across your desk shadow boxing with you or may interrupt your line of thought with their constant jabs and counter punches. "Oh, I know what you're getting at. I've been all through that. There's nothing in my relationship with my dad that has anything to do with where I am now." Often the comments are heavy with hostility and feel like a left hook coming out of nowhere, "You're not going to get me to react with that ploy!"

I find this brand of resistance to be most difficult. I also know how hard it is for a "counselor" to step out of that role, become the counselee, and not analyze everything that is going on from his psychological perspective. As a physician

I find being a patient a stiff challenge. I find myself evaluating all the data and the way the doctor is going about collecting them. It's hard not to try to guess what he's thinking and maybe harder not to let him know that I've already got the diagnosis. Given half a chance, I'll also advise him on the best treatment. So it is with the pastoral counselor trying to be just a hurting human being.

In addition to the problem of filtering everything through a screen of psychological expertise, the minister who is a counselor has his self-esteem tied up in that identity. That makes it twice as hard for him to accept the dependent position. I have found several factors important in working around that barrier.

First, I try to affirm the minister in his role as counselor. Remember he has a lot invested in that identity and has experience that can be helpful in forming a therapeutic alliance. I am genuinely interested in knowing about his professional life, asking what he enjoys most and has the most trouble dealing with. I may share some of my own areas of fear or weakness. I definitely let him know that I respect him for what he does. I have found that enlists him as a partner rather than setting myself up as a competitor who is out to put him down and prove my superiority.

I particularly remember a couple of ministers who fit this picture. One was a hospital chaplain who was a CPE supervisor and had been counseling as long as I. The other was a full-time counselor in a church. He was a former pastor who had a Ph.D. in counseling psychology and also had years of experience. Both came because of depression and were bewildered that they had not made any progress trying to overcome it. We talked first about their long and rich experience, the rigors of training, the joys of successes, and the deep hurt of the failures. I shared some of my own pilgrimage as a psychiatrist. In developing that sense of equality they were able to relate to me as a fellow struggler. That brought down the professionalism and we were able to explore their life histories in an open way. Coincidentally, both had conflictive relationships with their fathers. Neither had really had their dad's blessing and had denied that deep hurt. Their dads had died within the preceding two years, but neither man had grieved. They knew about grief work, but the pain of rejection had kept them from going through it. I was someone available whose respect would not be lost if they showed their tears.

Second, I avoid psychological jargon. I do this with all of my clients, but am particularly careful with counselors. The temptation is great for them to relate intellectually, and discussing theory keeps the relationship away from the inner struggles. If the ministers begin to talk in jargon, I will interrupt, "I'm not sure I understand what you mean by that, and I want to really get to know you. Try to tell me about yourself without expressing it in those terms." I find that people are more comfortable speaking English instead of professional jargon.

Third, in our group work I try to keep ministers from falling into a cotherapist role. I do this by focusing them on their own feelings rather than challenging their role or their interpretations. For instance, we had a woman in a recent group who did counseling in her ministry. She was good, sensitive, and insightful. Her questioning or interpretation was generally helpful to the other group members and I didn't want to lose that. I found, however, that she avoided dealing with her own pain. After she had made some comment to another person I began to ask, "Jane, that's a good point. How does it relate to you?" She slowly integrated herself into the group process, away from the counselor role, and into a peer position. We still benefited from her expertise, and she benefited more from the congeniality.

Finally, in our form of therapy which includes individual and group work, some counselors will attempt to limit their self-disclosure to the individual sessions exclusively. It's tempting to accept this as a compliment to my "superior ability" to deal with the problems, but this is destructive of the group process. I will ask about that pattern in our private time and encourage the person to be a part of the group. This helps to break down the professional barrier. At the same time, I use self-disclosure as a model in the group, thereby giving permission and encouragement to the others.

DEALING WITH FEELINGS

Tom is a minister in his midforties who came to therapy because of marital tension and trouble in his church. On both fronts he was being accused of insensitivity. Church leaders were saying he railroaded his own programs through them without hearing their ideas. His wife said she felt ignored. He never heard her or even cared to listen.

When Tom came to the Retreat he was understandably defensive. His perception was quite different: "I don't understand how they can say that. I've been working myself to death in that church. If I don't carry the ball nothing happens. I've tried letting other people be in charge of programs, but they never come through. The ideas they come up with would never work. I end up having to step in and rescue the situation every time. I remember when I first came, the finance committee wanted to get the budget pledged. I said, 'Okay, draw up a proposal and submit it to me. That'll be great.' You should have seen the disaster they called a plan. I told them how totally inadequate it was and had to start over from scratch. I wasted two weeks in the meantime waiting for them to come up with something. That's been typical. Now nobody even volunteers. I have to do it all.

"As far as my wife is concerned she's probably right about my ignoring her. She never makes any sense. Let me give you a typical example. Last year on our anniversary I had two very important meetings. One was with the building committee in our church and one was the executive committee of the conference. I had to leave early in the morning to drive to the executive meeting in another town so the night before I slept in the guest room, got up quietly and left without disturbing Alice. I left a note in the bathroom saying, 'Happy Anniversary.' I thought it was very considerate to let her sleep.

"That meeting lasted longer than I expected so I had to go directly to the building committee meeting at the church. I called Alice to tell her I wouldn't be home till after the meeting, but invited her to go out to dinner after I was finished. Well, that meeting went on and on. There were lots of important details to be worked out on our 1.5 million-dollar family life center. We didn't get through till midnight. By the time I got home it was 12:30 and I was beat.

"Then what did I find waiting for me? Alice in tears. You'd think she could be understanding for once, but no. She started in on me about how I didn't love her and how insensitive I was and how neglected she felt. Neglected! Can you believe it? I let her sleep late. I left her a note wishing her a happy anniversary. I called to tell her I wouldn't be able to make it home between meetings. I invited her to dinner out. She doesn't seem to realize that those meetings are no fun for me. They're work. I'd much rather be home with her or having a romantic night out. I only do those things because it's my calling. She doesn't seem to complain about our lifestyle."

On and on he went with point after point justifying his behavior. Time and again we would ask him what he understood about her feelings or the church members' feelings or even his own feelings. He would immediately begin the litany of facts that explained why he did what he did.

Tom is typical. Many ministers, especially men, have well-honed denial and intellectualization defenses. They are not only insensitive to other people's emotions, but unaware of their own. Yet their feelings affect their relationships. They become expressed as perfectionism, as anxiety, as outbursts of anger, as nonverbal hostility, and as depression.

As we worked with Tom we continued to focus on feelings. We would ask him what he was feeling. We would suggest a feeling a person in his shoes might have. We gave him feedback on his nonverbal feeling messages. We asked Alice to express her feelings as well as what she felt from Tom. We explored ways he might have been releasing feelings (such as his headaches and ulcer disease). Over and over again he would shift into facts, avoiding feelings. Another minister in the group began to see himself in Tom and really loved it when Melissa said, "Stick to the feelings!" He said, "I've always thought you had to avoid feelings and 'stick to the facts.'"

One day in group Alice was describing her loneliness and insecurity. Tom was listening with his usual filter. Someone in group asked him what he heard her saying because she

sounded as if she felt abandoned. That suddenly got his attention. He turned to her and asked with genuine concern, "Have
you been feeling unloved?" It was beyond his imagination
that she could feel that way, but for the first time he heard
her feelings and believed her.

It was only a beginning, but he went from there to becoming
aware of his own feelings. He discovered sadness, tenderness,
helplessness, anger, joy, hurt, frustration, hopelessness, jealousy, competitiveness, and fear (lots of fear). He also began
to connect how his feelings projected him into a rigid, controlling workaholism. He had been avoiding closeness in interpersonal relations because his inner feelings threatened to be
exposed.

For many ministers who come to you for help, therapy will
raise that same threat and the discomfort will raise the old
defense systems. One important ingredient to overcoming
that barrier is to reduce the fearfulness by creating a safe
environment. You need to give permission for feelings to be
expressed. The denial system was developed as a protection
against pain or rejection. The minister must begin to sense
that this relationship is different. It's safe here for me to have
feelings. I can even cry and still be accepted.

COUNTER-TRANSFERENCE

For someone who doesn't use jargon, counter-transference
is a noticeable exception to my rule. The term refers to distortions that a therapist brings into his relationship with a client
based on past life experiences. I think it may be a peculiarly
subtle barrier to successful counseling of Christian workers.
Whatever your religious background or spiritual position,
you're probably loaded with old tapes about "ministers."
Those distortions can significantly affect your attitudes and
expectations about your client from a church vocation.

One set of expectations can be that ministers are phonies
out there exploiting people for power and profit. When you
consider our recent history of Jim Jones, the Rajneesh Bhag-
wan, and countless television fund raisers, it's understandable
that such an attitude could prevail. Like it or not, it frequently

falls to the minister to promote his or her programs. Ministers are also involved in influencing thinking and motivating people to action.

As a people helper yourself, those attributes may create some discomfort in you. Like it or not, you influence ideas and behavior. You take money from those you help. Your conflictive feelings about that behavior in you may find expression in denial of your own guilt and emerging hostility toward the minister seeking your help. You may find yourself creating guilt in the minister or being highly suspicious. Either attitude can be a barrier to successful therapy.

A second attitude toward ministers is one of unrealistic adoration. Some people view anyone in religious work as a saint who can do no wrong. A counselor with this childlike awe and reverence will have trouble being an objective help.

When I was in training at the Mayo Clinic I saw many Roman Catholic clergy. Growing up as a Southern Baptist, I always viewed nuns, monks, and priests with a mixture of curiosity and respect. They seemed so truly pious in a positive sense. I'm sure the mystery of their orders and vestments created an aura of unreality to me. That was magnified by the Barry Fitzgerald–Myrna Loy portrayal on the silver screen which was as close to a real priest or nun I ever got.

Suddenly as a psychiatric resident I was being asked to evaluate a real flesh and blood nun. She was in post Vatican II modern habit, but was still a powerful stimulus to my old tapes. She had a crucifix, wore a habit, and, of course, a sweet Myrna Loy smile. She was not seeking help, but had been sent by the mother house. They said this serene, holy young woman was causing a lot of conflict with her sisters and the mother superior. For the first time in my life, I heard about life as a postulate and novitiate. I got an inside view of the stress in a convent. I found out that Julie Andrews was not your typical nun—nor was Sally Fields who was flying about at the time.

This sister was real. She had sexual feelings. She got angry and jealous. It was hard for me to separate her reality from my fantasy. How could the awe-struck, respectful little Southern Baptist boy hiding behind my Mayo Clinic name tag confront a nun with her hostility? Just how far is it proper to probe into a sister's sexuality? Dealing with counter-transference properly was critical if I was to be of any help to this angry, hurting young woman.

I did succeed with difficulty and even became friends with one of the local priests who helped me overcome some of my provincialism. I have known many Christians who held anyone in ministry in the same unrealistically high regard. To do so places the counselor in jeopardy of being only a childish admirer unable to deal with the humanity clothed beneath the vestments.

A more common distortion I see in the Evangelical church world is that of the adolescent recognizing the fallibility of a parent. At some time or another we all have to face that fact. Mothers and dads aren't perfect. The childhood fantasy of omnipotent parents has to go and with it some of the security that fantasy carries. Often the wishful ideal is not completely eliminated but is transferred to other parent figures. Clergy are obvious objects. They are powerful. They speak with the authority of God. They are dehumanized and even elevated to papal status (although Evangelicals would be loathe to admit it). In short, they become the perfect parent that was lost in adolescence. Now at last the emotional security is regained.

What happens when this new parent also fails? For some, there is a replay of the anger of adolescence. Betrayed again! The insecurity of facing life without an omnipotent protector and provider resurges. I see the results of this reaction time and again as the church responds to its wounded clergy with rage rather than love.

What happens when the counselor is the one struggling with the disappointment? We are not immune from the same overdetermined reaction.

Matt was the victim of that response. He was in a textbook midlife crisis when he became involved in an adulterous affair. He realized the sinfulness of his action and could not understand how he had allowed himself to do what he had so condemned in others. He got out of the relationship and truly repented, confessing to God, his wife, and the other woman.

He found forgiveness. He knew inside that he still needed help in understanding himself and in rebuilding his marriage. He went to a local "Christian counselor." He found himself virtually "stoned" with castigating condemnation. He felt the sting of Scriptures being hurled at him until his brokenness was complete. He was exposed before the church and given a penance to prove his penitence. I believe his was a serious sin, but I also believe the intensity of the response signaled an unresolved counter-transference phenomenon.

One other form of counter-transference is that unrelated to the client's vocation. Just because a person is in ministry doesn't exclude him or her from more routine distortions. I tend to dutifully see my mother in older women with big brown eyes and sweet smiles. Soft spoken southern gentlemen easily become my youth director who came from Georgia. Time and again I realize I am reminded of some former client and have begun to fit this present minister into a past mold. The facial features or tone of voice or body build can entomb this real person in the shrine of some departed soul for good or for bad.

SUMMARY

There are many barriers that can prevent successful outcome of counseling Christian workers. Being aware of them as you attempt to effectively minister to the minister is critical. Often, just the awareness will serve to remove the barrier, such as in your counter-transference. At other times identifying for the client that the feelings and attitudes are common will suffice. Sometimes more work is necessary in exploring the issues with the minister, searching out the roots, and correcting the myths.

Remember that for the Christian worker, coming to see a counselor can be a threatening event—career-wise and personally.

PART TWO

COMMON DIAGNOSTIC CONSIDERATIONS AND COUNSELING APPROACHES

CHAPTER FOUR

MARITAL MALADJUSTMENT

IT IS BEYOND the scope of this book to consider every possible emotional and mental disorder. In fact, other volumes in the Resources for Christian Counseling series will deal exclusively and extensively with various diagnostic entities. Needless to say, Christian workers are subject to any and all of the wide range of diagnoses.

Here I think it is appropriate for us to look at some specific symptom clusters that are more common to ministers. Even these aren't the exclusive territory of clergy. You may be dealing with these in other professionals or in your own life. I will try to relate them to the particular pressures of Christian workers and share some therapeutic considerations. I'll be discussing the problems we have dealt with most often during the past twelve years at Marble Retreat.

The apostle Paul had an accurate understanding of the conflict between marriage and ministry. He recognized the validity of spouses' needs and saw the inevitable tension they would create for Christians committed to ministry. In fact, he may have had a better grasp of the problem than most clergy today. That's why he recommended celibacy. He also recognized that not everyone could live the celibate life. So most clergy, other than Roman Catholics, marry and the stress begins. That's why over half of our guests at Marble Retreat have come because of a marital crisis.

There is still a basic commitment to marital permanence among clergy, so choosing divorce is not an easy option. Besides that, in many denominations a divorced clergy person will find ministry opportunities severely limited regardless of the circumstances of the divorce. Consequently the first open discussion (threat) of divorce provides motivation for counseling. It's amazing that many Christian workers seem willing to endure a rotten relationship for twenty or thirty years. Then let one or the other say, "I think I'll file for divorce," and the feathers fly.

We have identified four common patterns: 1. the neglected spouse; 2. the battle for control; 3. falling "out of love"; and 4. marital infidelity.

THE NEGLECTED SPOUSE SYNDROME

It is plenty hard to compete against the demands of a church for the attention of a spouse in ministry. Unless a mate squeaks louder, the cries for attention may go unheard. There are a lot of wheels squeaking for oil. Many ministers actually believe they'll be able to meet all those needs. They can't say no. There aren't many minutes and even less energy left after eighty- to ninety-hour work weeks for oiling the marriage machinery.

A complicating fact is that many ministers prefer it that way. They fit with Daniel Levinson's report in *The Seasons of a Man's Life*. Establishing a foothold in their professional life is just more important than family needs in the first fifteen to twenty years of ministry.[1]

Zackary and Joan came to the Retreat in a marital crisis after eighteen years of marriage. He was pastoring a "successful" church of 650 members. It was growing along with his reputation. In the meanwhile, their marriage had badly deteriorated. Joan felt abandoned and had become lonely and mad. She was furious at Zack and the church. All 649 other members had better access to his time than she did.

Ironically, he had started his ministry with firm resolve to keep his wife and family at the top of his priority list. In fact, he had conflict with his first boss over that philosophy. He gradually drifted away from that position in his subsequent church positions. His "family first" priority was lost completely when he became the senior pastor of his present church. The demands were so great he quit trying to hold the line. Besides the success felt good.

Often such a problem is enhanced by the wife's attitude toward ministry. She feels that her needs aren't important when compared to the church's. In a way she puts herself into a no-win position. If she demands attention, she feels guilty. If she doesn't, she feels abandoned.

Spouses handle the neglect in many different ways. It's important therapeutically to identify how each is responding. Since many ministers' spouses share a sense of "calling," they may feel guilty about wanting more attention. Some seem to be able to accept a supportive role, denying their own needs altogether. There are many more who try to do that, but with limited success. What happens then is that the feelings of neglect build to resentment and anger. That gets expressed through: 1. nagging for more time; 2. criticism of the spouse; 3. getting even by reciprocal neglect; 4. getting sick. All of these behaviors tend to drive the spouse further away.

Nagging

Proverbs says it's better to live in the desert alone than with a nagging woman (21:19). I was telling a wives' group this one time and one of the women blushed and moaned. I asked her what she was thinking. She said her husband had just taken an oil field job in Saudi Arabia.

The nagging wife needs to realize two things. First that

her nagging is an expression of anger. Most wives don't realize that. They may need help seeing nagging as "frustration," "aggravation," "irritation," or "hurt." Those emotions are easier to admit, since anger is so forbidden to many Christians.

The second important fact she must comprehend is its inefficiency. If she sees her nagging as the only stimulus that will get some attention to her needs, she'll have a hard time giving it up. She can usually come to see that it doesn't work very well. I frequently just ask, "How does that work for you?" Suddenly a light turns on and she realizes that nagging not only doesn't get her the attention she legitimately needs, but also creates hostility and tension. What's worse, being a nag doesn't serve as a release from the anger she feels.

In conjoint session or group therapy the husband can be prompted to share his inner reaction to her nagging. Most men say something like, "I just get tired of it. I say to myself, *I don't need this,* and I leave." Lots of husbands learn to say mollifying things like, "Oh, yes dear, I've been meaning to do that for you. I'll get to it right away." That's a lie! They aren't intending to do what she's nagging about. The verbal response is positive but leaves the wife thoroughly mystified. Their nonverbal message is the honest one. They forget all about her request and go to the church. It may also be enlightening to explore their past experiences with nagging people. Both partners may be quite conscious that they see their parents or in-laws or some sibling in those patterns and have a strong negative response built in.

The next step therapeutically is helping the couple develop some new communication patterns. We have found the book *Straight Talk* to be very helpful. As the Couples' Communication Program has discovered, by becoming aware of inner feelings and responses, the individual is helped to clearly communicate personal feelings in "straight talk" messages.[2] The wife is then able to talk about her feelings of abandonment and anger. She can express her need for attention and help. The husband is able to respond to her honest, verbalized feelings more clearly than to the nonverbal hostility he has been receiving in the nagging. Hearing each other accurately, they can begin to recognize underlying problems.

Barbara and Dan were a typical couple caught in the negative spiral of neglect and nagging. He was a burdened minister in an inner-city work with street people. The demands were incessant and the rewards few. As Barbara's feeling of being lost and lonely grew, she began to add her voice to those demanding his time. She had some real needs. There were repairs to be done around the old apartment they rented. She was isolated socially. They had only one car which he used, so there were many errands she needed him to run. Soon she had a long list of "honey-do's." It also didn't take long for most of the items to sit undone for weeks and months.

The more she nagged, the less she saw of Dan and the more angry she became. As they were able to openly talk together about their feelings, some interesting insights emerged.

Almost immediately they understood the pattern and saw hope in overcoming it. He validated her needs for his attention and caring. She expressed empathy for his overwhelming ministry demands. They began to feel like allies instead of enemies. That helped them look at deeper feelings and needs.

For the first time Dan was able to say that as an adolescent he had decided he was not going to listen to a nagging wife, like his mother. His dad gave him encouragement to disregard his mom's demands. The message he got was that women are whiners. Their complaints are just neurotic. They are better ignored. Dan thought Barbara was just living up to his previous image of a wife. He believed that any man worth his salt would avoid reinforcing the imaginary needs of a nagging woman. Eventually she would "grow up" and quit.

Barbara's expectation had been that a husband would be attentive like her dad. He was a handyman who was always eager to fix anything broken. He gave Barb's mother lots of attention and love. Barbara concluded that Dan didn't love her because he wasn't caring for her in those ways. When she realized that all men don't show love the same way, she was free to negotiate about getting repairs made and errands run. She and Dan found alternatives to expressing love and meeting needs that relieved pressure for both of them.

Criticism

A neglected spouse often becomes the number-one critic of her mate. Criticism can easily become the primary expression of the anger. Like nagging, it drives the husband further into his ministry tasks, intensifying the neglect. It's not unusual for the criticism to become public. Unlike other vocations, Christian ministry is often shared by a couple. They are with the church people together in work situations. When the anger is unresolved between them it's understandable for the wife to pick at her mate's performance. That doesn't happen to lawyers or physicians. Their mates don't come into the court room or surgical suite and begin to point out mistakes. The minister's wife is on hand to witness every error. What's worse, his work isn't guided by objective standards. Anybody and everybody can offer a critique, and criticism from the wife is the most stinging of all.

We try to help couples understand the feelings that prompt the criticism. The minister is better able to deal directly with his wife's feeling of anger because of his neglect than with her criticism of his ministry skills. As the wife realizes how damaging her criticism is, she's able to choose a "straight talk" expression of her feelings. The wife thinks her husband is impervious to her corrections. The miscommunication from him is that he doesn't care what she thinks. It is very helpful for her to understand his need for her praise rather than her advice.

When working with couples it is important to help them express their needs more clearly. Since mutual need-meeting is the most accurate marker of good marriages, it's critical that communication of needs be accurate. We have found this pointedly true in regard to criticism versus praise. There are times when each one is legitimate. Melissa and I have learned to give each other clear signals about which is needed. If I want her approval and praise (which is usually my need), I say, "What do you think of this idea I just had? I think it's divine inspiration." She says, "You're wonderful," which is what I wanted to hear in the first place. If I really want her advice or ideas I ask for them: "Melissa, I'm working on a paper for the conference this summer. I'm not sure if this sounds good or not. I need your advice. What do you think?" That way she can really know what need I'm expressing.

What often happens in marriage is that one partner wants approval, but asks for criticism. I figure most folks can find something to criticize in just about anything, so it's not hard for them to offer some advice on how to improve. When praise was really the need, the advice feels like a put-down. The critic may come away feeling helpful and loving while the mate is disappointed and downcast.

Retreat into Sickness

One of the most difficult patterns to deal with in the neglected spouse syndrome is psychosomatic illness. The anger and emotional tension are repressed from consciousness but get redirected toward the body. Almost any body system can be the target. The most common are the musculo-skeletal system (tension headaches, low back pain, stiff neck, general fatigue, even paralysis), the gastrointestinal tract (ulcer disease, irritable colon, diarrhea, ileitis), and skin (neurodermatitis), the cardiovascular system (hypertension, angina, migraine), and the genito-urinary tract (menstrual problems, vaginisms, orgasmic dysfunction, erectile failure). The symptoms are not "in the head." They are very real and there may be definite physical damage and malfunction.

The illness is reinforced by the secondary gains it produces. The sick person gets attention, care, and empathy—especially early in the history. When neglect has been an important factor in the genesis of the illness, it's easy to see how critical being sick can become. Unfortunately the response doesn't remain purely positive. It's hard to live with someone who is incapacitated. Before long hostility creeps in as the healthy mate feels more and more manipulated by the symptoms. Doubts begin to be entertained about the legitimacy of the complaints. Resentment of the expense of doctor bills builds. Finally, in more exasperating moments, accusations of malingering and manipulation escape.

The primary factor in effective treatment is acknowledgment of reality of the disorder. The sick person has his or her integrity on the line. If the illness is said to be imagined or there isn't understanding of how the body channels stress into various systems, the patient will feel accused of being a fake and liar. That only serves to intensify the stress and increase the patient's defensiveness. Emotionally patients must invest themselves in proving the legitimacy of the complaints. To overcome that response they must feel others acknowledge and respect their pain. Good medical care for control of symptoms by an empathic physician is important. Then they can be brought into the educational process of learning how their psyche (emotions) affects their soma (body). Their negative feelings can be identified, and they can learn to express them verbally and consciously instead of somatically. It can be a long and frustrating process of making that change.

Simultaneous work on improving the marriage in all areas can help. This would include communication, cooperation, spirituality, sexuality, and playfulness. I think it's especially useful to help these individuals learn to laugh and play again. Life has so often become a sad, serious drudgery. Bringing back some lightness and fun has a remarkably beneficial effect.

I broke my wrist this summer. It not only incapacitated me in countless little ways (like buttoning shirts and zipping my pants), but it hurt. That thing *still* aches at times. After a few weeks I realized I was really becoming a sourpuss. I was glum and irritable. I wasn't much fun to be with. I finally decided I didn't want to be that way. I began to be playful and make jokes. I was surprised at the difference that made in my healing.

Because of the dependency involved in dealing with an unwell person and the hostility that can so easily develop toward the neediness, it's helpful to take a team approach to these cases. Involve a physician, the mate, and a supportive group. This takes cooperation and direct communication so that you don't work against each other. It's especially important that medical input be carefully coordinated. If more than one physician gets into the act, overmedication and abuse of drugs can complicate the treatment. With a well-coordinated effort, the dependency is diffused and each person involved can maintain a more positive attitude. Especially the minister-mate who can more easily deal with the problem of neglect and avoidance that may be at the root of the psycho-somatic syndrome.

Retribution

There are lots of ways a neglected spouse responds. Those we've talked about are more or less unconscious, but there are also ways they can consciously choose to "get even." I think these are easier to cope with therapeutically because they are conscious choices.

The abandoned mate gets tired of being ignored. He or she finally decides one day that two can play that game. The means of getting even we have seen most commonly have been: neglecting housekeeping, refusing to cooperate with goals, spending money selfishly, refusing sex, staying away, and/or having an affair.

It's important to mention that these patterns are more threatening to a Christian worker than they might be in other marriages. The minister often feels his home and family are scrutinized. They feel the expectation to have model house-holds. It's frightening for the house to be unfit for entertaining drop-in church people. The spouse's refusal to cooperate to-ward goals may threaten success of a ministry project and, worse than that, raise questions in the minds of the church about the minister's marriage. Spending money extravagantly will likely have disastrous consequences. The Christian work-er's budget can't take it. Sexual and emotional withdrawal may not be recognized publicly, but may increase the minis-ter's tension, ineffectiveness, and vulnerability, indirectly af-fecting his ministry. Marital infidelity is perhaps the most threatening form of retribution. If discovered, it can end the ministry.

These counter-attacks are eye for eye and tooth for tooth. The neglected spouse feels unmet needs and reciprocates. This gets the minister's attention more directly, yet is still a destructive approach. Couples we have seen in this pattern have had a stubborn attitude. They have refused to give to each other and have each been determined not to give in first. Each partner also feels totally justified in his or her behavior.

We have found that an initial catharsis of the areas of hurt has been useful (if not essential) in getting past the standoff. As in many marital conflicts there is an accumulated backlog of resentment. The idea of forgetting the past and starting over with a clean slate is a good one, but without cleaning out the old hurts it doesn't seem to work well. Each person needs to feel his or her list of old hurts has been heard and genuine remorse felt for each wound. To do this, each partner has to acknowledge responsibility for contributing a share of the pain. Then comes the tricky part of listening *nondefensively* to the mate's hurts.

We have each person write a list of resentments. They then read those to each other with their goal being only to understand their mate's hurts and see the wounds from a different perspective. They each grant that, if given the opportunity, the other could defend his or her action, offering some rational (or irrational) justification. But no such defense is allowed into the conversation. Each must put emotions into neutral—except to feel the way his or her mate has been hurting in the relationship.

The next step is for each partner to express genuine regret and remorse about the other's suffering and to ask forgiveness. It's easier for the husband to say, "Forgive me for my contribution to your pain," than to take full responsibility. In fact, rarely is only one person fully to blame for a conflict. *So establishing blame is not the goal of the exercise.* The healing comes as each person feels heard and validated. A statement such as, "I see how you've been feeling and how what I've done has been painful to you. I'm sorry. Please forgive me," is a lot more effective than, "Let's just forget about the past and get on with life."

When the backlog is cleared out, the couple must move on to develop better communication skills and clearer awareness of each other's needs. While they work through *Straight Talk*, learning to talk to each other on a feeling level, we have them begin to work on their need awareness. We have each person write a list of his or her mate's needs and ways in which those can be met more completely. They then read the lists aloud to each other and make any appropriate additions or modifications. I think it's important that each one write the other's needs. That begins to change the focus from self to other. It also forces each person to give some thought to how to meet those needs. I insist that the lists be specific. It's common for people to write broad generalities that don't have much bite to them. A person can write, "She needs to be loved, so I'll show her more love," without giving it any real thought. If he writes, "She needs more of my time, so I'm going to take her to lunch every Tuesday and out for coffee every Friday night," he has thought about her. What's more, making a verbal confession of intent tends to solidify the commitment.

Sometimes couples are so unaware of each other's needs that they require some help in identifying them. For that reason I ask them to bring their lists back when they come to see me. If they only have one or two items each I suspect they don't understand the assignment or their mate. I will then talk with them about some important needs I've heard people share. Or I may tell the wife some of my basic needs as a man, and tell the husband some things Melissa has identified for me. We may then talk about differences in men and women or discuss ways their identified needs can best be met.

A useful book along this line is *How Do You Say "I Love You"?* by Judson J. Swihart. He points out four basic ways of expressing love and says that many couples miss the messages because they use different styles. For example, many men use material things to say "I love you" (e.g., buying flowers or a new washer). Their wives may be more verbal and be listening for the words rather than understanding the symbols. It's as though one were speaking Italian and the other Japanese. The meaning is never translated and each feels frustrated and unloved. When both can identify and communicate what says love to them there is a better chance of hearing it.

Don't take for granted that couples know these things. Many have taught the principles to others, but never really applied them personally. We've seen scores of Christian workers who have been in college, seminary, workshops, and counseling training, but don't recognize the dysfunctional behavior in their own marriages. It's safest to assume they don't know that their needs and expectations are different from each other, and that they've never talked about them together before.

It may be equally liberating and healing for you to give them permission to have needs. Many individuals in Christian ministry have been taught that they "shouldn't" have any personal needs. In fact it has been common for us to see couples who feel guilty for admitting they want attention, affection, praise, or sexual fulfillment. Yet their humanity, as well as their constant disappointment in life, is real.

There is one other interesting attitude that prevails about communicating needs. Most people cling to the infantile, magical notion that "If I am loved, the other person will know what I need and fulfill it without my having to say anything." The damaging corollary is "If I have to say what I need, it isn't worth anything when I get it." That premise may work well if everybody is adept at mind reading, but there aren't many good mind readers around. Even if I guess right some of the time, Melissa's needs keep changing. Some things that were important to her a few years ago aren't now, and some things that used to be insignificant now mean a lot.

Melissa's response to a need I have told her about is more meaningful than a spontaneous act of love. You may ask why. Well, when she does something because I've asked, she is expending energy on something that isn't second nature to her. The things she does spontaneously are part of her natural temperament or behavior. For instance, I'm a toucher. Melissa isn't. She shows me love in lots of wonderful ways, but it hasn't been natural for her to just come over and touch me. I tell her how important that is to me, and she responds by going out of her way to touch my arm or rub my neck or give me a hug. Now that's speaking my language! I could just keep quiet and pout and feel unloved because she doesn't intuitively know when I want to be touched. I'd rather be touched. On the other side of our coin, I don't naturally reveal my feelings. Melissa needs me to be more open so she'll feel a part of me. She's told me about that need on several occasions. I guess I should know it by now and just spontaneously tell her what I'm feeling inside. I'm ashamed to admit that I forget and don't do it as much as she'd like, but I'm delighted to admit that she'll remind me. She wants to be a part of the inner me. She could just keep quiet and wait and wait and feel left out. Instead she gets inside. I'm glad she does.

Summary

Dealing with the problem of the neglected spouse involves several important points:

1. Recognizing the feeling of each spouse.
2. Identifying the patterns of behavior and communication they've been using.
3. Clearing out the backlog of hurt and resentment.
4. Learning effective communication skills.
5. Becoming aware of each other's needs and having permission to place those ahead of ministry demands.
6. Educating the church or ministry group to the legitimate needs of the minister's family.

THE BATTLE FOR CONTROL

General Beauregard Lafayette is one of my favorite characters. You may not remember the general. He really never won any military battles. He is a basset hound created by the genius of the old Walt Disney Studios for *101 Dalmatians*. Beauregard is the top dog and constantly reminds his sidekick, Napoleon, of that fact.

In one scene there is great urgency for the hounds to get up and give chase to the villains. Napoleon gets excited, starts to move out saying, "Let's go." Beauregard steps on his tail and drawls, "Hold it! Hooold it! Ah'm the leadah head. Ah'll say when to go. . . . Ah right, Go!"

In many marriages I hear old Beauregard saying, "Now just a doggone minute. I'm the leader here. I'll say when to go." The problem is that "Napoleon" isn't about to sit still, while someone steps on his (or her) tail, and wait for the command.

Instead there is one horrendous commotion of yelping and barking and biting to see who's really the leader here.

Not only does the battle for dominance come in decision making but also in emotional submissiveness and it has some unusual dimensions in ministry couples.

Who Says, "Let's Go"?

The battlefields for control in decisions in clergy marriages are similar to those in other homes. Parenting creates its conflicts. Financial management is often a problem. Choosing activities for leisure time can be hard. Even selecting friends is fraught with difficulty.

To set the stage for the power struggle let's look at the personality and position of the Christian worker. People who are attracted to ministry are frequently nurturers with tendencies to be servants of others. As identified by the Thomas–Kilmann test, they commonly deal with conflict by avoidance or compliance rather than competition, collaboration, or compromise.[3] They tend to equate assertiveness with aggressiveness and use passive behaviors in fighting. Complicating the picture is the confusion regarding authority and power in ministry (see chapter 2). Christian workers frequently feel they have hundreds of bosses, each telling them what to do.

These patterns set up the clergy couple for control conflicts in their relationship. The avoidance-compliance style of conflict management tends to passively leave conflicts unresolved. The clergy person is quite likely to passive-aggressively refuse to make a decisive verbal stand, but proceed to control decisions by resisting a spouse's suggestions. In the meantime, the mate becomes so frustrated by the inaction and withdrawal that he or she is willing to do anything just to do something.

Complicating the picture is mate selection. The passive-compliant person is attracted to a decisive, strong individual. That assertiveness felt secure and comfortable in courtship. As married life progresses, it becomes more and more uncomfortable. The passivity that looked like sensitive silent strength seems more and more like quicksand.

From the outside looking in as seen by the church members,

the character traits may look like they did to the clergy couple during courtship. His passivity looks like a soft, sensitive servanthood. He is praised for his warmth and sweet spirit. Her assertiveness and organization look like efficiency and are affirmed as a complement to his warmth. That perception locks them further into their tension. They each feel affirmed by others while seeing their mate as the bad guy. It's also hard to face the conflict when the church world is looking on, expecting a model marriage.

I just got a call this morning from a typical wife. She has a responsible job and helps support her husband in his ministry which pays very poorly. She has tried to get him to do something about the problems in their marriage for years. He just says, "Oh, everything will work out. Just give it time." She's been reluctant to admit that they need help and they can't afford to pay for counseling. So they are stuck in their power struggle. She gets forced into making decisions which he then sabotages. The pattern is quite common and is expressed in all areas of clergy marriages.

Parenting is frequently a good guy–bad guy show. The minister refuses to set limits or participate in discipline. The mate is stuck being the heavy. Needless to say, the kids side with the minister parent and learn to play both sides to get their way. When the family feels the unfairness of the goldfish bowl existence, both parents may try to compensate by being easy on the children. The resulting tension and conflicts become daily battlegrounds for an interminable fight for control.

Family finances take on the same chaotic style. There may be alternating approaches as each partner tries to manage the money. Often the assertive mate takes control by default after the clergyperson has refused to be responsibly involved. Then both resent the other. The minister feels dominated and powerless while the spouse feels stuck with trying to make ends meet. When a joint checking account or, even worse, credit cards enter the picture all sorts of games begin. The passive-aggressive possibilities of charge accounts staggers the imagination. Not uncommonly the responsible partner finally gives up and tries to get even.

A beleaguered minister needs a supportive marriage and

family as a retreat from the stress of ministry. When a battle for control is raging, there is no repose. Where to go on vacation, what to do on an evening off, what TV show to watch, what food to eat, whether to invite friends over, when to go to bed and what time to get up, what kind of car to drive, where to live, and who gets to use the bathroom first—all become laden with win–lose implications. For the "loving Christian family" that creates unbearable dissonance.

Who Says, "I'm Sorry"?

Another facet of the battle for control is who takes on the role of peace maker. In most dysfunctional families one person is designated to try to prevent complete dissolution by appeasing the others. This may be the pattern adopted by the more assertive or by the more passive person in the marriage. The one who says "I'm sorry" is either the one who is most dependent or is most threatened by possible violence.

For the dependent person, the anxiety of separation overwhelms considerations of winning in a conflict. In counseling, a dependent person will commonly describe a childhood experience that involved being controlled by withdrawal of affection or a traumatic early separation. These events sensitize a person to being deserted emotionally or physically. In marriage, conflict and anger often produce temporary withdrawal and distance. That feeling of alienation awakens all the old anxiety in a dependent person. It seems the only way to relieve the fear is to give in and make up. Often the giving in is an "I'm sorry" through clenched teeth with a lot of resentment built in.

In therapy, we frequently hear people confess the intense pain and bitterness felt at having always to be the ones who give in. Exploring with them their feelings of dependency and the roots of trying to keep the peace at all costs is helpful. There can be a new awareness of their adult reality as they see their behavior in light of their childhood fears. The *old tapes* can be replaced by fact. The ineffective marital patterns of conflict resolution become available for change.

Stanley came into counseling because of tension and anxiety. He had frequent headaches. His stomach was upset much of the time even though he lived on antacids. Every morning he had diarrhea before going to work. At times his anxiety would send him home early in the evening, particularly if he had some meeting to attend. He hated conflict and would give in quickly to avoid the stress. At home he did everything he could to appease his wife. Quick to accept blame for any problem, he was constantly apologizing.

Under the frazzled, subjugated surface, Stanley was furious. He was angry at the church for demanding too much, he was angry at his wife for never admitting she was wrong, and mad at himself for not having the courage to confront anyone. When Stanley was a child, his mother had completely abolished his aggression. If he ever expressed anger in any form, she would send him to his room and withdraw all affection for days. She'd say, "How can you expect me to love you when you are such an angry, bad boy?" He transferred his fearfulness of her withdrawal to all of his adult relationships. The idea of confronting conflict was terrifying. Yet the anger remained and was giving him headaches, intestinal problems, and sleepless nights. He had also withdrawn sexually.

When Stanley and his wife realized what was going on, they experienced almost immediate relief. She didn't like his being so weak and giving in so easily. She never knew what he was struggling with inside. She had some work to do on her own pride and attitude of superiority, but began to be able to see areas where she could say, "I'm sorry." Stanley was like a new man the first time he heard those words coming from her lips.

Just as the threat of separation is highly controlling for some, the possibility of violence can be for others. The basis of that fear rests either on growing up with a violent person in the home or on an awareness of violent impulses within. With the current media emphasis on abuse in the home, individuals are now recognizing the effects of violence in their childhood. Those nightmare events are so scary that most people supress the memories completely. A common report is "You know, it's funny, but I don't remember anything before age twelve." As you continue to probe, memory retrieval is enhanced. At first a trickle of recollections of violence begin. As the person feels it is safe to report the terror, a flood of life-threatening assaults may emerge. I have wept with men and women as they have relived their horror.

We've heard of parents threatening each other with knives or guns; dads who came home drunk and beat up mothers with fists; an older brother who tied his little sister to the bed and sexually abused her on many occasions; a parent who would completely lose control and whip a child until blood flowed. One person even told of witnessing his mother's murder by her estranged husband. It has been remarkable how effectively many individuals are able to divest those scenes of feelings and report them initially as though they happened to someone else. The feelings of horror are there, however, and the slightest hint of anger sends the person scrambling for cover. Saying "I'm sorry" to keep the peace seems like a small price to pay.

For some, the violence is within. I asked Joe why he avoided conflict so completely. At first he didn't know except he just didn't like to be in an argument. I asked if he was afraid of the other person's hostility. Did he think he'd be hurt? He didn't think so. It never bothered him to get hit playing sports, but he had quit sports in high school. Was that because of the aggressiveness? He didn't know, but the coaches really tried to talk him into playing. He had the reputation of being hard hitting and very competitive. I asked him if that bothered him about himself. He began to look anxious. He said he didn't want to hurt anyone.

"Did you ever hurt anyone?"

"No." But there was a fearful look in his eyes as he said it.

"Were you ever afraid you were going to hurt someone?"

That did it. Joe began to sob and told me about almost hitting another kid with a lead pipe. They had been in a fight after school and he went completely out of control. Some other guys pulled him away just before he attacked the other boy with the weapon he'd seized in his fury. That episode had hurled him into passivity and compliance. The fear of becoming murderous again dominated his dealing with anger. Inside Joe was still a competitive, aggressive man, but he chose to become depressed rather than learn to be safely assertive. He was restored to wholeness as he disconnected his normal adult anger from his adolescent rage. He allowed the Lord to keep his anger within limits while he could express it verbally.

The battle for control in a marriage may feel like a fight only to the partner who is quick to give in. The spouse may have no idea that the "I'm sorry" is hiding deep fear of separation or violence. All the while the individual who gives in feels controlled and dominated. The resentment builds. The relationship suffers.

For the Christian worker there is the additional tension regarding anger. It is useful to explore the minister's theology of anger. I have found it helpful to point out the difference between feeling anger and acting it out destructively. I teach that our anger is a God-given emotional response. The limbic system is the part of the brain that produces our affective tone. When certain stimuli are perceived as threatening, we feel afraid or angry. That response has no moral "oughtness," but is like our stomach growling when we're hungry. There's no right or wrong to it. The threat is perceived and our limbic system neurons signal "anger."

Learning to deal with anger in a healthy way involves two things. The first is becoming more secure and mature as individuals. Then things that happen to us may not be perceived as threatening. I'm sure I have "mellowed out" as my kids say. Things that once would have really bothered me don't any more. The more secure we feel about ourselves, the less threatened we are. The Bible teaches that as we become like Jesus our life will show the fruit of the Spirit, which includes patience, kindness, and self-control. There is the real hope that we will honestly feel less anger as we mature.

The second approach to anger is learning to express it in a nondestructive way. When I feel angry, I try to discharge it safely. If the relationship is an unimportant one, I may release the anger by simply telling Melissa later about feeling angry toward the third party. When the relationship is closer and my feelings are going to affect us, I try to talk with the other person directly. I use first person messages, owning my feelings. I may say, "Melissa, I'm having some feelings I need to talk about. I really am struggling with my anger over what just happened. I feel like striking out at you, but I don't want to do that. I just want you to know I'm feeling put down (or frustrated or controlled or rejected or hurt) right now." That sort of statement can be heard nondefensively and we can talk about what happened. Melissa can come to understand why I feel the way I do, and I can become aware of how she is feeling. Usually that is all it takes for the anger to be dissipated. We may both ask forgiveness for something we did to contribute to the conflict. I believe that's what Scripture means when it says, "Be angry, and sin not" (Eph. 4:26, KJV). Talking it out leads to restoration and that's what redemption is all about.

Who Says, "It's Time for Sex"?

In his book *Money, Sex, and Power,* Richard Foster says, "Sexual intercourse is not a given, something that somehow miraculously takes care of itself once we enter marriage. It needs nurture, tenderness, training, education, and much more. When two people enter into sexual intimacy, there must be a lot of emotional, spiritual, and physical give-and-take." [4]

"A lot of emotional, spiritual, and physical give-and-take." Nowhere in marriage can a battle for control have as severe effects as in sex. Nowhere is a Christian couple more totally dependent on each other than for sexual fulfillment. Nowhere in life do we become so stripped of pretense and frightfully vulnerable than in sexual play. And nowhere is there a more powerful symbol of mutuality and oneness than in sexual intercourse.

For these reasons it is critical to understand a minister's sex life. We have had many hurting, stress-ridden clergy who felt that their marital intimacy had been one of the most significant factors in their professional survival. There they felt affirmed as a person. There was supportive love. There was release of tension. On the other hand, we've had Christian workers with the opposite experience. Because marital sexuality was a battleground, they felt powerless, angry, vulnerable, and tense.

We have found many reasons for the warfare over sexual control. One is ignorance. Some individuals with strongly fundamentalist upbringings are uneducated about sexuality. Since they don't understand their sexual differences, they don't learn the intricacies of the give-and-take. The partner's sexual desires feel like selfish demands. Giving and withholding sexual favors becomes an expression of power or anger rather than of love. One wife had told her husband that his desire for sex was abnormal. He was a pervert and she would tell him when they ought to have sex. That wasn't helping their feeling of oneness. When she learned about male sexuality, her whole attitude changed. She no longer saw him as a sinful person, but as a normal, loving husband with strong sexual drives. Likewise we've had many men who were totally ignorant of their wife's sexual response pattern. They became demanding and self-centered because they had no idea how to make sex enjoyable for their mates.

When ignorance is the problem, education through good books, such as *Intended for Pleasure*, and retraining through sensate focusing can be enough to end the battle. This technique allows a couple to enjoy each other sexually and learn how to please each other sexually. It is especially useful in abolishing negative habits.[5]

A second cause for the sexual power struggle among Christian workers is their inability to resolve conflict. We commonly hear a husband complain that his wife isn't available to him sexually. He feels manipulated by her use of sex. Only when he gives in to her totally in other areas of their relationship does he feel that she gives in to him sexually. Her apparent disinterest causes him to doubt his manliness. He may ultimately decide to give up sex altogether rather than face the humiliation of sexual rejection.

The wife's perception is that the relationship is most often marked by anger and conflict. Nothing is ever really resolved, but her husband expects her to be passionately responsive when he wants to make love. She can't understand how he could be shouting at her after dinner and wanting sex a couple of hours later. For her, sexual union isn't an avenue to resolve conflict, but a celebration of emotional harmony.

Teaching such a couple better communication and conflict resolution will bring their sexuality out of the combat zone.

A third reason sex becomes a battleground for couples in ministry is their closeness in a common work. Sharing of some sense of ministry was reported as one of the uniquely positive features of clergy marriage by Dave and Vera Mace.[6] Probably more than any other profession, both wife and husband are actively involved with the work. What can be a unifying force can easily become divisive. When a husband and wife share in ministry, there are more opportunities for competition, irritation, and relational fatigue.

When a couple comes to feel competitive in their work a win–lose dynamic is established. Their sexual relationship may serve as an extension of the competition. This can even find symbolic expression in their sexual techniques. One husband complained that his wife had to be in control in their ministry and even had to be "on top" when they had sex. I don't believe that positions for intercourse necessarily symbolize control or power, but in their case it did for him.

It is hard for any couple to work together without becoming irritated from time to time. The more they are involved with each other, the more likelihood of disagreements. Living with more incidents of annoyance creates sexual distance. Sexual closeness and cooperation are enhanced by romance, and an aspect of romance is to adore and cherish the beloved. When you have come at cross-purposes at ministry tasks several times during the day, it's hard to feel adoring and romantic. We had a missionary couple a few years ago whose areas of responsibility were poorly differentiated. He would make a decision she didn't know about and would unwittingly countermand. She would tell an assistant one thing only to find he contradicted her an hour later. They would go to bed exhausted and furious at each other. Neither felt very loving.

Melissa and I work together as group cotherapists three hours a day. We don't feel in competition (usually) and rarely find ourselves at cross-purposes. But we do suffer from overexposure. In the intensity of the group and with our style of self-disclosure we sometimes find ourselves emotionally drained. At those times it is hard for either of us to find emotional support in the bedroom. We both feel totally drained and want the renewal and tension relief that sexual intimacy can bring, but neither has the energy. It takes a lot of give-and-take for us to sensitively meet each other's sexual needs. We could very easily begin to keep score, and the sexual war would be on.

Better definition of ministry roles and built-in time apart can help reduce the feelings of competition and fatigue for those in Christian work.

Finally, clergy couples can also get into a control battle over sex because the minister's wife may feel otherwise power-less. The clergy wife sees her husband as the hero of the church. There he is on a pedestal and runs the show, but she feels herself playing second or third fiddle to "the minis-try." His desires and schedule often dominate their time and she feels unable to influence the system. As a result, she may hold onto the only thing she feels she can control—entrance to her own body.

She may feel unimportant except as a sexual object. It is no wonder that she may want to exercise power there. This pattern may not be operating consciously. Her unhappiness can be expressed somatically through pain during intercourse (dyspareunia or vaginismus) or other disabling physical symp-toms. To her husband it still feels like control.

Reordering of priorities and decision-making structures can easily give the wife a new sense of belonging. We have found that wives want to be good sexual partners, not only for their husband's enjoyment, but for their own. It is such a pleasure professionally to see that begin to happen as the "emotional, spiritual, and physical give-and-take" improves.

In counseling Christian workers it's important to explore their sexuality. Ministers are often treated as though they were neuter, but of course they're not. Many are living with doubt and guilt regarding sex, and feel they have no place to talk openly. The old taboo about sex seems to find its last stronghold among clergy. It has become perfectly acceptable to talk about sexuality in church. Few hesitate to seek help from their minis-ters regarding sexual matters. The church is finally taking its proper place in sexual education for youth and adults. But strangely the minister may be unwilling to talk about his or her own sexual problems. There may not be a battle for control, but a quiet desperation that can be turned to joy. (See "Sexual Dysfunction," chapter 6, p. 215).

Additional Therapeutic Considerations

I have mentioned the need for direct communication, for improved understanding, for better conflict resolution techniques, for education regarding parenting, finances, and sexuality, and for exploration of developmental imprints in changing control fights. There are some other areas you might want to probe. You might want to investigate role models and expectations and also bring understanding about the issue of submission.

A person's ideas about power and control in marriage are primarily derived from the role models of childhood. Like it or not, most of us bring into our marriage a strong expectation based on our parents' relationships. Many people unconsciously strive to repeat those patterns. Whatever we grew up with feels like the way marriage should happen. Even when there was unhappiness and conflict, the script is familiar and is hard to change. A spouse frequently lashes out, "You're just like your father (or mother)." We don't want to face the truth of that accusation. A woman may detest the nagging or dominance of her mother, yet find herself repeating the pattern. A man may preach against a husband being a dictator (like he saw his father being), yet become just as heavy handed.

Few of us stop to look at ourselves or to find healthy role models. We are taught English literature and computer science, but very little about being husbands and wives. Seminarians are taught hermeneutics and epistemology, but not how to have oneness in marriage. Instead the old images hang on to haunt us. We may recognize the destructive nature of the modeling and determine to be opposite, yet still not achieve the balance that is so important.

First, have the couple identify what its role models were. Have them talk with each other objectively about both sets of parents. At times there are critical blind spots that need to be seen.

Frank spent a great deal of time talking about his parents. He painted a picture of a warm, close relationship that was pretty ideal. We were all surprised when his wife asked, "Who are you talking about? You're not talking about the dad and mom I've known for twenty years." That was the first time he stopped to examine his childhood myth about Dad and Mom. As we listened they began to describe a whole different model than the one he had imagined. As it turned out, the real one had molded his attitudes about male dominance and superiority far more than he had realized.

To successfully approach this issue you'll have to deal with the Christian's ideas about honoring one's mother and father. I say two things in counseling to help reduce any feelings of betrayal. First, that we are not "blaming" parents for anything, but trying to come to better understanding. I usually grant that they were undoubtedly doing the best they could with their knowledge and abilities. Second, I tell them that it does not bring honor to parents to repeat their mistakes. I ask, "Would you want your children to stay locked into some of your negative patterns? Do you feel that would bring you 'honor' or 'dishonor'?" In fact, I acknowledge that if I were to meet their parents, I would probably like them, even after I got to know them fully. I still like my own even with their faults. That approach usually prepares them to take a new, adult look at Mom and Dad.

After clearing that hurdle and finding a true picture of their parents, the next step is to see how their own marriage is being affected by those systems. I have each one make a list of his or her expectations of marriage. I ask them to include what they thought a husband or wife should be like 1. as an emotional confidant; 2. as a helper at home; 3. as a provider; 4. as a lover; 5. as a parent; 6. as a spiritual partner; 7. as an intellectual companion; 8. as a playmate; 9. as a friend. Then I have them share their list with as much specific detail as possible. This exercise identifies areas of disappointment. They may need to adjust their expectations to reality or begin to adjust their behavior to fit the expectations.

Couples are usually surprised when they discover how much each partner has superimposed the images of a parent onto a mate. I've discovered how many ways I had unconsciously expected Melissa to be like my mother. I love them both, but have found out they are very different women. As I have consciously and objectively adjusted my expectations, I relate more accurately to Melissa without the "mother filter" distorting my vision.

At times I will bring a little humor into the counseling situation by drawing up resignations for each to sign—resigning from being each other's parent and resolving to get to know each other as real people.

As their old family patterns are explored, it may be necessary to talk specifically about their attitudes and beliefs about 1. power, 2. control, 3. decision making, 4. men, and 5. women.

Another vital area when dealing with power is submission. There has been a lot of emphasis on the biblical teaching about authority and submission in recent years. Many Christian workers in evangelical groups have become locked into a rigid, legalistic system that spells out a strict hierarchy of authority. These systems can be abused and carried to extremes that seem to miss the spirit of love that permeates the Bible. John Howell's book *Equality and Submission in Marriage* presents a healthy, balanced view.[7]

In teaching about submission I use two concepts. First, there is power in submissiveness. Richard Foster has good discussion of this "creative power" in *Money, Sex, and Power*.[8] In *The Road Less Traveled,* Scott Peck also develops the idea of maturity and love being self giving.[9] Long before these writers, Paul admonished mutuality of submission in the Ephesian letter (Eph. 5:21). Neither husband nor wife could take Ephesians 5 seriously without giving self up in love and respect to each other. We allow our insecurities to propel us into a quest for power. As we become confident of who we are in Christ, submission takes on an entirely different and powerful dimension. It is a free act of the will that preserves autonomy.

Second, submission is related to mutuality and oneness. I use the analogy of our human bodies. The brain may be the data center and direct the action of the rest of the body, but it can't ignore the other parts.

I strained a muscle in my back the other day shoveling

snow. I really do love the winter here. The snow-covered mountains in the moonlight are something everybody ought to see at least once in a lifetime. But this year we had ninety-six inches of snow in November and December. That's eight feet of snow. That's a lot of shoveling. So I strained a back muscle. Well, my brain kept getting the message while I was shoveling. "Ouch! Hey, that's beginning to hurt! How about finding another way to do this or wait awhile!" Did my brain listen? No. It said, "I'm in charge here. Just quit complaining and keep working." Now my brain can't ignore my back any longer. There are constant messages every time I move that remind my brain it made a mistake.

I think marriages and families and even churches should work with the same mutual sensitivity that our bodies have. The brain needs input from the skin and muscles, oxygen from the lungs, and sugar from the intestinal tract. A husband needs the female perception his wife can add. A woman needs the ideas and direction her husband can give. Both need to be sensitively aware of their children's needs and the whole family will benefit from submissiveness to the Lord.

Many couples marry with intentions of becoming "one," then spend the next fifty years or so fighting about which "one" they'll be. It's a lot more fun to learn to listen to each other and for each one to give of self in submission.

Summary

Power struggles within clergy marriages are common and are related to the indistinct authority structure in the ministry, to the inability to deal effectively with conflict, and with role models and expectations from childhood.

1. Help the clergy couple to see the battle for control they're fighting and to understand the underlying reasons.
2. Negotiate a truce.
3. If you teach them to resolve conflicts creatively you will open an entirely new way of looking at life.
4. A balanced, mature view of submissiveness can bring a fresh spiritual dimension to their marriage.

FALLING OUT OF LOVE

"I'm just not in love anymore."

Many of the couples I see are not in a crisis situation. They are civil to each other. Neither one has been unfaithful. They still do caring things for each other. Basic respect is intact. No problem with trust, but something is missing. Maybe one or both partners feel they're just going through the motions of marriage. There's no excitement, no romance. They've "fallen out of love."

Is this an important problem or just a part of the normal marriage cycle? For those who risk talking about it, there seems to be real pain. The longing for emotional connectedness is still there, languishing deep inside. Some can look back nostalgically to a time when they felt alive in the relationship. Others are hard pressed to describe any period in their marriage where the intimacy existed. The yearning for something more was always there. I believe this is a serious problem for many married couples including those in ministry.

To understand, we need to look at four distinct but connected issues: stages of marriage, stages of the adult life cycle, stages of ministry, and the meaning of love.

Stages of Marriage

Sociologists have described marital relationship in terms of the common life tasks involved. The effects these stages have on the husband–wife interaction can contribute significantly to feelings of closeness, intimacy, and romance.

The first stage is courtship. In our studies of couples, the vast majority (over 90 percent) report physical attraction as the primary factor that brought them together. This is decidedly related to a self-centered drive for sexual fulfillment. I like the way the *Living Bible* describes Adam's response to Eve: "This is it!" (Gen. 2:23). Something chemical happens. We "fall in love." Then we try to get to know the other person during courtship. There is little evidence that much objective evaluation really happens. David Mace says he thinks premarital counseling is of doubtful benefit.* The lovers are convinced

---

Southern Baptist videotape series, "Marriage Enrichment."

that they are made for each other. Any underlying doubts are either denied, ignored, or rationalized. Almost all couples can recall some romantic feelings of excitement during this phase. However, when those private doubts become reality the romance may fade.

The second phase of marriage is establishing the commitment to each other. After the wedding the work of adjusting to life with this stranger *begins.* In this phase, patterns of dealing with conflict and meeting of needs are established. Hopefully, the couple has enough individual maturity to work out healthy patterns of giving. That doesn't happen very often. Usually each individual begins to regress into immature, even infantile, ways of getting his or her own way. Depending on the degree of stress, their experience of romance may be preserved or disappear totally from the scene. As we shall see, the adult life cycle and ministry stages also affect their development of intimacy.

The third stage is variable depending on child-bearing decisions (or accidents). The arrival of the first child has dramatic effects on the marriage relationship. Some husbands feel abandoned as the demands of an infant invade their territories. These feelings, left unresolved, may form a pivotal point in the union with a gradual distancing as each partner pursues different goals. Both husband and wife, feeling a loss of intimacy, blame the other and compensate by investing their energies in other directions. A more mature response to those natural feelings is for the couple to recognize them and not allow resentment to develop. Time can be made for romance to be preserved.

The fourth stage, parenting through the years of childhood, is marked by considerable preoccupation with the needs of the children. Frequently the mother carries the primary load and pure fatigue may interfere with meaningful involvement between husband and wife. The father may allow himself to be excluded from child raising responsibilities, further alienating himself emotionally from his wife. Those are tough years on a marriage, and maintaining the primary marital union is difficult. They coincide with stages of ministry and manhood that easily detract the father's attention. When ministry is shared by husband and wife, the time and emotional demands of career and children leave little energy for the marriage.

The fifth stage, the adolescent years of the children, relieves some of the physical demands of parenting as the kids liberate from the family. Peers become the primary focus instead of family. Fortunately, most (about 70 percent) adolescents move through those years with minimal turmoil. We have a picture of great stress because of the tremendous energy, lability of emotions, and potentially devastating daily problems. Couples may find themselves brought closer together as they cope with the individuation of their teenagers, or they may find themselves divisively at odds. This stage can provide a positive moving together as a basis for the phases to come.

The sixth stage is the emptying of the nest. There are considerable changes during these years. The marital union is in the spotlight again. The duet is on. Some couples have forgotten how to harmonize after having worked for twenty or twenty-five years on opposite wings of the stage. This is often when the confession of "nonlove" is made. The responsibility for children is lightened. There is a sudden shift of attention, and it's hard to ignore the reality of what remains of the marriage.

The seventh phase covers the declining years. Health may fail. Dependency increases. Friends and siblings begin to die. If the marriage has survived, one mate is likely thrust into a care-taking role for the other. Yet these can be satisfying years of a culminating oneness. Deep intimacy and communion may mark those last years. I am seeing my own parents enjoy more closeness in this phase of their marriage than they've had in years. I think they have fallen more and more in love in the last ten years.

Stages of the Adult Life Cycle

Daniel Levinson has described seven more or less distinct phases of the adult male life cycle: 1. leaving the family, 2. entering the adult world, 3. settling down, 4. becoming one's own man, 5. the midlife transition, 6. middle adulthood, 7. older age.[10] These correspond with Erikson's last three "ages of man," where the developmental tasks are to develop intimacy through commitment, to be generative through productivity and creativity, and finally to arrive at ego integrity with a comfortable sense of wholeness.[11] For both men and women these phases of adult life affect the marriage profoundly.

The first stages call for a movement beyond the self-centered uncertainties of adolescence. A person's adult identity is tested primarily in his or her ability to form lasting commitments. Marriage is one of those. In a very exciting sense, a person pledges his or her life to another. The risk of fusing the newly established boundaries of self with the loved one is both frightening and exhilarating. In *Intimate Strangers,* Lillian Rubin has an interesting discussion about intimacy which she calls the approach–avoidance dance, the intricate tango of merging of individuality while preserving the unique identities of each person.[12] This similar giving of self is occurring as a woman pursues a career or pregnancy and as a man establishes himself in the adult world of work and parenting. Erikson terms failure at this stage "moving into isolation." Hence a marriage will be marked by a romantic, energetic fusion of personalities or a sullen withdrawal into self.

The next stages, from entering the adult world to the midlife transition, encompass generativity. Adult responsibilities are embraced and an individual becomes a productive member of society. Not only are children produced and nurtured to become responsible members of the culture, but also acts of love toward others promote the well-being of the community. Here a couple either progresses toward self-giving mutuality or regresses to an immature self-centeredness. Erikson calls that failure "stagnation."

Levinson identifies four critical issues faced by men in the midlife transition: 1. integrating his masculinity and femininity, 2. facing his need for intimacy, 3. accepting his own mortality, and 4. adjusting to the process of aging.[13] Frequently these emotional tasks draw a man into himself in introspection. He may inventory his life and decide to make drastic changes in order to reintegrate himself. At this point his marriage may offer a secure platform for his transition or may appear detrimental to these tasks. This is particularly true regarding his need to have more emotional intimacy and to accept his "female" qualities. These characteristics can enhance his marriage and contribute to a deepening of the romance if there is a safe foundation for the transition. If not, he may abandon the marriage, hoping to find fulfillment elsewhere.

Erikson's last stage corresponds to Levinson's middle adulthood and retirement. Here a person becomes mentor for the younger generation. He or she has comfortably faced the midlife issues and can face decline and death with assurance and peace. Ideally there is ego integrity, a sense of wholeness as a person. A marriage of two people who have successfully achieved this is marked by a comfortable oneness. They are no longer threatened by the needs of the other, but can relinquish their own "rights" for the benefit of others.

A romantic union in this life stage bequeaths a hopefulness to the succeeding generations and stability to society.[14]

Stages of Ministry

Our work has shown ministry cycles that seem to mirror some of the life changes in marriage and adulthood. Early ministry is a time of enthusiastic idealism—commitment to the task of changing the world. The naiveté of seminary days, newly wedded bliss, and the early adult transition are quickly challenged by the reality of church life, the invasion of infants, and the stress of ministry demands. It has been found that there is a peak in ministry dropouts about ten years after seminary. *Ex-Pastors* data show that a majority of their participants had left ministry within twelve years.[15]

Those who survive this period (which corresponds to the early thirties transition) move into a more comfortable phase of ministry. Idealism tempered by reality and ministry skills honed by experience move the clergyperson into a productive period of responsible adulthood. There is still a sense of optimism about ministry "success" as the couple moves through their thirties. They have probably had upward moves once or twice by their midthirties. These years are hard on the marriage, however, since primary energy is invested in ministry goals and raising children. This is the most critical time in a marriage as far as "falling out of love" is concerned. What happens for a couple relationally during this period sets the stage for coping with the midlife transition.

Fifteen to twenty years into ministry, a clergyperson is facing adolescence in the children, midlife transition, and a serious time of questioning in his or her professional life. She or he may feel the need for rest, perhaps even a change. A few fortunate clergy have the chance of a six- to twelve-month sabbatical. Unfortunately most are not so blessed and move toward burnout. The minister must face the reality that upward mobility is topping out. Most individuals begin to realize they are going to be frozen where they are. Churches will soon begin to disqualify them on the basis of their age. They may feel a pressure to make a change now or never. Yet these are hard years for moving their children. These concerns may become a preoccupation that complicates the midlife transition. The feeling of being trapped professionally can easily spill over into attitudes about the marriage. There is a second peak of career change in this period.

After the unsettled years of their early forties, most clergy enter into a time of comfortable productivity. They have learned to say no. They know their strengths and weaknesses. The fear of letting others share in ministry gives way to confident leadership. With the nest emptying at home and the midlife sense of generativity and integrity emerging, there is energy for an investment in marital intimacy. A time of recommitment can lead to a meaningful renewal of romance. If successfully established, this will carry over into retirement years. When negative aspects of the relationship become emphasized, there is growing loneliness and alienation.

Table 1, which I adapted from Levinson [16] to include the stages of ministry, summarizes the life stages I've discussed. Understanding the relationship between these life stages may help a couple maintain or rebuild vitality in their marriage. That's easier to do if the myths of "falling in love" are replaced with the reality of loving.

Item	Stage 1 (18-21 years)	Stage 2 (22-28 years)	Stage 3 (29-31 years)	Stage 4 (32-39 years)	Stage 5 (40-42 years)	Stage 6 (43-59 years)	Stage 7 (60 years and over)
Individual stage	Pulling up roots	Provisional adulthood	Transition at age 30	Settling down	Mid-life transition	Middle adulthood	Older age
Individual task	Developing autonomy	Developing intimacy and occupational identification; "Getting into the adult world"	Deciding about commitment to work and marriage	Deepening commitments: pursuing more long-range goals	Searching for "fit" between aspirations and environment	Restabilizing and reordering priorities	Dealing effectively with aging, illness, and death while retaining zest for life
Marital task	Shift from family of origin to new commitment	Provisional marital commitment	Commitment crisis; restlessness	Productivity: children, work, friends, and marriage	Summing up: success and failure are evaluated and future goals sought	Resolving conflicts and stabilizing the marriage for the long haul	Supporting and enhancing each other's struggle for productivity and fulfillment in face of the threats of aging
Marital conflict	Original family ties conflict with adaptation	Uncertainty about choice of marital partner; stress over parenthood	Doubts about choice come into sharp conflict: rates of growth may diverge if spouse has not successfully negotiated Stage 2 because of parental obligations	Husband and wife have different and conflicting ways of achieving productivity	Husband and wife perceive "success" differently; conflict between individual success and remaining in the marriage	Conflicting rates and directions of emotional growth; concerns about losing youthfulness may lead to depression and/or acting out	Conflicts are generated by rekindled fears of desertion, loneliness, and sexual failure

Intimacy	Fragile intimacy	Deepening but ambivalent intimacy	Increasing distance while partners make up their minds about each other	Marked increase in intimacy in "good" marriages; gradual distancing in "bad" marriages	Tenuous intimacy as fantasies about others increase	Intimacy is threatened by aging and by boredom vis-à-vis a secure and stable relationship: departure of children may increase or decrease intimacy	Struggle to maintain intimacy in the face of eventual separation; in most marriages this dimension achieves a stable plateau
Power	Testing of power	Establishment of patterns of conflict resolution	Sharp vying for power and dominance	Establishment of definite patterns of decision making and dominance	Power in outside world is tested vis-à-vis power in the marriage	Conflicts often increase when children leave and security appears threatened	Survival fears stir up needs for control and dominance
Marital boundaries	Conflicts over in-laws	Friends and potential lovers; work versus family	Temporary disruptions including extramarital sex or reactive "fortress building"	Nuclear family closes boundaries	Disruption due to reevaluation: drive versus restabilization	Boundaries are usually fixed except in crises such as illness, death, job change, and sudden shift in role relationships	Loss of family and friends leads to closing in of boundaries; physical environment is crucial in maintaining ties with the outside world
Ministry Stages	Call to ministry	Idealistic enthusiasm	Disillusionment	Upward mobility	Questioning of ministry goals	Mature productivity	Facing financial insecurity of retirement

Table 1 Stages of Marriage, Adulthood, and Ministry

Falling In or Out of Love

What is falling in love anyway? Scott Peck in *The Road Less Traveled* has given us the clearest discussion of love I have read. His section on love is required reading for couples who have "fallen out of love." [17]

If, as Peck proposes, we all fall out of love, why are some marriages alive and well while others are dead? That is best answered by identifying how love has been acted out in the relationship. Jesus said, "Where your treasure is, there your heart will be also" (Matt 6:21). If we see treasure as something we value highly, in which we invest ourselves, we see that a treasure can be another person. As we choose to invest our time and energy into the well-being of another, our heart (or feelings) will follow. I believe that is the essential principle on which positive emotional tone is maintained in a marriage. When two people continue to show caring for each other, their feeling of love will follow. That does not mean they will never be unhappy with each other. It doesn't mean they will always have ecstatic emotional highs. It doesn't even mean they won't "fall in love" with another person. It does mean they can experience individual growth while having their needs for intimacy met. I have observed that they may continue to enjoy the romantic feelings of being in love as they choose to really love each other in the sense of commitment.

Floyd and Harriett Thatcher, in their book *Long-Term Marriage,* give some important considerations for preserving a loving relationship. These include: learning to resolve conflict, developing interests for each partner outside of the marriage, working on communication skills, sharing spiritually, and keeping the sexual relationship active.[18] These positive actions can help a couple realize love in their marriage. There is no way that this can be done without effort. Those in Christian ministry are usually loving people who have invested their lives in showing love to others. That same giving of self must be channeled into their primary human relationship.

I encourage even the most disheartened couple to reinvest in each other. We have seen hundreds of marriages find real renewal through some basic hard work. The steps toward building back a marriage aren't easy, but we believe they are a good option to divorce or lonely coexistence. We have found the process a lot like growing a flower garden in the Rockies. I say in the Rockies because the natural conditions are extremely hostile—perhaps like the fallen state of mankind being basically opposed to oneness.

1. Preparing the soil. It takes a tremendous amount of back-breaking work to make a flower bed. We mostly have rocks. That's why they're called the Rockies. There is not one place you can sink a shovel without hearing the crunching sound of resistance. First you have to dig out the rocks, and so it is with a marriage. The rocks of bitterness, resentment, and self-centeredness must be removed.

Besides taking out rocks we have to add a lot of things to make the soil rich enough to grow plants. We put in peat moss and manure and specific chemicals that are lacking. A marriage relationship needs good drainage to keep it from becoming too wet with stagnating water. It needs fertilizer, input that will stimulate closeness such as touching, talk, and time. At times there are specific ingredients lacking in the personalities of husband and wife like positive attitudes about sexuality or willingness to trust.

2. Planting the seeds. It's important to plant the seed of the flowers you want. For a marriage, this means identifying the qualities that are desirable and sowing seeds for growth in those areas. These may be spiritual seeds of prayer or Bible study to produce the fruit of the Spirit. They may be psychological seeds of love, acceptance, and support to enhance better self-understanding and confidence. They may be intellectual seeds of instruction about financial management or sexuality to grow more effective behavior in these important areas. They may be physical seeds of diet and exercise to produce healthier bodies.

3. Cultivating the bed (no pun intended). As the plants grow it is critical to keep the weeds pulled and to keep the soil loosened around the tender plants. A marriage needs to keep the weeds out by learning to resolve conflict and deal with negative feelings that arise. It's also important to keep the ground from becoming too tightly packed. Loosen things up with some fun, recreation, and humor. Improving the sexual relationship will also help the plants to grow and flourish.

4. Protect the growing plants from the environment. There

are lots of elements here in the Rockies that can devastate our flower beds. Chipmunks, rabbits, and deer can trim back a promising petunia patch in one short snack. The temperature can drop below freezing even in July. The natural vegetation can grow into the flowers using up their food. A marriage is equally susceptible to environmental threats. Other relationships, the demands of ministry, and lack of warm, supportive friends can destroy the tender young plants before they get established.

When we can successfully accomplish all these steps we have the exhilaration of seeing fragrant, colorful blossoms greet each day. It is worth the effort. Every Christmas we receive scores of cards which remind us that our efforts are being rewarded. Marriages that were dead are alive and flowering again.

Summary

Falling "out of love" is a common experience. The normal stages of marriage, adult development, and ministry contribute to the growing apart. Couples must work to maintain a sense of "romance" and vitality in marriage. Since the marital relationship is the primary support for ministers it warrants the investment. Things that help a couple renew their love are:

1. Spending time together in interesting activity.
2. Learning to communicate.
3. Being creative in the relationship.
4. Sharing spiritual ideas and experiences.

INFIDELITY

Many of the Christian workers who come into counseling are propelled by an adulterous affair. I'm sure you know of some pastor whose ministry was terminated because of marital infidelity. In our experience at Marble Retreat only two individuals have consciously set out to be sexually promiscuous. Both had serious problems with their sexual identity. The others have looked back with amazement that it could ever have happened to them. Women and men alike have begun their marriages with a firm commitment to faithfulness. Both have had a firm belief that adultery is a sin. Consequently, they have suffered deep disruption of their identity structure after becoming involved extramaritally.

You might think that individuals with those ideals and working in Christian ministry would have a more solid protection from this problem. On the contrary, there are aspects of the ministry that increase vulnerability to infidelity.

In the first place, our world has rapidly changed regarding restraints on sexual promiscuity. Men and women are encouraged to "find themselves" through sexual encounters. The ideal of premarital chastity and marital infidelity is passe. Our culture entices us to realize our "full potential" as individuals by enjoying our sexuality through multiple partners. In movies, television, and real life our celebrities model sexual relationships as casual encounters with no apparent negative results. Ministers are not exempt from the subtle influence of these pervasive messages. I remember one young woman pastor who had been involved in an affair. She was really confused about the morality of her involvement. The man she had had sex with had convinced her that her ideas of sexual faithfulness to her husband were old-fashioned. She came to question whether biblical principles were still valid. Yet she was relieved that the guilt she had felt could be handled through confession and repentance.

One more vocationally specific factor is the minister's role in society. As a people-person, the minister is deeply involved emotionally with hurting people. Those in ministry are available to men and women who have many unfulfilled relational needs. They are seen as warm, caring, sensitive individuals. One of the critical needs in our impersonal society is for intimacy. A common complaint in marriages is the lack of sensitivity by spouses. Husbands, particularly, fail to provide their wives with a sense of emotional closeness. The minister looks very attractive as someone who will listen and understand. The developing closeness creates a danger for sexual involvement. So their caring role and their warm personality place ministers in jeopardy.

Another specific reason for increased vulnerability is the similarity between spirituality and sexuality. In both there is a lowering of interpersonal barriers, an encouragement of intimacy, and increased openness to profoundly moving emotions. Both provide a setting for intense physiologic response and a blurring of ego boundaries. A sense of oneness with those who share the experience is common. Touching, holding, and hugging are frequently a part of the encounter. Some people I've known have spontaneously compared their deepest spiritual moments to sexual orgasm. Involvement with adults of the opposite sex at this sensitive interface enhances the possibility of sexual intimacy.

From my experience, I'd identify yet another danger—the angry seductress. Some women carry a deep, inner hatred for men and a compulsion to gain control over them. Frequently they were rejected or abused by their fathers. Often they learned in childhood and adolescence that sensuality is their most effective weapon. Consciously or unconsciously, they form a pattern of destructive conquests of men while they appear to be helpless women who need a strong man to care for them.

What man of the cloth is not eager to help damsels in distress? Yet many pastors who have ridden to the rescue find themselves seduced, exposed, and expelled in short order. The "helpless damsel" sometimes even garners the love and compassion of the church. She plots her next assault while the last unsuspecting minister is still trying to remove the tar and feathers. One such woman we heard about had been the hapless "victim" of sexual advances by the last three pastors in her church. All had left in disgrace, their ministries nullified.

A minister is a particularly enticing target for this kind of woman. With a man of God, she can act out her hostility toward men in general, authority figures, symbolic fathers of society, and even God the Father all at once. It gives a gratifying sense of power. She again proves the male to be weak and inadequate.

There are also purely personal factors that contribute to a minister's vulnerability to adultery. Those who have grown up as Christians may begin to wonder what they've missed out on. They hear the intimate details of others' sexual lives. Their experience of having had only one sexual partner may begin to look rather unexciting. This is particularly true as the midlife transition approaches. If their marital sexual relationship is boring and unfulfilling they may be tempted to ask, "Hey, what have I been missing? I wonder what it would be like to have a lover?"

Some may have been plagued by questions of their sexual identity or adequacy. Men in ministry frequently find themselves in a female subculture. They work primarily with women. Their daily tasks are more intellect- and emotion-oriented. They are immersed in the symbols of "mother church." They can easily come to look for some affirmation of their manliness. Performing sexually is certainly that.

Other men with puritanical backgrounds may have what's called the madonna-prostitute complex. They have been so ingrained with sexual taboos that they see sex as totally sinful and vulgar. In their mind they know that marital sex is morally pure. Unconsciously, they feel that a wife and mother is too wholesome to enjoy sex. Only prostitutes or loose women could really be involved in something as lewd and carnal as sexual intercourse. These men may actually be unable to function sexually with their wives yet be quite active with an adulteress.

I have previously discussed (chapter 2) the vulnerability of youth workers and evangelists to sexual encounters. It is certainly important for Christian workers to understand this danger and take precautions against becoming involved in an affair. I have outlined some specific danger signs and ways to protect against adultery in "Avoiding the Scarlet Letter" (reprinted as Appendix 1).

You may not have an opportunity to help prevent the problems. You're likely to be consulted only after the fact. Your task will be to help a clergy couple work through the problem to renewal and restoration of their marriage. Here are some important considerations I have found through our experience.

Removing the Roadblocks to Reconciliation

I have often been amazed that there can ever be reconciliation after a mate has committed adultery. The wounds are deep and destructive. Yet in the Christian community there seems to be a remarkable willingness to attempt to repair the damage and rebuild the marriage. However, some common barriers do emerge to complicate the process. These must be avoided when possible and dealt with decisively when they appear.

1. Anger and unforgiveness. Anger is almost always a part of the picture. Interestingly, it will be present in both partners. The injured spouse has every right to be angry. That's apparent, but the offending mate may be just as angry. Mad at having been found out. Angry about the areas of disappointment the marriage had held before the affair. Anger toward self for being so stupid (to have become involved in the affair or to have married in the first place), and increasingly hostile that the spouse can't just let the whole thing drop.

The anger may progress through unforgiveness to bitterness. These attitudes are the most formidable walls to reconciliation. If they are not torn down, they will form an impossible barrier to any meaningful restoration of oneness.

At times it's necessary to evaluate a person's unwillingness to forgive. There can be many reasons at work. Some feel that forgiveness is equivalent to approval of the behavior. I've heard many Christians express the idea, "If I don't continue to show how much I condemn that action, my mate (or a child or friend) will think I am giving my consent to the sin committed." The unforgiving spouse needs to see that attitude as judgmentalism and let go of it. I also point out that people who live under condemnation frequently become totally frustrated that they can't live up to the expectations for holiness. In effect, they ultimately decide, "If I'm going to be hung as a thief, I might as well steal."

Another reason for unforgiveness is that to relinquish the hurt is letting go of a powerful means of control. Some people use guilt as their most potent force to manipulate others. To have such a "prize" hurt can give them tremendous leverage. That's hard to give up. One husband whose wife had committed adultery ten years ago continually reminded her of how deeply she had hurt him. He often told her she had no rights in their marriage, since she had broken her vows. In counseling he frankly admitted that he enjoyed the power that he had over her. He was afraid if he forgave her she would no longer be guilty and wouldn't do what he wanted any more.

Needless to say their marriage was miserable for both of them.

2. Pride. If either partner is controlled by self-righteous pride, reconciliation is practically impossible. When infidelity occurs there has been an obvious failure in the marital commitment and both husband and wife must honestly face some responsibility. If either is too proud to accept part of the burden of guilt and a share in the accountability for change, the process will likely prove too heavy for the other to bear alone.

For men and women in ministry, there is an ever present temptation to spiritual pride. They do try to live a righteous life, and they justifiably feel that they pay a personal price for their obedience to God. They may be able to show loving acceptance to your "generic sinner," but facing the sin of their own spouse is a different issue. They have been able by their superior spirituality to remain faithful in spite of the stress in the marriage. Now, here is their mate caught in adultery. They'd be surprised to discover that their attitude is like the Pharisee who prayed, "Oh, Lord, I thank you that I'm not like this sinner."

If you detect such an attitude you might explore whether or not it antedated the adultery. It may have been there and been a significant source of hurt for the unfaithful spouse. The pride must be dealt with spiritually so that love and grace can invade the marriage.

3. Fear. There is usually some fear related to reconciliation. The injured party will naturally be afraid to trust. The guilty mate may be afraid that significant change will not occur or that the spouse will hold the sin over his or her head in a controlling way. There may also be fear regarding exposure. Any of these areas of fear can create enough anxiety that reconciliation is threatened or blocked.

Get the couple to talk about their fear with each other—first in your presence and then in private. Using "straight talk" messages makes it easier for them. The anxiety can be owned without coming across as an accusation toward the mate. For instance, if an unfaithful wife is afraid her husband is going to punish her with his anger she can say, "Honey, I'm so afraid your hurt will cause you to be angry with me forever. I don't know if I can handle that in a good way."

Otherwise, she might be pushed by her anxiety to say, "You're angry with me! You're never going to let me live this down. You're still punishing me all the time." Those statements are much more likely to produce defensiveness and counter-attacks.

You might also focus on the fear that each has so he or she can identify the specific things the mate does that prompt fear. Understanding the fears as normal responses to their situation can reduce the negative impact. Enlist their cooperation with each other as they deal with the fears and reassure them that the fear will be time limited.

4. The third person: An unavoidable ingredient of an affair is the lover. What may happen in that corner of the triangle is entirely unpredictable. One thing that is predictable is that the continued presence of the other man or woman will create significant tension. Often the unfaithful spouse must deal with powerful feelings of responsibility toward the lover. It may seem ironic but the concern for the lover may be just as intense as for the spouse. It is imperative that those impulses to minister to the former lover be squelched and that particular ministry turned over to someone else. Contact must be cut off entirely.

I have found this to be so important that a geographical move and job change may be advised. I have known several ministers who stayed in their church with their lover still a member. Even when that was comfortable for them, their spouses who knew about the relationship had a much harder time with their fear and mistrust. In any case, the minister must be barred as a pastor or counselor to the former lover. Objectivity has been lost. If there are other staff members, they can provide the pastoral care. If not, another church should be sought either for the minister or the member involved.

5. Old patterns of relationship. When the marital relationship always had negative patterns, these may become serious barriers to reconciliation. For instance, a parent–child pattern that must change if a couple is to achieve a healthy mutuality in their marriage.

To identify the destructive patterns I ask each one to make

a list of the areas of conflict or hurt. Each writes one list from his or her own perspective and one of what he or she thinks the mate will say. It is not too surprising that each is usually fairly accurate in knowing what the other will say. They've heard it often. Helping them understand why they've been relating to each other in those ways may be new for them. Also teaching them some positive alternatives will be encouraging.

6. The cost of the affair. This factor varies considerably with the situation. I have just been counseling with a couple who has been very fortunate about the fall-out of his affair. No one has found out. His lover has admitted her sin and relinquished her claim. There was little emotional involvement in the romance. The sexual encounter was less exciting and less satisfying than his marital sex. The husband had not used lies and deception. There were no gifts given or money spent on the romance. All of these circumstances are unusual. It is much more common that the unpleasant consequences create significant financial or social costs. These produce serious resentment in the injured spouse. The depth of the resentment varies proportionately to these "costs" of the affair.

There is a critical balance necessary in dealing with this problem. On the one hand, the hurt spouse needs to express any anger about these costs. On the other, little can be gained by seeking some accounting of everything that was done. It is better for the unfaithful mate to confess that he or she was guilty of taking important emotional and material resources from the marriage, to ask forgiveness, and recommit to faithfulness.

7. The counsel of the ungodly. There are many dangers in what counsel is offered. One danger is that an injured wife may be extremely vulnerable to becoming romantically involved with a male counselor. One wife said she felt so lonely and rejected that she could have easily fallen into the arms of any caring, warm man. If a counselor of the opposite sex is consulted, it is important that objective professionalism and a high moral standard be maintained.

Counselors may also create a barrier by continuing to advise retribution or an uncompromising attitude toward the spouse. It is very easy to find counselors (even "Christian counselors") who readily recommend divorce rather than the hard work of reconciliation. Certainly we must remain loving and accepting toward those whose lives have been shattered by divorce, but I think the desire to show love has at times pushed counselors into a soft position about divorce. The secular press abounds with books advising divorce when marital bliss has dimmed. I think it's time to stand firm for marital permanence. That stand will involve costly commitment to working through conflict.

Overcoming these barriers to reconciliation is a first step toward the tough work of restoration, and it is necessary for successful growth toward oneness.

Reconciliation After Infidelity [19]

Not long ago a young couple was in my office for counseling. They were working through a serious marital crisis—infidelity. A few months before she had discovered his involvement with another woman. She confronted him and he confessed. They wanted to quickly move away from the pain, so he pledged to never see the other woman again and asked her forgiveness. She said, "I forgive you," and life moved on. Now, after several months, they were confused and angry with each other. For reasons they didn't understand things weren't rosy between them. She reiterated her forgiveness and he kept telling her to forget it, too. Somehow that wasn't enough to bring healing.

What they had done was only one part of the very difficult process of reconciliation. There is more to rebuilding a relationship than just forgiving. In counseling couples facing this struggle there are some specific steps I find helpful.

Many of the couples I see have never stopped to consider their options. They have made up their minds one way or another without any discussion. I think they need to talk together about the choices.

One choice, of course, is quickly to say, "I'm sorry and I forgive you," and then go right on with whatever inefficient system was in effect before the affair. That doesn't seem very attractive to me—or to most couples in crisis.

A second option is divorce. This may seem very attractive to both husband and wife, but because of their Christianity the possibility hasn't been thoroughly discussed. It may be the unspoken fearful thought that lurks in the corner like a monster. You need to help them broach the subject.

There are some apparently positive aspects of divorce. The most obvious is relief. When a relationship has been unsatisfying or frankly destructive, it feels good just to move out of the pressure cooker. When infidelity has occurred, the prospect of pursuing the new romance may be enticing. Finally it may seem attractive to move away from a stalemate in any direction, and divorce seems the easiest way to do this.

However, there are significant costs of divorce that also need to be considered. As I counsel couples I try to make them aware of these consequences. After the initial relief or the excitement of a new romance, most people face a period of grief that can last a year or more. Depending on the circumstances in the individuals' lives this depression may be very severe. Recently we have walked through a divorce with a friend. For her, the degree of hurt was quite intensive and she is only now coming out of it after two years. Even now, certain things that remind her of her former husband can start the flow of tears all over again. Her ex-husband had developed a romantic attachment while continuing to pay lip service to his love and commitment to his family, so the sudden announcement of divorce completely surprised her. He moved in with his lover so did not feel the initial grief. His grief came later, as he realized the loss of his closeness with his children.

Another result that I see is a loss of self-esteem. This is particularly true of the abandoned mate who is left feeling a deep sense of inadequacy. They frequently begin ruminating on the question: "What's wrong with me that I couldn't hold my mate?" That blow to their self-concept adds to the weight of depression. This damage will often persist into future relationships making self-disclosure and trust more difficult.

My friend Ken Bekkedahl, who pastors in Aspen, has lots of opportunity to counsel divorcing couples. One aspect of divorce he always points out is the financial devastation that occurs. He meets with the man and says, "Do you think you can afford to divorce? This may bankrupt you!" By then he has their attention and can go over their individual financial picture looking at what a divorce will cost. Aside from the legal fees, which can be minimized, maintaining separate houses, at times expensive moves, and loss of job are only the beginning. The complications come as children's needs become more expensive or a second mate and step-children enter the picture. Money may not be a good reason to stay married, but it may be a good incentive to reconsider a decision to divorce.

One other long-range effect of divorce that has been deemphasized in our divorce-prone world is the dissolution of the nuclear family. The problems for children of divorce are real and lasting. Their initial confusion, sense of abandonment, and grief is often expressed in school problems, drug and alcohol abuse, depressive withdrawal, delinquent behavior, and suicide.[20] Their long-range ability to form committed relationships is reflected in the increased incidence of divorce in children of divorced parents. With remarriage there is frequently a sense of further loss of the parent and feelings of rejection.[21] There is also a higher incidence of child abuse (particularly sexual) with step-parents.[22]

A further common complication with children is their discipline. Children quickly learn which parent they can manipulate, and both become more vulnerable to manipulation. Let's face it, nobody wants to always be the "bad guy"—especially not when the "good guy" is the ex-mate. We have friends who divorced some years ago and are now struggling with a son entering adolescence. I should say the father is struggling. After being the custodial parent for several years, he now sees his son migrating toward the mother who sets no limits on his behavior. Needless to say, the teenager would much rather be with his mother. Now, at a time when he needs some secure limits, he is manipulating the situation to support his total freedom.

Even as young adults, children of broken homes often say they wish their parents had not divorced.[21] Their lives continue to be more complicated as graduations, weddings, births, even funerals can become logistic nightmares.

I want couples considering divorce to look beyond the immediate relief of tension or their desire for personal pleasure to seriously consider the cost.

Realizing that divorce is a costly alternative can be a practical motivation to choose recommitment to the marriage. Coupled with the unmistakable position of Christianity regarding the permanence of marriage, there is little question of the preference for reconciliation.

I am often asked whether or not I ever advise divorce. Only under the most extreme circumstances, such as physical abuse, alcohol/drug dependency, or absolute refusal by one partner to work on the relationship, have I recommended divorce. I even think "staying together for the children" is not all bad. Our culture has placed such a high value on personal pleasure, comfort, and fulfillment that the legitimate needs of others, including children and society, have been ignored. I have known many couples who "stayed together for the children" —choosing to give them stability rather than strife, continuity rather than confusion. Not infrequently I have seen such marriages grow into close, mutually satisfying relationships as life goes on.

Making a definite choice and communicating the recommitment clearly is a critical step in the reconciliation process. There must be no question about the willingness to work toward oneness. That decision can be communicated in countless ways. It is important to know what says it most effectively between your clients.

One couple I know did this very effectively. Her main doubt was in his faithfulness since his affair. His primary area of mistrust was whether or not she would continue to be more affirming and less critical of him. They recognized these problem areas and made a part of the recommitment to work especially hard to allay these fears of their partner. He began to take her out with him more and to let her know his schedule. Rather than seeing that as control on her part he saw "checking in" as an investment in the marriage. She began to compliment him and express her gratitude for the nice things he did. She also refrained from being her usual negative, critical self. That was hard work for both of them, but those were the specific ways they could communicate recommitment best. The whole process of reconciliation is based on this step. If either person adopts a "you go first" attitude it will falter or fail.

Understanding the Hurt

Often the guilty partner would like for the whole sticky situation to just disappear. I've heard some men say, "Well, I came back. I chose to stay with you, so let's just forget it happened and get on with life. It's not such a big deal." It is a big deal, however, and it is critical for the partner who has been betrayed to sense understanding from her or his mate. Hearing the hurt and communicating understanding about it are essential for working it through.

This process is similar to completing the communication cycle. It gives the hurt person the valuable feeling of having really been heard and understood. Since the hurt goes both ways you can help each party identify with the other. I may ask the husband, "How did it feel to you when you were ignored (or criticized or deceived) at some time in your life?" As that feeling is recalled it is easier for him to respond in a nondefensive way to his wife's similar hurt. I may interpret for a wife how I believe her husband has been feeling in their relationship. He may have never been able or willing to communicate his feelings to her. Many wives have said, "You know I never thought he felt that way, but I can see now how he did."

There are many different dimensions to the insult felt. Some are unique to each individual and couple (e.g., violation of very private aspects of a relationship shared only by that husband and wife). Others are more universal. Of these, perhaps the most critical is the break in trust that has occurred. Marriage is built on trust and commitment to faithfulness, so when one partner commits adultery the foundation is seriously shaken. How severely the trust is broken depends on several factors. One is the level of dependency of the spouse who has been betrayed. For some individuals the betrayal does not create high levels of insecurity and anxiety. Just because of their inner strength they do not see the unfaithfulness as life threatening. Others may have very deep dependency needs and are left feeling completely vulnerable and defenseless. Another important determinant is the life experience and expectation of the spouse. If a person grew up in a home where infidelity was common, the expectation of faithfulness may not be strong. There can even be an expectation for infidelity.

Another significant variable is the length and quality of the marriage. If the relationship has been marked by conflict and disappointment, the final blow of unfaithfulness may not be too surprising. In such marriages there's not much trust left to be broken. If there had been many years of deeply committed devotion, the shattering of trust will be devastating. Similarly, the nature of the adulterous relationship affects the consequences. If it was essentially a "one night stand" which was quickly ended, the break in trust may not be very deep. If the affair was a prolonged one, there would be more instances of deception and betrayal creating a wider breach in trust.

Let me emphasize, however, that under any circumstances the breakdown in trust is a serious part of the hurt. Perhaps the first question the spouse asks is "How can I ever trust again?" The injured mind begins to doubt and question every absence. Suspicion and disbelief move in where trust and confidence were once in control. These are natural, expected, and difficult feelings to deal with for both partners.

A second important injury is to the self-esteem of the spouse. The fact that the unfaithful mate chose to stay in the marriage has very little effect on the level of insult felt. The overriding questions are: "What's wrong with me as a woman (or man) that I couldn't hold my mate? Am I inadequate as a person? Have I lost my physical and sexual attractiveness?" No matter what is said to the contrary, the fact that speaks loudest is "My mate chose someone to replace me!"

It is impossible for me to fully describe the inner pain and disruption of identity that is created. It is remarkable how much of our sense of who we are and what we're worth becomes enmeshed in the marital union. We really do become one flesh and a spouse still faithfully committed to the relationship feels that a large part of self has been brutally torn away.

Sadly, many extramarital affairs take place during the mid-life transition. That is a time of reassessment of value and direction. For both men and women there is a growing concern about aging and physical appearance. Men may be more concerned about strength, stamina, and sexual performance while women are worried about sags, bulges, and wrinkles. It is also sadly true that the lover is often a younger and more sexually attractive female or a more successful, powerful male. In both cases the inner doubts about self-worth are reinforced in the betrayed spouse.

Another aspect of the damage to self-image is the shame and embarrassment felt. It would seem that those consequences should be felt exclusively by the offending person, but not so. Practically every betrayed spouse reports a heavy sense of embarrassment. They often become withdrawn and isolated. They begin to imagine what others are saying about them and find it difficult to go out socially. They feel as if they are being blamed for their mate's unfaithfulness. In fact, they may truly blame themselves.

A significant part of the feelings to be worked through is the sense of guilt. It is important that whatever guilt is present be dealt with through forgiveness.

Hand in hand with the guilt is anger! This may be the last feeling to surface. Not infrequently the initial response is disbelief, then hurt, then self-doubt and recrimination, then guilt, and finally anger. Allowing the anger to surface and be expressed may be very threatening. In the wake of an affair the marriage may be so insecure that both partners are afraid to express anger for fear of driving the mate away completely. The anger is present, however, and needs to be expressed. It's important to realize that anger is not a sin and can be dealt with without destroying anyone. I try to prepare couples for the anger and reassure them that it can be worked through.

Some of the more individual, private areas of pain are: the loss of the sense of exclusivity in the relationship, the invasion of special places, music, and memories by the image of the lover, the death of dreams of the future, erosion of respect of the mate as parent to the children, and a sense of abandonment by God. Any of these may be a part of the hurt to be healed. It is important to explore all these areas and talk about them together.

This part of reconciliation was the most difficult of all for Bill and Kathy. They were unbridled romantics. A significant part of their feeling of being married was sharing in a wild romance. They sent each other cards and flowers. They had their favorite mood music always in the background. They regularly did unusual, spontaneous things like walks on the beach in the rain or picnics in the snow. When Bill discovered that Kathy had been sharing some of their most romantic experiences with another man, he was devastated. It became a terribly hard thing for him to bring that back into their relationship, and yet it had been and remained a critical aspect of their oneness. Kathy understood his hurt, but felt punished when he stopped doing the special things.

Applying Forgiveness

God has given us an effective way of dealing with even the severest kinds of emotional injury. Recognizing the damage and anger, communicating it directly to the offending person, and choosing to forgive is the pattern we have been given. This is essential. Forgiveness needs to be understood in spiritual, emotional, and physical terms.

Spiritually, we are commanded to forgive so that we may be forgiven. As long as we hold onto unforgiveness, we shut ourselves off from God's forgiveness. We set ourselves up as judges of those who have hurt us and become spiritually blinded to the reality of our own imperfection before a holy God. The result is a growing coldness and loss of love. Healing does not occur in such a climate.

Emotionally, forgiveness allows us to invest energy in the relationship. We cannot move toward intimacy without taking the risk to make that investment. An individual who does not take that risk becomes trapped in self-centeredness, bitterness, loneliness, and despair. Our own need for love and intimacy demands our choosing to forgive. It is critical that we understand forgiveness as a choice, an act of the will—not a feeling. As in love, we decide in forgiveness to act in a specific way. We decide to relinquish hurt rather than reinforce it.

That brings us to the importance of understanding the physical aspects of forgiveness. To do this one must understand the way the brain works neurochemically. In essence, it has been shown that memories are stored as physical structures, protein molecules. They are present in our brain cells and remain permanently. Each time a specific area of the brain is stimulated, a particular memory is recalled. Memory traces can be retrieved by making thought associations that select precise neuronal pathways to bring the stored memory into consciousness. When a specific memory trace is replayed repeatedly that recording is enhanced and more easily brought to awareness. We are familiar with this process in "memorizing" facts. We go over and over some information until it is readily recalled. The same thing happens with emotionally charged memories, whether positive or negative. If we have been hurt, the event and its associated feelings are deposited in our nerve cell computer. We can then either review that memory, rehearsing it into a vividly enhanced mental image, or we can choose not to allow its repetition, relegating it to the unconscious. That mental, neurochemical act is forgiveness. The memory is still there, but when life stimuli bring it to mind we choose to extinguish it rather than reinforce it. So the forgiveness is not a one-time, magical act that removes all memory and pain, but a continually repetitive choice. The outcome is a freeing up of brain energy and neuronal pathways for reconciling behavior and positive thoughts.

I tell couples about this aspect of forgiveness. It fits with their personal experience so it helps them see forgiveness as a volitional act instead of a feeling. It also helps them remain hopeful rather than sinking into despair when the old memory comes to mind. They can see forgiveness as a process rather than an instant cure.

Controlling Curiosity

The next step is a very difficult one for the injured spouse. It calls for overcoming a strong natural drive. In couples I've counseled after adultery, I find a universal curiosity about what happened. All the whens, wheres, and hows become compelling questions demanding answers. In my experience, hearing the answers only intensifies the feelings of rejection. Learning the facts creates visual images of the mate with the lover that must then be overcome. Some of the specifics may destroy important positive associations of the marriage. For instance, if a couple has enjoyed a very private, meaningful romantic attachment to a favorite restaurant, that beautiful shared tradition may be shattered by knowing "they" went there together.

Asking the questions also tends to alienate the guilty spouse. To be queried repeatedly about what happened intensifies the guilt. It can also serve to reinforce the positive memories of the love affair and enhance the feelings of protectiveness toward the lover.

I was recently counseling a man who had been unfaithful to his wife. He was telling me that one of the most difficult things for him was keeping quiet when his wife was so focused on the other woman. She was asking questions constantly about her in a judgmental, demeaning way. She'd ask, "Well, did your 'girl friend' do that better than me?" He knew he had done wrong and he understood his wife's angry feelings, but the truth was that he had deep, positive feelings toward the other woman. Hearing her attacked not only made him feel angry and defensive, but lowered his respect for his wife. It also made it harder to forget his "girl friend." That sort of reaction can be avoided if the injured spouse confines the curiosity to sessions with a counselor.

Rebuilding Trust

This takes effort by both husband and wife. The offending mate must make special efforts at reassurance of faithfulness. This means letting his spouse know where he is and with whom. It means reserving special looks and expressions of affection only for her. It means finding time to be alone together. It means being truthful and keeping commitments. Some of these behaviors may feel unnecessary or even like being controlled, but they are important if trust is to be rebuilt.

For the betrayed spouse, rebuilding trust includes accepting what her mate says without expressing doubt through accusations. When doubts arise, she may need to make first-person feeling statements about her problem with mistrust and anxiety rather than accusing "you" statements. That really sounds different. She can say, "I'm still having a hard time with my doubts and fears. I want to trust you, but my anxiety sometimes pushes me into mistrust." The alternative is, "Where have you been? You don't care if I'm alone and worried! You've been to her (or him) again, haven't you!" On the receiving end, those statements feel very different and will probably elicit a very different response. The first style can be heard with empathy. The second is sure to produce defensiveness. The first helps rebuild trust. The second confirms the mistrust.

I recently received a letter from a man who had successfully rebuilt his relationship with his wife. He said the thing that helped him most was her attitude of trust. Even at times when he did things that might have aroused her suspicion she didn't accuse him. He found himself wanting to keep her informed and avoid making her worry. His attitude changed from feeling threatened to feeling grateful. His gratitude was expressed in his concern for her. That reinforced her choice of showing trust. It wasn't an overnight miracle, but a steady successful process.

Focusing on the Positive

.There is a song from the forties that says, "Accentuate the positive, eliminate the negative." How can a couple "accentuate the positive" when a marriage has been disrupted by infidelity? One way is to recall the many positive shared experiences of the marriage: remember the initial attraction felt for each other; talk about the special events enjoyed together; look at the struggles they have come through together; think of all the acts of love that have been given and received.

As a counselor, you can help them "accentuate the positive" qualities of their mates. At a time like this, it's much easier to see the glaring faults. Remind them that they have to live with and be one with whichever aspect of their mate they choose to emphasize. When focused on the negative, one must try to live with a diminished person. When they accentuate the positive, they give themselves the best possible qualities to relate to.

The positive can also be accentuated by keeping a sense

of humor. The seriousness of the situation can become over-whelming. Being able to step back from self and look for the humor in life helps lighten the burden. The main principle to remember is to laugh at one's self instead of at the other person. There is a fine line between humor and hostility and it's easy to cross that line and ridicule a mate. Then the fun's over!

In counseling I find it very helpful to diffuse the gloom and heaviness by gently sharing some foolish or ludicrous be-havior of mine in a situation similar to that of the couple. For instance, I have worked hard to overcome being passive-aggressive. At times I have silently refused to do something that I agreed with Melissa needed to be done. My refusal to repair the screen so I wouldn't be "hen pecked" continued to let in the mosquitoes. They bit me just as much as anyone else. Usually confessing such ridiculous behavior touches a responsive chord in those I'm counseling and they can see the humor in their own patterns.

Accentuating the positive also extends to moving into the future together with optimism. Rebuild dreams. Be excited that the level of oneness can be deeper than it has ever been. Have faith in God that even from this painful, sinful event, His Spirit can bring good. (I have seen that happen many, many times.) Help each person see the prospect of working out changes in self as well as in the relationship as an exciting opportunity for growth. They need to know that the intense feeling of hurt and loss can be replaced by joy and peace, and even by being "in love" again.

Developing Mutuality in Need Meeting

Dave and Vera Mace have found that marital happiness is related most directly to mutual need meeting.[23] To the degree each partner feels his or her needs being met, the marriage seems fulfilling. When either mate is not feeling satisfied, the focus tends to be increasingly on the sense of disappointment. The unmet needs loom up in the mind as giants blocking the path to happiness. The dissatisfaction is usually expressed through criticism or withdrawal. Neither contributes much to effective change.

In working toward reconciliation it is important for each

partner to communicate areas of disappointment, but not to remain focused on them. Rather each must begin to focus on the needs of his or her spouse, looking for ways to more effectively meet those needs. When this is done it becomes mutually reinforcing. Each person begins to feel more cared for and less frustrated. The tendency toward being a score-keeper of hurts is decreased and the excitement of becoming a better mate is enhanced. Applying the principles of love from 1 Corinthians 13 should be emphasized repeatedly.

The conclusion of the matter is that the sin of adultery is forgivable. Relationships can be restored and often reach depths never before realized or thought possible. It's not easy, but neither is marriage—under any circumstances.

Summary

When infidelity has interrupted a marriage there are significant barriers to rebuilding the relationship. These include: anger, pride, fear, the third person, old patterns in the marriage, the costs of the affair, and the counsel each person has been given (or continues to be given).

Overcoming these barriers open the road to restoration. You can help a couple to:

1. Consider the options and make a definite clear-cut commitment to reconciliation.
2. Work through the hurt and apply forgiveness as a positive volitional act in obedience to the Lord.
3. Squelch curiosity about the affair.
4. Rebuild trust, focusing on positive elements in the marriage and developing mutuality in need meeting.

CHAPTER FIVE

DEPRESSIVE ILLNESS

DEPRESSION IS a normal emotion. It is a response to loss, loss of a loved person, loss of a prized possession, loss of a dream, loss of position, even loss of self-respect. It is also a common result of illness. Most people with a cold or the flu experience a degree of depression. It's a common side effect of many medications and alcohol. It may be related to anger that is repressed. Some types of depression are genetically determined, biological disorders.

I think it is safe to say that everybody experiences depression at some time or another. A report by the Institute of Medicine estimates that nine to sixteen million Americans suffer from depression at any one time.[1] Most depressions are self-limited and don't require treatment of any kind. At times, however, the symptoms of depression can become so severe that the person is not able to continue to cope effectively with life's demands. That's when treatment of some kind is needed. As a general rule, a thorough medical evaluation is essential since depression is frequently related to organic factors. Treating the underlying abnormality may relieve the affective disorder. If not, further treatment may be needed. The most effective treatment approach has been a combination of medical, psychosocial, and spiritual approaches.

I will be discussing primarily the psychotherapeutic management of depression. It is wise to keep in mind, however, that antidepressant medication may be useful. Even electroconvulsive treatment (ECT) given judiciously for some types of depression is the treatment of choice. It is important to see depression as the common affective expression of many different illnesses which may overlap each other in any one person. Neither the cause nor the treatment is simplistic. In the discussion to follow I will be isolating the various factors, but ask you to realize that they often interact. Don Baker's personal story of depression is an excellent description of its complexities as reported in his book *Depression*.

In the Christian workers who have come to Marble Retreat, depression has been by far the most common symptom. This is different from the general population where anxiety reactions, including agoraphobia and panic attacks, equal depression.[2] The types of depressive illness have varied, with most being burnout which has depressive symptoms, and dysthymic disorder (depressive neurosis). Both of these have features that are intensified in highly committed Christians. Burnout is related to trying to live up to unrealistically high expectations which is extremely common among the clergy. Depressive neurosis is related to unresolved anger or guilt which tends to be handled poorly in the Christian world.

We will look at several different variants of depression, their causal factors, and treatment. We'll also consider the risk of suicide among ministers and how to evaluate and deal with the suicidal person.

BURNOUT

Freudenberger popularized the term *burnout* in 1980 and called it "the high cost of aiming too high." [3] Since that time it has been a common topic of concern among those in ministry fields. Before the diagnosis was coined, ministers with burnout were probably just called "depressed" if they sought any treatment at all.

I remember the first burned-out pastor I saw in 1977. He was in his late forties and had been in pastoral ministry for twenty-five years. He said, "I'm tired out. I feel like I've been a fighter plane flying missions or waiting, revved up on the runway all the time. I could never turn the motor off. I never finished the work. There has always been more than I could do. Always out there on the runway. Always with the engine running wide open. I just can't take off any more."

His story has become a familiar one. Ministers who are worn out. I receive many calls from clergy who say, "I think I'm suffering from burnout. How can you tell if you're burned out?"

The diagnosis is not hard. Although it is not an approved diagnosis in the American Psychiatric Association's Diagnostic and Statistical Manual, it seems distinct in its presentation. There are definite depressive symptoms. These include: fatigue, difficulty becoming motivated, loss of enjoyment and enthusiasm, withdrawal, sadness, loss of appetite, sleep disturbance, and trouble making decisions. There may be various physical symptoms as well. The onset is usually gradual with fatigue or loss of interest coming first.

In evaluating burnout you will find a preponderance of perfectionistic individuals who are workaholics. They fit into Freudenberger's original description. They are idealistic and compulsive. Ministers who suffer burnout are very committed and are unable to say no. They are frequently trying to gain a sense of approval, usually of a parent.

Adam was a typical burnout. He was forty-two and in his third pastorate. He was the oldest of three siblings and never felt he could please his father who was the dominant parent.

He was an overachiever in all areas—academically, athletically, socially, even financially. He tried everything to get his dad's blessing. Nothing seemed to work. He was an honor graduate in college and seminary and was widely acclaimed in his denomination. He won an "Outstanding Young Man in America" recognition in his first pastorate. His churches grew and he continued to move up.

When he finally came to a standstill with burnout, his church was still doing great. No one suspected the turmoil that raged inside. He was disillusioned and felt like a terrible failure. He became withdrawn and irritable, finally refusing to go to the office.

His wife, Susan, had been seeing the increasing depression, but he masked it extremely well at work. She kept asking him what was wrong and suggesting he get help but only met with defensiveness.

When he could go no more, he was lovingly urged into therapy. The hardest thing about that for Adam was for his father to hear about his "breakdown."

There is an ongoing debate in psychiatry about whether or not there is a difference in endogenous depression which has no external causes and exogenous or reactive depression related to life stress. The evidence is at best conflicting. It certainly seems that burnout is a form of depression that shows a combination of internal and external causes. I find that burnout results from trying to meet demands that are perceived to be greater than one's ability to meet them.

The pivotal aspect of that formula is the person's continued effort to meet the demands. For ministers, in general, the demands are overwhelming, yet many arrive at a balance in their approach to the work. They don't continue to push themselves unrealistically. For the person who succumbs to burnout there is no balance. The drivenness inside intensifies the pressure outside. There is no rest because self-worth has come to hang in the balance. As with Adam, there is something to prove through the high goals—the impossible goals—that are set. These individuals seem to be on a relentless course toward self-destruction. They can't stop. Perhaps on a deeply unconscious level the conflict is between proving dad was wrong and proving he was right. There seems to be no way to get his final blessing so finally achieving failure is an ironic solution.

The treatment of burnout is fourfold. First, the person must be allowed to rest. Removal from responsibility is essential, since a significant part of the syndrome is fatigue. A supportive environment is important where love and acceptance are available. Good diet and recreation are important. The opportunity for spiritual renewal in a noninvasive way is necessary. Keep in mind that the personality of these ministers tends toward compulsion. That means they will likely begin to attack any treatment "schedule" with their same perfectionistic goal orientation. Enforced nonactivity is essential. A heavy emphasis on spiritual discipline will only reinforce their feelings of guilt and failure.

Second, the basic underlying drive to achieve must be evaluated. When it arises from a low sense of self-worth and need to gain parental approval, as it usually does, the fallacies in that system need to be identified. The person must come to realize that his worth is established firmly and securely by God. It isn't necessary to have the parental blessing to assure value. In most cases it's also impossible. Either the parent has been giving approval that wasn't heard, or never gives praise or affirmation to anyone. Burnout victims may need to talk with their parents about the feelings of disapproval or nonapproval they've had.

This process of self-acceptance can be enhanced as you give your love and acceptance. In the therapy setting the client is removed from his usual performance–reward system and can begin to comprehend grace as unmerited favor. I have found touch to be very helpful. I give these unhappy ministers a big hug and tell them they are all right. They frequently cling to that embrace from the depths of the hurt child within.

Praying with them for the healing love of God to surround and penetrate their being may be appropriate at some point. I usually evaluate what their spiritual feelings are first. When they are guilty and perhaps angry at God, I don't want to increase those feelings by coming on with an immediate "spiritual fix." I have found they first need to sense acceptance on a human level. They need to feel a freedom to express their negative spiritual thoughts then to be loved back into God's arms.

Scriptures that describe God's love and grace become meaningful as safety and acceptance are established. I have found the story of the Prodigal Son especially applicable. These children of the Father have not been in a far country sinning, but they've never recognized God as a loving Father waiting to embrace them. Like the older brother, they've been trying to earn a love that can't be earned. Now they have come to the point of total bankruptcy like the Prodigal. Now they can realize emotionally that they are loved in spite of themselves.

The third treatment factor is modifying their behavioral patterns. They will need help from their mates as well as church leaders or ministry colleagues to make the necessary changes. These include learning to let go of control. Allowing others to share the load is hard for them. They must learn to prioritize demands and say no more often. They need to learn to play and to rest. There must be a growing awareness of their own need for spiritual feeding and renewal. Involvement of the spouse in the treatment process is very helpful. Encourage the couple to establish a support group that can reinforce the changes and confront old patterns. And point out Jesus' ability to get away from the needs of the masses and to have fun with his friends.

A fourth dimension of treatment is to improve the person's ministry skills. As we have reflected on the causal factors of "trying to meet demands that are perceived to be greater than one's ability to meet them," we have dealt with the expectations placed on self and ways to reduce the demands. At times a person may be actually unprepared for some areas of ministry. The choice is to drop those as role requirements or to get training to do them effectively. It is surprising to me how often clergy are poorly trained to meet some ministry demands. They know theology, but may have received little instruction in practical skills, such as dealing with conflict or managing money and time.

One pastor who was here recently because of burnout had done well in his ministry until coming to his present parish.

He was met with a few powerful, obstreperous, critical people who thrived on conflict. He had always avoided conflict at all cost. This time the cost was almost his ministry. He realized that he needed to learn to confront in an assertive way and found a conference dealing with that topic. Not only did he register, but he convinced one of the difficult members of his board to go with him. I see that as a very positive approach to a personal deficiency.

Most ministry boards are accepting of the need for continuing education. Christian workers can be encouraged with your recommendation to enlist their boards' support for useful training. Some denominations or conferences have funds and scholarships available as well. The burnout crisis has everybody's attention and can provide a point of readiness for change in lots of ways. The congregation's awareness of its minister's needs is one of those ways and should be utilized for everyone's good.

Summary

In conclusion, let me enlist you in educating ministers and laypeople alike about the possibility of burnout. Help them take action to avoid it by:

1. Finding self-worth through God rather than production.
2. Learning to prioritize and set realistic limits on demands.
3. Taking time for personal spiritual renewal.
4. Establishing good health habits of diet, rest, and exercise.
5. Accepting limitations and working in areas of strength.
6. Improving ministry skills when necessary.
7. Maintaining an emotional support group including spouse and friends.
8. Keeping a sense of humor about life and especially about self.

A helpful resource on burnout is available from Ministers Life Resources.[4] Another is the special issue on burnout of Fuller Seminary's alumni publication.[5]

I believe burnout is a preventable illness. Every effort toward reducing the pain it brings should be pursued.

DYSTHYMIC DISORDER (DEPRESSIVE NEUROSIS)

A second type of depression that Christian workers seem particularly susceptible to is neurotic depression. This depression is less related to current life stress. The roots extend far into childhood and are entangled with painful conflicts. The emotional conflicts have been repressed and are no longer conscious, but the feelings remain destructively active. People with dysthymic disorder may recall a lifetime pattern of depressed mood. Their adolescence and adulthood has been punctuated by episodes of gloom. Their moodiness may be apparent to those closest to them, but may remain an undisclosed misery that no one else knows.

The reason Christian workers may be more prone to dysthymia is that the unacceptable feelings involved are anger and guilt. Those go hand in hand and seem very non-Christian. When anger comes into consciousness and is unresolved it produces anxiety and guilt—anxiety because the hostility induces murderous thoughts. Becoming aware of an impulse to destroy another person is frightening. Realizing that rage is lurking within produces guilt. Those feelings become mutally reinforcing. The guilt creates more anger.

When it is first generated in childhood, the anger is directed toward the person who initially created the turmoil. The mind asks, *Why should I feel guilty and take the rap for this? I didn't do anything to cause this mess. I shouldn't feel guilty. I'm justified in my rage.* But that is too threatening to a child. He or she is totally dependent on the adult care givers. Then the anger is turned back toward self and the guilt becomes attached. Now the rage that was so threatening, the rage at mother (or some other significant person) that prompted destructive ideas, is repressed. The mind handles it by removing it from consciousness. What's left is the misdirected anger at self and the guilt of being such an unloving child. The process may be conditioned in a very short time interval, particularly if the parent uses guilt and shame to control the child. You can see this happening in a three- or four-year-old. Already the anger that might have exploded in the "twos" begins to change its face to self-deprecation. The anger becomes shame and guilt and, more and more, the child is putting self down. She or he becomes sullen and inhibited.

The system may be initiated from guilt rather than anger. If the child is shamed for certain thoughts or deeds the weight of the guilt can create anger toward the judge and the system. It is painful to feel guilty. Nobody enjoys that pain and anger toward those who create the guilt is a natural result. Then the cycle, fed by anxiety over the possible outcome of the anger, begins to roll again. It becomes a downward spiral carrying the person into deeper levels of self-recrimination and despair.

The sad thing is that the anger may have been quite understandable or minor. The child feels angry because the parent ignores some feeling or need for attention. The anger may stem from what seems to be unfair favoritism toward a sibling. Those feelings happen regularly in the course of a family's interactions. They can be handled without becoming convoluted. The anger can be identified and listened to and talked about with forgiveness asked for and given. Instead the parent may be too busy and simply silence or punish the distressed child, leading to confusion and guilt. The danger lies in that response becoming the usual pattern.

It is also sad that the guilt a child carries is often false guilt. No real sin has been committed, yet the feeling of guilt is assumed and accepted. There are all sorts of life events that children can't understand. Because a child's thinking is egocentric, the universe becomes interpreted through those filters. A relative's death, mother's premenstrual tension, the parent's separation, little sister's accident, World War III, and the national debt all become the responsibility of "me." It's frightening to feel like the omnipotent center of the universe. It's unfortunate when some hapless child carries a sense of responsibility for some disaster throughout life, but it happens a lot.

I said Christian workers seem more susceptible. The reason is that anger has been badly misunderstood in some churches and Christian homes. Consequently, those raised with a strong taboo against anger are likely to repress it. As a guilt-laden child becomes older and learns about *sin,* the "natural" explanation for this discomfort inside is found at last. "It is because I'm a sinner that I'm so bad." Unfortunately, confession, repentance, and grace work best for real sin. When the guilt is false guilt attached to a non-sin it seems to escape God's grace. I have seen some Christian workers who were motivated into ministry primarily as a way to work out the guilt and gain salvation. That's a no-win work trap. There's no wonder that it ends in depression and despair. That's what happened to Bernie and to Jana. Their different stories are not uncommon.

Bernie came to the Retreat several years ago because of his depression. He had become withdrawn and practically nonfunctioning in his pastorate. He was tearful much of the time and guilt ridden. He felt like a failure as a pastor, as a husband, and as a father. He couldn't understand why his family and church members stayed by him. He felt they just didn't really know what an awful person he was. He wasn't exactly sure what he had done that was so terrible. He was plagued at times by lustful thoughts toward beautiful women and at times yearned for some material luxury or pleasure. He had always confessed such feelings and yet continued to feel guilty. God seemed distant and condemning. His prayer life was cold and ineffective. He had seriously thought of suicide. Once, a month before I saw him, he had even taken his hunting rifle down from its rack and held it in his hands for several minutes. He put it up knowing that was not a solution he could choose.

Bernie's life history was a fascinating story. He was the unplanned and unwanted baby, eight years younger than his four siblings. They grew up on a farm and times were tough. It was at the end of the Great Depression. His father had lost his land and he became bitter working as a tenant farmer who could barely feed the family. Another mouth to feed was unwelcomed.

Dad's bitterness and pessimism pervaded the family. The mother was strained and overworked. She had little time to give her children attention and affection. Bernie's two brothers and two sisters felt the weight of the parents' unhappiness and focused their anger toward Bernie. He came along about the time their life seemed to fall apart, so they naturally assigned the blame to him. He was the constant target of their hostility.

Bernie's initial story about those miserable circumstances was remarkably sterile. He gave the facts as though it had all happened to someone else. In fact, his first account had great gaps before age thirteen and fourteen that he didn't remember at all. He gave the bare facts of years and ages and names—few specific events and no feelings.

As we probed the history of his depression, he began to identify earlier and earlier bouts of loneliness and sadness in his life. Eventually, he saw that he had always felt worthless and guilty. That realization seemed to unlock a room he had closed off in his mind. The pain of his childhood had been securely walled off. Unfortunately, the guilt kept seeping its way under the door and pervading his life. The anger he had felt at the unfairness of his life remained unconscious. We soon discovered why.

Once, when he was eight and his next oldest brother, Bill, was sixteen, they were sent out to work on the irrigation ditches. They took their shovels and started out to the fields. As usual, his brother began to criticize him. Bill told him what a worthless runt he was. Bill accused him of being to blame for their oldest brother, Bob's, getting a beating the night before. He became vulgar and started taunting Bernie about sexual acts that Bernie didn't even understand. On and on it went as they worked on the ditch: "You can't do anything right. When are you going to quit being such a baby?"

Bernie began to flush with rage as he told the story. He remembered how angry he felt. He kept thinking how he'd like to kill his brother. Finally, in a bullying outburst, Bill pushed him down into the ditch and laughed at him as he struggled out, wet and muddy. Bernie began to sob convulsively as the images came rushing back. He charged blindly at Bill and swung the shovel with all his might. His mind was filled with the sight of the blood gushing from Bill's head as the shovel landed. Then everything went blank in Bernie's memory. He vaguely remembered running to the house and getting a terrible licking for what he'd done. The most vivid thought was that he had killed his brother. His feelings of worthlessness were confirmed. He was a terrible person who didn't deserve to live. That became the inner truth in Bernie's unconscious that controlled his life. "You don't deserve to live."

It was interesting that during the working through of these feelings Bernie reported having had a recurrent dream. This time there was a new twist to it. He had often dreamed of being in an old two-story house, like the farm house they lived in when he was eight. He would go upstairs to a certain room, but it was always locked and he would awaken with feelings of fear and frustration. Just after remembering the attack on Bill he had the dream again. Only this time the door was open and he went in. There in the room was his family and Billy with a bandaged head. The family was happy to see him and asked where he had been.

Jana's story is similar yet different. She also came to counseling because of depression. She was a single missionary on medical leave because of her symptoms. She was depressed, but her hostility came through very clearly. She was sarcastic and critical and very cold toward the men in the group. When confronted, she denied any feelings of anger.

Jana was an only child and the apple of her father's eye. As she entered adolescence she remembered her mother's being increasingly jealous of the attention and affection Jana got from Dad. She could endure Mother's put-downs and innuendos because Dad would defend her and tell Mom to lay off. As a blossoming young woman that felt good.

Then one day she came home from school and walked into a violent argument between her parents. Her mom had discovered there was another woman in her father's life and now he was packing to leave. Jana felt as if he were being more unfaithful to her than to Mom. They had been close. He loved her best. Now there was another woman he was choosing. Jana's world collapsed. Her dad completely deserted her. He didn't have room in his life for a teenage daughter. His new wife wasn't much older than Jana, who was left to live with her mother's bitterness and rejection. Not much changed between them except that Dad was no longer her champion. She gradually began to accept the blame her mother heaped on her for the collapse of the marriage.

Her anger toward her mother was readily available. They weren't together more than an hour before they were at each other. However, the inner rage at her father was not as conscious. She still needed the fantasy of his total love. But the hostility was there. He had abandoned her. She had not had a meaningful relationship with any man since.

Both Jana and Bernie viewed God through their childhood eyes as someone you can't really trust to look after you. Bernie felt he didn't deserve to be loved. Jana wouldn't risk getting close and becoming vulnerable again. As they became aware of the dynamics in their emotional development and learned to deal with them consciously, they were able to change their view of God and accept His love and grace.

In treating dysthymia I have found uncovering the repressed feelings and memories to be critical. It's important to do this in a gentle, supportive way. You must remember that psychological defenses, such as denial, repression blocking, projection, and transference, are protection against pain. One of my teachers at the Mayo Clinic used to tell us about a Brazilian gourd. He said it was about the size of a person's head and contained five thousand seeds, all geometrically arranged. He'd pause, then say, "It's very easy to scrape out all those seeds. . . ." The implication would slowly dawn— it's not so easy to put them all back in. So it is with a person's repressed feelings. Anyone assaultive enough can break down defenses and scrape out the anguish. Putting it all back together in a healthy reintegration is not so easy.

Allow the person to come into those dark shadows of self slowly, in the presence of someone safe. Ask tentatively what is there. Don't assume you already know. That's the wonder of doing psychotherapy. No two people are alike, and you are being privileged to see another human soul laid bare before you. What an unfathomable honor. What an awesome responsibility. At times you'll be afraid to look and want to close your eyes to these shadows and what they hide. And yet you can't. You must face and feel and share the pain. What a gift to receive—and to give.

The most fruitful areas to explore are: early memories, rela-

tionships with parents or parent substitutes, feelings and interaction between siblings, how anger was expressed, how love
and affection were demonstrated, early sexual experiences and
attitudes, feelings about the emerging self, fantasies and
dreams, traumatic events such as separations and illness, and
the spiritual pilgrimage. Depressed people are also relieved
to broach the subject of suicide. It has almost always been
somewhere in their thinking. Exposing it to the light is a
relief.

After uncovering the feelings and providing that catharsis,
it's important to bring healing to those areas of pain. One
of the most useful tools we've found is having the person
write out the conflictive feelings to the important other. Writing the memories and emotions on paper externalizes them
and defuses their explosive potential. The letters need not
be mailed, indeed some can't be for the person has died. Some
may be mailed and open the door to meaningful communication. I have each person read the letter(s) to me aloud to
evaluate what feelings they have touched and hear any areas
for further work.

I have found group therapy to be extremely useful in the
psychodynamic approach. A feeling of mutual support develops. Areas of memory and painful feelings are stimulated by
the stories of others. Transference patterns (like Jana's with
men and Bernie's with siblings) emerge. Group members are
able to bring insights that Melissa and I may miss. For our
own survival, the most important feature may be that intense
feelings are diffused into the group rather than directly focused on us.

I also use prayer to assist in the uncovering of painful memories and in their healing. I pray privately for each person
and for myself to have wisdom. I may pray with the person
for the Holy Spirit to reveal the areas that need His healing
touch. And finally, we pray together our thanksgiving for the
experience of walking together through the valley. Dr. William Wilson has discussed the use of prayer in therapy as a
significant force toward healing.[6]

There is one other very important ingredient to treating
depression. That is to restore hope. As I have said, depression

is a self-limited disorder. A bout might last days to weeks to months, but unless suicide intervenes the person will recover. Color will return to life and the dull gray existence is over. Let them know that they *will get better*. From inside the valley there can appear to be no hope. Your word and presence with them will give them the courage to go on.

Summary

Ministers are particularly prone to dysthymia because of their tendency to repress anger and guilt. Dealing with this neurotic syndrome entails work on the early life roots.

Some important considerations are:

1. Gently explore painful childhood memories.
2. Give permission to "honor your father and mother" by breaking negative behaviors.
3. Group therapy will frequently provide a supportive, dynamic setting for working through early conflicts.

GRIEF

It has been my joy to open the garrisoned gates of grief for many depressed clergy. I say joy, not in the sense of a happy day at the beach, but in that unspeakable touching of two souls in a moment when aloneness is breached. In those brief encounters we have shared our tears and held on to each other and to the sweet sadness that surrounded us, closing out the world.

In *A Severe Mercy*, Sheldon Vanauken discusses grief in these terms: "The death of any familiar person—the death, even, of a dog or cat—whether loved or not leaves an emptiness. The great tree goes down and leaves an empty place against the sky. If the person is deeply loved and deeply familiar the void seems greater than all the world remaining. Under the surface of the visible world, there is an echoing hollowness, an aching void—and it cuts one off from the beloved. She is as remote as the stars. But grief is a form of love—the longing for the dear face, the warm hand. It is the remembered reality of the beloved that calls it forth. For an instant she is there, and the void denied." [7]

Grief is the love that brings forth the reality of the beloved and denies the void, the emptiness of the loss. But what if the grief is denied? Then there accumulates a greater void and emptiness. The losses multiply the void until a portion of the self collapses into the void in depression.

Ministers are set up by their role to deny grief. They are the ones who bring solace and spiritual strength to those who mourn. It is remarkable how many times I have heard a story like Dave's.

Dave had watched his wife die a long and agonizing death with cancer. He was pastoring a church and they had teenage children at home. He felt he had to be strong. He wanted the community to see that Christians had no fear of death and wanted to provide stability for his children. He never cried. He never missed a day at work. He spoke briefly at her funeral. He never mourned.

Years later he was depressed and couldn't figure out why. In talking about her struggle into death he suddenly collapsed into deep sobs of sadness and pain. His long overdue grieving began.

Hal not only lost his wife, but, a month later, a daughter in an accident. Like Dave he remained in control, never dealing openly or even privately with the emptiness suddenly thrust into his life. He maintained his composure during therapy except for a few seconds that tears filled his eyes. That was enough to tell him he needed to grieve. He went home for time alone with picture albums that he had steadfastly avoided since the deaths. The grief work was started.

George was a garrulous, jovial pastor who could not understand the bouts of sadness he was experiencing. He was the "religious one" in his family and had preached his mother's funeral without shedding a tear. People remarked about how strong he was. He has been very close to his mother and talked everything over with her. Now she was gone and he had denied the loss. He suddenly realized that although he said her death hadn't bothered him, he had been unable to go to the cemetery where she was buried. He had visited his sister's house across the street many times, but would not go near the grave. He tearfully confessed his fear. He felt that if he ever started to grieve he'd never stop crying. He was able to cry and to talk about how much he missed "Momma." It was hard because "big boys don't cry and grown men don't ache for their mommas."

I could go on. It is important in assessing depression to ask about the losses and specifically how the minister grieved. At times all it takes is your permission for him or her to cry to open up a delayed grief reaction and begin the healing of the depression. It can be a painful experience for you both, but one that brings a joyful oneness you will cherish.

In therapy for grief there are several aspects to keep in mind. You won't always see Kubler-Ross's steps of grief (i.e., denial, shock, protest, and acceptance), but it is helpful to have an awareness that grief is a process. It commonly lasts from six months to two years. In the loss of children, and to a similar degree mates, the feelings of loss may never be entirely gone. Don't try to cut short the process because of your own anxiety and discomfort. The person grieving must walk through the darkness.

John Claypool has given us a moving description of grief in his personal account of the loss of his daughter. *Tracks of a Fellow Struggler* takes its theme of hope from Isaiah 40:31 which says, "Those who hope in the Lord will renew their strength. They will soar on wings like eagles; they will run and not grow weary, they will walk and not faint." Claypool reminds us that there are times that "walking and not fainting" is all we can really do, but that the Lord is faithful to His Word. He will help us walk and not faint.

A second point to focus on is the anger and guilt that may follow the loss. There may be anger at being abandoned or because of unmet needs in the relationship. Unresolved anger may be left over from conflicts with the deceased or there may be anger about the provisions of the will. Some people allow their expectations about grief to prevent them from expressing the negative emotions which then can grow into bitterness and depression.

My first encounter with such melancholia was as a college sophomore. I was selling Bibles door to door and was invited into the house of a reclusive middle-aged woman with about a thousand cats in her small apartment. She began an hour-long diatribe about her dead husband and the evil he had done to her. They didn't teach us at sales school how to get "out," only how to get "in." I quit for the day after that experience, and I didn't even sell her a Bible. Her anger was overwhelming.

Guilt can be equally crippling. I suppose most everyone can see things they failed to do for a loved one who died. Usually a person is able to find balance between those regrets and the positive aspects of the relationship. Those who get hung up in their guilt are often those who had angry feelings toward the dead person. On an unconscious level they may feel that their anger contributed to the death. They may have even consciously wished the person dead. It's important that those feelings and impulses be seen in the daylight. Those are normal feelings that don't have magical powers. What does have power is the guilt unconfessed and God's grace to cover the guilt.

I have been talking about loss in terms of death of a loved one. Other losses can be just as critical in the etiology of depression. Ministers are assailed with losses year after year. They see many friends come into their lives only to move away. Their own tenure is frequently short. They lose dreams as ministry goals are thwarted. They may lose self-respect under a barrage of criticism or after forced resignation. All such losses call for some grief work—talking about the hurt and anger, the emptiness and sadness occasioned by the loss.

Nowhere is listening more important than in dealing with grief. Learn to sit quietly and patiently. Hear what the person is saying. I've heard so many people say the most helpful thing to them in their time of grief was a friend who was just there. No platitudes or sermons were given. No cheerful banter to lighten the mood. Just their presence.

Job says, "Listen carefully to my words; let this be the consolation you give me" (Job 21:2).

Summary

Pastors are susceptible to delayed grief reactions because of their need to be strong in the face of loss. Help them:

1. Recognize that grief is a healthy emotion.
2. Express the aspects of grief—anger, guilt, and loss.
3. Realize that all of life's losses (dreams, goals, friendships, etc.) create grief.

MAJOR AFFECTIVE DISORDERS

A discussion of depression is not complete without some mention of this group of illnesses. It includes: manic–depressive (or bipolar illness), unipolar depression, and psychotic depression related to organic disease, hormonal changes, or child-birth. These mood disorders are severe and seem to be primarily determined by a neurochemical imbalance.

Manic–depressive illness and unipolar depression are both recurring cyclical disorders that have a strong genetic component. In the bipolar variety individuals oscillate between bouts of depression and bursts of euphoria. These cycles have occurred as rapidly as every twenty-four hours but usually cycle in several month intervals. The manic phase is marked by energetic overactivity. There is a grandiose expansiveness that gives manics a "hail fellow well met" aura of charisma. They may give away new cars or invest in gold mines. They sleep very little and talk nonstop. Their light-heartedness is extremely superficial. They can become violently irritable in a second and their combativeness is frightening. I recall one man who became suddenly assaultive in the hospital and had broken one doctor's jaw and knocked a large policeman unconscious before being subdued by eight big men. The point is that these people are potentially dangerous physically and economically to themselves and their families. They need to be hospitalized as quickly as possible. They are not usually cooperative about being controlled, so involuntary admission is often necessary. Don't hesitate to suggest or institute that process.

Both bipolar and unipolar illness can be well controlled in frequency and severity by medication. Lithium and antidepressants are effective in combination and may need to be continued indefinitely.

Psychotic depressions are those in which the afflicted person has delusional thinking (i.e., irrational thoughts). These illnesses are often related to some organic pathology such as hypothyroidism, pancreatic disease, uncontrolled diabetes, various states of chemical intoxication, drug/alcohol abuse, or child-birth. These individuals also need to be hospitalized for diagnosis and treatment. Correcting the underlying disorder brings them back to sanity and out of the depression.

It is important for you to become familiar with psychiatric hospital facilities and physicians in your area so that you can confidently refer a minister who might have one of these syndromes.

SUICIDE

The only significant threat to life in depressive illness is suicide. Recent epidemiologic reports identify approximately thirty thousand suicides in the U.S. per year making it the tenth leading cause of death.[8] There are probably many unreported suicides in which an automobile is used as the instrument of death. Suicide incidence is lower among population subgroups with active religious affiliation and is low among Christian workers. We only know of one suicide that has occurred in those who have been to Marble Retreat since 1974.

Although suicide is not common among clergy, it is always a risk in any depressed individual. In a recent study reported in the *American Journal of Psychiatry*, Dr. Jerome Motto developed a list of prediction variables that is of some use in identifying high risk individuals.[9] These are listed in Table 2.

It is most important to hear his caution about using these indicators. When dealing with a potential suicide, each case is the most important statistic. Every case must be taken seriously. Use the high risk variables only to increase your understanding of circumstances that may affect an individual's life, but not as a checklist to eliminate a person from the risk of suicide.

One item that is not included clearly in the variables Motto considered is the degree of "hopelessness" the person has. Beck, in a recent study, found that very few individuals who score low on the hopelessness scale of the Beck Depression Inventory commit suicide. On the other hand, many people

Variable	High Risk Category
1. Age	Risk increases with age
2. Occupation	Executive, administrator, owner of business, professional, semiskilled worker [are at higher risk]
3. Financial resources	Risk increases with resources
4. Emotional disorder in family	Depression, alcoholism [in family add to risk]
5. Sexual orientation	Bisexual, active; homosexual, inactive [increase risk]
6. Previous psychiatric hospital admissions	Risk increases with number of admissions
7. Result of previous efforts to obtain help	Negative or variable
8. Threatened financial loss	Yes [distinct increase in suicide risk]
9. Special stress	Severe [stress associated with high risk]
10. Sleep (hours per night)	Risk increases with number of hours of sleep per night
11. Weight change, present episode	Gain loss 1% - 9% [seen in high-risk individuals]
12. Ideas of persecution or reference	Yes [these thought disorders are associated with higher risk]
13. Suicidal impulses	Yes [high-risk individuals admit having suicidal impulses]
14. Seriousness of present suicide attempt—intent	Unambivalent or ambivalent but weighted toward suicide [tendency toward greater risk as seriousness of attempt increases]
15. Interviewer's reaction to subject	Risk increases with negativity of reaction

Table 2   Set of Predictors of Suicide Risk

who score high do not commit suicide. So if the individual does not report feelings of hopelessness the likelihood of suicide is quite low.[10]

It is not clear whether Motto's "emotional disorder in family" includes the person being evaluated. Alcoholics and drug abusers have a statistically higher rate of suicide.

There are several myths about suicide to be dispelled. One is that if a person talks about suicide he or she is not likely to make an attempt. On the contrary, most people who commit suicide have told someone that they are thinking about it. Another is that the topic shouldn't be mentioned around depressed people. That might "give them the idea." A third is that people seriously depressed don't kill themselves, only those who are recovering and have more energy available. It is true that early recovery is a particularly dangerous time, but it's not true that during severe depression a person won't commit suicide. A fourth is that a family history of suicide increases the risk. This is not true and the absence of a family history should not be interpreted as decreasing the risk.

What can you as a counselor do to minimize the risk of suicide? I have listed several actions that are useful.

1. Ask about suicidal thoughts. When a person is depressed there is always the possibility of suicide. It may relieve some pressure for them to be able to talk about it. Is there a history of previous suicide attempts? Multiple attempts certainly alert you to the degree of disturbance in a person's life. Whether they have been minor "cries for help," such as a scratch on the wrist, or serious attempts, they indicate that person's range of coping skills to be low. Has the person made specific plans as to how, where, or when to do it?

2. Assess the person's sense of hopelessness and begin to modify it positively. Reassure them of the eventual outcome of their depression (not necessarily that all their stress will end; it may not). Let them know that you care (and others if you know that) and will be with them. Begin to evaluate their ideas and conclusions about themselves and help them to correct false assumptions. If they are unbelievers, share the hopefulness of knowing Christ.

3. Make a "suicide contract." Have the person pledge to contact you before making any suicide attempt. I have had many such contracts and the clients involved have honored

them explicitly. It reminds them that someone cares and will be available if needed. Some of these have been unable to reach me by phone and, while waiting for several days, got over the impulse to kill themselves.

4. Take precautions to remove the most dangerous possibilities. For instance, if a person has a gun, take it away. If they are intoxicated, don't let them drive, and keep someone with them.

5. Take the person to a hospital if there is no other practical way to watch them.

6. Don't be afraid to refer the person to a more experienced professional during a crisis.

7. Take steps toward alleviating stress. For instance, if a person is out of work, help him or her find new direction toward employment. Some denominations have career assessment and placement officers (Appendix 2). If the person is alcoholic, recommend Alcoholics Anonymous. If there's a physical illness, get medical attention. If there are marital conflicts, make efforts to begin counseling.

8. Establish a support network. Many ministers are isolated individuals without a circle of friends. Spouses and other ministers can form the nucleus of this important asset.

For further reading about suicide, I recommend Don Baker's *Depression* and Gary Collins's *How to Be a People Helper.*

CONCLUSION

Depression is a common symptom in Christian workers. Since there are many variations in types and severity of depression, it is important to carefully evaluate each individual. Begin with a thorough medical examination.

Assessment of causes includes investigating areas of anger, guilt, and loss. The family history, developmental history, and pattern of the depression are important in diagnostic and treatment considerations.

General health measures, particularly diet and exercise, are useful in overcoming depression. For burnout, rest and removal from stress is critical. For depression related to losses, grieving is essential. For dysthymia, evaluating emotional conflicts and dealing with anger and guilt are primary.

Medical treatment with antidepressants can speed up the recovery and should always be considered as an option.

Finally, suicide is a serious risk in all depression and must be investigated.

CHAPTER SIX

DYSFUNCTIONAL PERSONALITY

THERE IS A SPECTRUM of personal traits and behaviors that cling to us in our humanity, like beggar's lice to my hiking-boot laces. On one end of the scale, these traits are expressed in those little habits that annoy us in others but aren't really a problem in ourselves (like being a little late for everything). At the other extreme are serious patterns that disrupt relationships (like alcohol addiction or child abuse). Some of these personality characteristics seem particularly common in Christian workers and contribute heavily to ministry conflicts. They can be altered and their alteration makes a significant change in relationships, vocational effectiveness, and inner peace. The traits and behaviors we see most often are: poor self-esteem, passivity, perfectionism, explosiveness, sexual dysfunctions, and addictions.

POOR SELF-ESTEEM

What do you like most about yourself? What came to your mind first? Maybe you've always liked your hair or your body shape or the color of your eyes. Maybe it's your easy-going attitude or sense of humor. Perhaps it's your analytic ability or intellect or creativity. There are so many things we can enjoy about our self-hood.

I'm sad that a lot of people are unable to think of a single thing they really like in themselves. A lot more have a hard time actually saying, "I like this in myself." It seems that some Christians have the notion that it's sinful to accept anything about themselves. Our most frequent task in therapy is breaking through the defensive walls people build up to protect a fragile self-esteem. In *I'm OK, You're OK*, Tom Harris estimated that 95 percent of adults have a pervasive feeling of being "not okay." [1]

How a person really feels inside is not always evident from appearance or achievements. I recall a *New Yorker* cartoon years ago that pictured an aristocratic older couple in tux and evening gown sipping martinis by the grand piano in their penthouse suite. He had a look of despair on his face and was saying, "Oh, Mabel, I'm a complete failure. I failed as chairman of the board at Chrysler. I failed as secretary of state. I failed as presidential adviser. . . ." The sense of not being good enough cannot be easily displaced by accomplishments or prestige. One of the most beautiful women I've ever known was once the representative for her state in the Miss America Pageant, but she had the "too's." She felt that her selection was a mistake. She was really "too tall" and "too shy" and her nose was "too long" and her personality was "too blah." How we see ourselves may be unbelievably different from the way we appear to others.

Helping a person come to the point of self-acceptance is the most healing thing you can do. I think it's bringing light into their darkness, sight to their blindness and liberating them from the prison of their fear. It is doing the work of Jesus in bringing light, sight, and freedom that creates wholeness in a fallen world.

We begin the process by giving acceptance and love to the broken person. I suppose we do this by our willingness to listen to them and showing concern for their hurts. We let them know that we respect them for giving themselves in ministry which we know is hard work. We feel with them. At times that means we cry; at other times, share their anger. Often it is in laughter and frequently with a silent touch of the hand. This love and acceptance for who they are right now forms the platform for helping them change. In the safety of acceptance their defenses begin to come down and they can risk exposing the fear and pain and uncertainty.

I discovered early in my counseling career the idea of *readiness.* People grow in stepwise fashion. At times, there is a giant step to great new heights of maturity. At other times, only a tedious inching upward. But nothing happens until the person is ready to risk the growth. Not everyone who comes into counseling is at the point of readiness. Providing the security of acceptance may enhance readiness. I have also found that readiness can't be rushed or forced. Walking with someone hand-in-hand is more effective than pushing hard from behind. Most people don't respond well to a kick in the rear although you may feel inclined to do just that.

As I observe some of the defense systems a person has, I will begin to identify them. I'll ask how these defenses are working. For instance, if a person is abrasively brash, keeping others at arm's length, I might say, "You seem to send signals of anger that keep people at a distance. How does that work for you?" I may ask next how it feels to be close or why they want to maintain the distance. This is done as a process. I may only make the observation of the defense in one exchange and ask the questions in a later session. Eventually the person begins to see some of the protective devices he has created to keep people from getting too close. Then he must ask what he's afraid of. That question leads to the realization that he doesn't want people to really know him because he doesn't like himself. One of the goals of therapy is for the minister to become aware of his underlying problem with self-esteem.

The next step in the process is understanding the genesis of the negative self-concept. I have people make a list of things they believe about themselves and where each idea came from. We'll do this for every area of the ego structure: body image, intellect, relational skills, emotions, spirituality, sexuality, and creativity. I have them go back to the earliest messages they remember. This exercise is often very enlightening. Many individuals never stop to investigate their beliefs about who they are.

One of the negative aspects of my self-concept had to do with body image and sexual identity. There were many old "tapes" that I played to myself that reinforced feelings of inadequacy. The earliest memory was an early Christmas. I must have been three or four. An uncle who was big and gruff and had a black mustache seemed to delight in terrorizing me. I didn't understand that he was a practical joker. I only felt the shame and humiliation. That Christmas he gave me a pair of little girl's pink panties. I still remember blushing and running from the room crying. My next images are of being generally fearful of the "bullies" in school. Their aggressiveness seemed calculated to increase my feelings of being weak. At recess I would be the last one chosen for the ball team. I was not at all athletic and remained thin and asthenic till I was twenty. I just realized that I've been avoiding the most painful words—sissy and effeminate—but that's how I felt about myself as a male. I found many ways to compensate and felt good about myself in general, yet deep inside I had a poor level of self-esteem as far as my masculinity was concerned.

That is the sort of insight you want to model and encourage. When I give that example in therapy, many men identify immediately. There are similar negative messages in most areas of a person's identity.

After identifying what the belief is and where it originated, establish what is true and what isn't. For me, it was true that I was nonathletic and thin and a sissy. My conclusion wasn't true. I had erroneously concluded that I wasn't a "man" because I didn't go out for football.

Melissa has come through a very liberating process of identifying the lies she had believed. She tells our groups that she had the notion that her worth as a person depended on her being "sweet" at all times and getting skinny. (I wish I could have given her my skinniness.) The being sweet she could usually do, but as she says, "I could never quite get the hang of being thin." Consequently, she felt inferior or worthless. She finally realized that she would never attain worth by being thin. "Thin" was a moving target that she could never hit. Her lie was not that she was overweight but that her worth was inversely related to her dress size.

Those early messages are believed because they are repeated frequently by big people important to the dependent child. A little kid doesn't have the emotional and intellectual capacity to evaluate rationally what's being said. Unfortunately most folks continue to let that "little kid" inside control their life. When the adult looks squarely at the lies, they can be seen for what they are and can be discarded. When the old feelings of inadequacy begin to come into consciousness they are labeled as lies and not pursued in thoughts or feelings.

However, those messages and the conclusions we derived from them have been played over and over many years, and they will return. I still get that old inner rush of anxiety when I'm invited to join "some of the boys" for hunting or fishing or playing ball. It's only momentary and I am not controlled by it like I used to be. That's because I've replaced the false conclusion in my thinking. I no longer let my thinking go from, *Oh, no, I'm not good at athletic things* to *I'm not much of a man* to *What if they find out?* to *They might give me pink panties.* Now I know I'm a man—still not very athletic, but fully masculine—comfortably male. What's more, my worth as a person is firmly established on something immovably secure.

I know that my worth is fixed on God's love for me. He made me and loved me enough to die for me at Golgotha. I can't do anything to increase my worth or to destroy it in His eyes. Jesus said, "Which of you . . . can add one cubit unto his stature?" (Matt. 6:27 KJV). I see people trying to add cubits (or take off inches) to become worth more. It can't be done. Here's the Good News that even when we were impertinent sinners, Christ died for us. Now you can't do anything to improve on that. And that's the truth that needs to be programmed into the mental computer to take the place of the lies.

We have found *Your Erroneous Zones* by Wayne Dyer and *Do You Hear What You're Thinking?* by Jerry Schmidt to be helpful reading in this process. Scripturally, Psalm 139 and Jeremiah 1, which tell of God's knowing us and loving us while we were still unborn, remind us of who we are. The Good News of salvation by faith, a gift from God, seals it. We don't have to work our way into worth.

It's exciting to see the change that occurs when a person moves off the sand of self-hate on to the rock of self-love. That new stance enables them to take their eyes off of self and begin to be the channel of God's love to those around who are still sinking in the sand. What a transformation of ministry. Only when we truly love our selfhood as God does can we truly love anyone else.

Establishing a minister's real value also provides the foundation for working on behavioral change in all of the following problem areas.

Summary

Establishing an individual's sense of worth is foundational to mental health. We use a cognitive approach to:

1. Identify distorted ideas about self.
2. Recognize the roots of poor self-image.
3. Replace negative conclusion with the truth of God's love and acceptance.

PASSIVITY

The Hollywood stereotype of the man of the cloth is a pale, limp-wristed, bespectacled wimp who is afraid of his own shadow. As Carlyle Marney put it, most ministers don't have the confidence "to say boo to a church mouse." [2] I can't decide whether seminary and Christian theology take assertiveness out of a minister or if church vocation attracts passive people. I suspect it's the latter.

Christian work is not physical labor. The church world is an environment of love and nurturing. It requires a person of compassion and sensitivity. At least on the surface, it doesn't seem to have the cut-throat competition of the business world. It lacks the physical pain and blood of medicine and the adversarial battles of law. Instead, one finds music, art, and ideas. For a passive young person seeking a vocation, it looks safe. One even enters by submitting to God's call.

Needless to say, Hollywood is wrong. Not all Christian workers are passive, nor is all passivity deleterious. But many are—and some is. The negative expressions of passivity you will see are passive–dependency and passive–aggression.

Passive–Dependency

Passive–dependent people simply refuse to take initiative. They force others to make decisions for them by their indecision. Often the spouses feel the most tension from the passivity and begrudgingly make decisions in their behalf. At times, the system seems to be perfectly okay with passive–dependent people, but more often they resent the "parenting" role others take. Their anger is matched by those who feel controlled by their inertia. They are trapped by their insatiable desire to be taken care of.

Larry and Becky came to the Retreat because of a marital crisis. Larry had become emotionally, but not sexually, involved with his secretary at the church. It was Becky who had insisted they come for counseling or she would leave him. Larry was a quiet young man in his midthirties. He had very little to say and seemed happy to let Becky do his talking for him.

Becky was not quiet. She was a highly verbal, very angry young woman. She recited at length Larry's areas of failure climaxing the story by saying it was like having another child instead of a husband.

In private, Larry began to express his fearfulness about life. He had been totally dominated by a perfectionistic father until Becky took over. He learned early in life that he could not do anything well enough to suit his dad. He dared not make a decision. It was much less painful to hear the com-

plaints about his passivity than to take initiative and be casti-
gated for that. He really hadn't intended to marry Becky,
but she seemed to know what was best for him. Anyway it
was a way to escape his dad. He didn't realize he was just
trading parents.

Now he was in love with his secretary who treated him
"with respect." On closer inspection, it became apparent that
she was a mothering sort of woman who was attracted by
his helplessness. If Larry had been a little more assertive he
would have traded Becky in on a replacement parent. Then
the pattern would have repeated itself.

Treating the passive–dependent person is hard. You often
feel like Br'er Rabbit and the tar baby. He just sits there saying
nothin' till you whop him with your other foot, and that gets
stuck too. Pretty soon you are immobilized by this immovable,
helpless, controlling blob. The first step is to help the person
see that remaining in dependency is not the easy way out.
Life doesn't just have to happen by default.

Passive-dependent people can come to see that truth as
they understand the development of their dependency. They
must face the fact that their parents failed to give them care
and approval. They often fit with the dependency pattern
of children raised by domineering parents. They are left feeling smothered and inadequate—a vulnerable place to be as
an adult. When one is raised by a controlling parent, it is
threatening to admit mistakes. If the parent becomes angry,
the "protection" might be withdrawn. It is liberating for them
(and their parents) for the old dependency to be broken. When
they realize they have been imprisoned rather than in protective custody, they will more readily risk freedom.

It is critical to enlist the cooperation from the spouse and
other important people who have to quit taking the responsibility. You will also have to refuse to make decisions for passive–dependent clients although they will attempt to put you
in that position. You must firmly but gently put the ball right
back into their courts.

Assertiveness training can be helpful to passive–dependent
individuals. These workshops are usually done in small groups
and each person gets to practice taking a positive stand on

various issues and under role-played circumstances. This may be their first positive experience in asserting themselves and will help them begin to move out of self-centeredness to show caring and love for others. That's on the road to wholeness.

Passive–Aggressive

The other destructive pattern of passivity is passive–aggressive behavior. This is seen in such nonactions as procrastination, uncooperativeness, tardiness, forgetfulness, and stubbornness. Ministers who are passive–aggressive are often in a silent power struggle with strong lay leaders. Their basic problem is not with unmet dependency needs and insecurity, but with how they handle anger and conflicts. Rather than deal directly and honestly with negative feelings, they play a frustrating game. On the surface of a disagreement, they appear (by silence or assent) to agree with the other person's ideas or desires. They then go about having it their own way. They express anger by their refusal to comply. They ultimately win the battle for control while avoiding the discomfort of confrontation. If challenged about their behavior they will smile and apologize for "forgetting" or "putting it off" or "not understanding." Their methods generate tremendous frustration in everyone who opposes them.

There are two keys to successful therapy with passive–aggressive people. The first is for them consciously to recognize and own their hostile feelings. If they continue to deny responsibility for their oppositional stance, they stay locked into the old game. Since you as their therapist will probably be the recipient of their passive–aggression, you can begin to identify it as it happens. Tell them how it feels to you to try to relate to them. Point out the anger you feel from them and explore their feelings toward you as a parent-figure in their life.

A common developmental history reveals parents who were ambivalent about discipline. Rather than setting clear cut limits and enforcing them consistently, they vacillated. There was likely a lot of nagging about what the child didn't do, but in the end the parent would give in. A child quickly learns what's going to happen and how to get its own way.

You can observe this training program daily in the supermarket. Up and down the aisles the three-year-olds are intimidating their parents into giving in. They grab things from the shelves. They refuse to come or follow. They stage stubborn sit-down strikes if thwarted. All the while their fathers or mothers are likely threatening to take them to the car or give them a spanking. Do you see terror in their eyes? No! They've learned that these are idle threats. They control the situation by doing exactly what they want or by passively resisting the demands of their parents.

Occasionally I see a parent actually say no and mean it. The kid is given a spanking or has to take the sugar crunchies back to the shelf or is even taken out of the store. When that happens and I recover from the shock, I commend that parent verbally on the spot.

Melissa becomes embarrassed and disappears when I respond to the negative patterns. I may stop a child, get his eye contact, and say, "Did you hear your mother? She said you can't have that." The startled child and startled parent sometimes complete their shopping without any more hassles. I may even point out to the parent the training they are doing. Perhaps that is a bit obnoxious, but, if it saves some kid from being passive–aggressive as an adult, maybe it's worth it.

You can do the same thing with your passive–aggressive clients. Help them see how the training program went in their childhoods and that they're not still stubborn children in a battle for control with "parents." It's not a flattering picture. Most adults will want to change it.

The second key is for them to learn to confront conflict directly rather than passively. Basically this involves becoming aware of their own feelings and expressing them verbally. You can teach the "straight talk" technique of owning the feelings and saying them in first person statements.

I had to learn this communication style as an adult. I don't like conflict and tended to use passive–aggressive methods of circumventing it. I've now discovered that I can be honest. I say, "I'd like to express some thoughts and feelings I'm having. I disagree with that idea. I think I feel unheard regarding this issue. . . ." Those statements avoid using accusatory or demeaning "you" messages. The "You're wrong about that" or "You never listen" style creates defensiveness and starts World War III. Disagreement doesn't have to intensify the conflicts. Even the anger can be talked about openly without destroying relationships. Some of my closest friends now are those with whom I've had direct confrontation in times of disagreement.

Needless to say, the passive–aggressive person may have to start cooperating with the desires of others from time to time. That seems to be a necessary part of mature love. The Ephesians 5 principle of submitting one to another is a distinct call to mutual respect and self-giving.

Summary

Passive individuals are sometimes attracted to ministry by its "softness." Their passive–dependency or passive–aggressiveness create inefficiency and frustration.

1. Identify the origins of their passivity.
2. Deal with their underlying fears.
3. Teach them to become comfortably assertive.

PERFECTIONISM

In a good and proper Evangelical homiletic style, I'll be alliterative and continue the discussion with another "P" topic—perfectionism. Perfectionists may be overrepresented among Christian workers. Particularly in more legalistic circles of ministry, the rigidity of the perfectionistic personality fits right in. Now if I were a perfectionist, I'd never let that last sentence stand. It is "wrong" to end a sentence with a preposition, and that's the way a perfectionist views life. Things are right or wrong, black or white. There is a correct way of doing everything. There is a place for everything and it should be in its place.

A perfectionist's conversations are sprinkled with "shoulds" and "oughts." "Sprinkled" isn't really a good perfectionist expression. It implies a spontaneous, unmeasured use. That won't do at all. One ought be more precise. I should have said "punctuated" rather than "sprinkled." I imagine you get the point.

Another tendency of the perfectionist is to see issues at

their extremes. Life is polarized. It is difficult for the perfectionist to contemplate compromise or change. They have an almost palpable anxiety about not being right. When the thought of relaxing a little is brought up, they immediately jump to the opposite end of the spectrum and imagine becoming lazy, inept, slovenly, and probably sinful.

Perfectionists are hardest on themselves. Most will confess they've never quite lived up to their own standards. Unfortunately those around are also under scrutiny. Colleagues and family members live with constant criticism and a sense of failure. No one is very happy.

At the root of perfectionism is anxiety. There is an inner fear of loss of control. Frightening inner impulses *must* be contained in a tight box. Whether the impulses that require control are aggressive or sexual is not easy to get at and perhaps not necessary to establish. Feelings, both positive and negative, are shut in along with the unfriendly drives. What is left is the control, the box. It is rigid and logical. The intellect overcomes emotions, choking them out.

The perfectionist is also striving for acceptance. Approval has been conditional relative to performance which has never been good enough. The impulse within is often anger toward the task masters. Those psychic jailors are the voices of self and parents who have made being lovable out of reach.

Treating perfectionism is built on the groundwork of a wholesome appreciation of self-worth. Without this foundation, the perfectionist will continue to try to find the logical, legalistic formula for being good enough to be loved. Paul's discussions of the law and grace appeal to the logical mind and are helpful in relieving this bondage (Romans 1–8).

Perfectionism can also be helped by a behavioral approach to decondition the compulsive behavior. James Joliff's tape series, *Too Much of a Good Thing,* is an enlightening and useful tool for deprogramming.[3]

Ultimately the perfectionist has to let God be God, accepting his or her own humanity. He or she is still of value and is loved, and can't improve on what God has done. The rigidity must then give way to balance and the person can begin to live within the gray areas of life without anxiety.

Summary

Perfectionists in ministry are hard to work with and hardest on themselves. Build their basic sense of self-worth and move them away from polarized thinking.

PUGNACIOUSNESS

There is perhaps no behavioral problem more ego alien to Christian workers than having an explosive personality. Those I have seen with this complaint are fearful, guilt-ridden individuals. They live in fear of losing control and becoming violent. They are laden with guilt because of the hurt their eruptions produce.

The story is usually similar to Ron's.

"I don't understand what comes over me. The slightest little thing can just set me off. It's as though I have no control over my actions. One minute I can seem fine and the next I may be shouting obscenities or slapping someone. Then it's over and I feel terrible. How could someone who is a minister be like that—so out of control?

"I've been that way as long as I can remember. In school I'd get into fights. I'd lose my temper if anything frustrated me. I used to build model airplanes, but I really didn't finish many. If the slightest thing went wrong I'd smash the thing to bits. I'm still that way. The other day I couldn't get the power mower to start and before I knew it I had smashed it with a hammer. If someone pulls out in front of the car I become furious. So far I've only cussed them out, but I'm afraid one of these days I'll ram into them with my car.

"I don't usually hit a person, but there have been a couple of times that I've shoved Joan across the bedroom or slapped one of the kids in the face. That's really scary."

There are several important considerations in evaluating explosiveness in a person. First, get a collaborative witness to describe what happens. *Rarely,* explosive outbursts can be a form of seizure disorder. This is very uncommon. Seizure-generated behavior is less purposeful and more randomly directed. The person seems unconscious of the surroundings, and there may be some confusion after the attack. There may also be some other neurological signs or symptoms, such as the onset of headaches or abnormal sensory experiences just before the attacks (e.g., a strange taste, feeling, or sound). If there is any question of a seizure disorder, it is reasonable to have a neurological consultation perhaps including an EEG (electroencephalograph or "brain wave test").

Similarly, blood sugar abnormalities should be considered. Hypoglycemic attacks can be manifested by almost any unusual episodic behavior. Many people with low blood sugar describe feelings of marked irritability. Those episodes are usually accompanied by sweating, some lightheadedness, tremulousness, and fast heart rate. A good medical evaluation may lead to the cure.

Second, find out how the person normally deals with anger and attempt to identify roots of the rage. Ordinarily the person will be aware of a smoldering hostility inside. The rage is often related to early life trauma. This may be abuse or abandonment and leaves the person with a frustrated anger toward the world. It doesn't take much to tap into the reservoir.

Although there is an inner awareness of the rage, the minister may not know it shows. I recall that Ron thought he was seen as a gentle, light-hearted man. The therapy group pointed out to him ways that his anger showed. His humor was biting sarcasm. His muscle tone was tense. He was in constant restless motion. He seemed exasperated with his wife and others frequently. He was surprised that it was so apparent and began to understand why people seemed to avoid him.

Third, ask about a history of childhood abuse. Most explosive people were themselves abused. Sometimes those painful memories are repressed and some probing is necessary to uncover them. Their early abuse not only created a rage at the unfairness of life, but also became a model of response to frustration. It seems helpful to the client to be able to tell about those episodes to someone who cares. They may have either assumed their experience was "normal" or that it was bad to expose their parents' abusiveness.

In treating explosiveness make a three-pronged approach. Deal psychodynamically with the underlying rage. Use a behavior modification approach to the outbursts, and apply spiritual truths to developing wholeness in the person.

Psychodynamically, the person can come to integrate the repressed early rage and identify the legitimate target. Ron began to recall his very early sense of being abandoned. He was literally deserted by his father and practically abandoned by his mother who became alcoholic early in his life. She would escape into her alcoholic stupor leaving him to fend for himself. He related his memories with intense anger and hurt. The release of those feelings was helped by writing letters to both parents and going through those feelings in therapy.

For several ministers the question, "Who really cared about you when you were little?" has opened a gate into their feelings of being neglected. At times others have said, "I can't cry for myself, but I sure cry when I watch certain movies." The common theme of the movies seems to be a warm, loving relationship between an adult and a child. The image of a loving parent awakens the sadness inside over their own lost childhood.

Behaviorally, there are many useful techniques. One has to do with their "critical interval." That is a term that has been applied, particularly in violent-prone individuals, to the time lapse between a negative stimulus and the response to it. Ordinarily as a person matures that interval becomes longer and the consequences of various responses are considered. In the violent prone the critical interval is very short. They tend to act first and ask questions later. They can begin to increase the response time and learn to question the consequences. The old idea of counting to ten coupled with an understanding of their heightened reactivity is put to good use.

The second behavioral approach is more preventive. Have the clients make a list of situations that commonly stimulate them to an explosion. They can then begin to anticipate such situations and either avoid them or change them. Some changes involve talking about the threatening situation with other people who may be involved. A few years ago a pastor who was explosive shared with his wife the list of things that seemed to set him off. She was surprised at most of the things on his list, but was willing to change the things she did that bothered him. They also found that just talking about some issue decreased its impact on him. He would say, "Honey, I know this is totally irrational, but I often feel enraged when you crunch candy or carrots. I know that's silly, but could you try to avoid crunchy things when I'm around?" She was quite happy not to crunch in his presence.

A third behavioral technique is for the person physically to dissipate the anger. Working with clay, hitting a punching bag, playing racquetball, or running can burn off some of the energy generated by the rage. These are not a cure for the underlying cause, but they can help modify how intensely the feelings are being expressed.

Spiritually, a Christian can take hope in the possibility of a life brought into maturity in Christ. The fruit of God's indwelling Spirit includes self-control, and that hope is encouraging for the explosive personality. One missionary was liberated when she realized that she had a choice in how she reacted to frustration. She had always felt victimized by her rage. Realizing that her mind was subject to God's Spirit suddenly released her from the bondage of a life-long response pattern that seemed outside of her control. Now she is able to talk with God about her choice of responses and feels empowered to make mature choices.

There is also spiritual release through forgiving those who created the traumatic life experiences. Forgiveness includes first facing honestly the hurt and anger, then choosing to release them. Lewis Smedes's book *Forgive and Forget* gives a thorough discussion of forgiveness.[4]

Finally, explosive personalities in Christian work are overwhelmed by guilt. They need the reassurance of forgiveness from others and from God. The principles of confession and asking forgiveness apply. Living under the guilt only adds to their anger, so this spiritual truth brings healing from both of those negative emotions.

A remarkable witness to me is that without Christ explosive people are often violent criminals. It is a testimony to God's healing power that the Christian with this problem of anger and impulse control is under conviction to change. The non-Christian is often completely sociopathic, feeling no remorse and not the slightest desire to control the violence.

Summary

The explosive personality in ministry lives with tremendous pressure and guilt.

1. Identify the source of their underlying rage.
2. Teach appropriate ways to express anger, expand the "critical interval" and avoid stress.
3. Bring spiritual healing for the rage and guilt.

SEXUAL DYSFUNCTION

Christian workers are sexual. As far as I can tell, they have normal sexual drives, a healthy interest in sexual pleasure, and the problems that are common to human sexuality. Some even struggle with developmental arrests creating immature expressions such as pedophilia, incestuous behavior, and homosexuality. Effective treatment of sexual dysfunction may require special techniques and long-term involvement that may be beyond your interest or expertise. It is important, however, for you to give the minister you are counseling the opportunity to talk about sexuality without fear of condemnation.

To do that adequately you need to be knowledgeable enough to talk about sex comfortably. If you find it difficult to talk frankly about erections, orgasm, the penis, clitoris, or vagina, you need to first work on your own sexual feelings. I would recommend several books on sexuality. Dr. Joe McIlhaney's new book, *1250 Health Care Questions Women Ask*, is a must for anyone counseling women. Even if you are hesitant or uncomfortable, you can reach for Dr. McIlhaney's very thorough and clearly written book and read to your client (male or female) his answers. Dr. Ed and Gaye Wheat's *Intended for Pleasure* is also quite complete. It covers the anatomy, physiology, psychology, and techniques of sex adequately for most problems. Masters and Johnson's studies, *Human Sexual Response* and *Human Sexual Inadequacy* give the most in-depth, clinical descriptions of human sexual function. Unlike the other two, they are written from a non-Christian perspective. Lillian Rubin's *Intimate Strangers* and Richard Foster's *Money, Sex, and Power* would also be helpful.

Your attitude and feeling about sex will set the tone for your client's willingness to deal with sexual issues. If you find, even after reading and discussing sexuality with colleagues or your mate, that you are uncomfortable approaching the subject I would recommend some counseling for yourself. Otherwise you may regularly avoid this critical area. As I so frequently say to ministers, don't be afraid to get help. If you feel reluctant to do sexual counseling, identify a competent person to refer to.

I'd like to briefly discuss the common areas of sexual dysfunction and treatment approaches.

Taking the Sexual History

In all areas of sexual dysfunction taking a thorough history is an important therapeutic tool. It is a genuine act of love and perhaps the most important step toward healing. For most people, sexual feelings and fantasies are a secret, shadowy section of their identity. Sexuality may remain confusing and fraught with fear and guilt. You have only to reflect on the power and mystery of sex in your own private world to know its importance.

As a part of the general history, I simply ask about their current sexual adjustment. "How is your sexual relationship?" is adequate to open the door. I usually ask two additional questions if the response is a noncommittal "okay." I ask, "What do you think your mate would say to that question?" and "Do you have any questions or problems with sexuality you want to discuss?" I have found that men, for all their bravado about sex, are more reluctant to admit concerns than women are. Asking about their wives' feelings and opening the door for questions allows them a less direct, maybe safer way to approach the subject.

If the responses by both husband and wife (and history from both is important) indicate a good sexual adjustment I drop the subject. If there are problems, I pursue the topic in depth in a later therapy session with a thorough sexual history.

For the complete history, begin at the beginning. Explore the attitudes about sexuality, the body, and nudity in the family of origin. These set the foundation for everything that happens later. You can help the client identify these by asking about affection and touch, about sexual talk or absence of it, about modesty, about sleeping arrangements, about the value of boys versus girls, about pregnancies and babies, and about toilet training and diapering of younger siblings (or about their own if they remember). At times a person will have no specific impression about the family message regarding sexuality until these questions prompt their memories and associations.

I ask next about the earliest memories of sexual experiences or fantasies. All you have to do is be around three- to five-year-olds to know they have a rich and active sexual curiosity. They are "on the make." The little boys are wanting genital stimulation and the little girls are learning to be seductive. You'll find that many people will recall playing "doctor" or "mommy and daddy" where there was undressing and comparing anatomy. Some vaginal and penile manipulation is not rare. Penetration of the vagina with various objects or attempts at intercourse also occur. The importance of these events is in their effect on the person's subsequent feelings about sexuality. They may be entirely positive or create questions, fears, and guilt that interfere with their sexual responsiveness.

Similarly, later sexual experiences, including incest or abuse, are explored. It is now clear that brother–sister and father–daughter incest is not uncommon. Even more prevalent is stepfather–daughter involvement. Investigate other males living with or frequently visiting in the home, such as uncles, cousins, and baby sitters. Some form of sexual abuse by older boys is not uncommon in males. This usually involves being forced to commit fellatio or be the recipient in anal intercourse. It is rare for boys to be used by adult women, but not rare for older girls to initiate them into sexual activity.

Not all incestuous or abuse events are perceived as traumatic. The result seems to depend on the relationship with the other person and the degree of violence or force involved.

217

One negative effect can be guilt over having enjoyed the sexual stimulation and perhaps encouraging the encounter. I have had many women in counseling who were incest "victims" who knew somehow that the relationship was wrong, but enjoyed the special attention and the sexual pleasure. Some have been aware in adolescence of feeling in competition with their mother for the dad or step-dad's affection. When there are deeply negative feelings of resentment, fear, or guilt, these need to be talked through to resolution.

Although I have generally found that it is not pivotal in a person's sexual attitudes, I ask about their "sex education." Needless to say, all of life is an education in sexuality, but learning about reproduction is more encapsulated. One reason for asking about this is to discover whether or not the individual feels that he or she has an adequate understanding about sexual anatomy and physiology. There may also have been strong taboos about sex that have created "hang ups." One common one is the horror stories taught Christian girls in an attempt to maintain their chastity: Boys are only interested in one thing and will drop you once they've made a sexual conquest. Sex is really a nasty, unpleasant, carnal activity. God will punish you if you become sexually active, and so forth. Unfortunately, these messages aren't modified to allow marital sex. Subsequent adjustment may be difficult. Feelings about masturbation and homosexual experiences can also cause problems.

Courtship experiences can have significant effect on marital sexual adjustment. There may be guilt about premarital sex— even with the spouse. Either husband or wife may blame the other for having pressed for intercourse. The forbidden pleasure aspect of premarital involvement may intensify the excitement and passion of premarital sex making marital sex seem disappointing. There may have been a previous lover who was more skilled and brought excitement not present in the marriage. These are subjects most couples don't discuss unless they are brought up as angry accusations in arguments.

Finally, marital and extramarital history should be explored. Don't assume there has been no adulterous affair. Ask. If there has been, evaluate the effects it has had on the marriage.

Be sure the person recognizes the sin, has confessed it before God, and has received forgiveness. Some counselors feel it's always necessary to confess to the spouse and receive forgiveness there. I am not convinced of that and don't see distinct scriptural guidance in that area. I have certainly seen incidences where such a confession led not to healing or marital growth, but to lasting hurt and bitterness. Ideally, I know it shouldn't, but we are human and imperfect. If there has been forgiveness from God, repentance and a renewal of obedience to God, and a restored commitment to the marital partner, I'm not sure the relationship is helped by the confession.

In evaluating the current marital sexual history, try to identify areas of concern or inadequate adjustment. Remember, there is no standard of performance. Each couple is unique in its frequency and technique. A session to discuss sexuality with both husband and wife may clear up long-standing problems. This is especially true when the couple doesn't talk to each other about sex. Teaching the husband about the female response curve is often the solution to their maladjustment.[5]

Frequently, ministers and their spouses thank me specifically for giving them the opportunity to deal with problems in their sex life. It seems so risky to expose this personal area that most people suffer in silence. Just taking a good history brings relief and hopefulness to your clients. Learn to do it well, but don't practice on your spouse unless you have a comfortable degree of openness in this area or a mutual agreement that some experiences can remain private.

Now let's look at areas of dysfunction and their treatment.

Orgasmic Failure

The "success" of sexual relationship has been practically equated with achieving orgasm. For men, having orgasm with ejaculation is certainly the focal point of sexual function. For women, having an orgasm may not be as critical. Many women don't regularly (or ever) reach orgasm, yet feel quite satisfied with the closeness and affection involved in their sexual life. Ann Landers's recent survey seems to support this.[6] Many women I have counseled don't know if they have ever had an orgasm. Of these, some have been distressed about it, some have been curious about what they've been missing, and some have seemed unconcerned. Men unable to reach climax may not want to talk about it, but are usually significantly upset.

If both parties are mutually satisfied with their sexual relationship, I may ask about orgasmic failure and offer to look into that if they want to. If they aren't motivated to work in that area, I reassure them that it isn't necessary. I encourage them to enjoy their closeness and intimacy and not worry about what anyone else may experience. In trying to push a couple into fuller sexual release, you may just create anxieties that diminish their sexual satisfaction. I guess my attitude is "If it ain't broken, don't fix it."

At times the husband may be the one distressed because his wife is inorgasmic. The pressure to perform adequately as a lover weighs heavily on men these days. With so much written about women being capable of multiple orgasm, the titillated male fantasy can begin to get carried away. If the wife is not experiencing several orgasms, the man may begin to question his potency. Clear communication is critical in this area, but often absent. Because of the male focus on climax, it is hard for a man to believe that his wife may be really satisfied if she is not orgasmic. I have come to believe that a woman may be sexually fulfilled without reaching climax. When that is the case, the necessary treatment may simply be to help the husband accept what his wife says. His pleasure will be enhanced by relieving the pressure to perform great feats of sexual prowess.

If there is orgasmic failure and mutual concern about it, evaluate it fully. First find out about the inorgasmia. Has it always been present? When did it begin? Is it always present? Under what circumstances did it start or does it now occur?

Primary orgasmic failure is a term applied when a person has never achieved a climax. Causes can be physical (e.g., diabetic neuropathy), but are rare. This is usually a psychological problem and related to psychosexual development. These problems will be revealed in the detailed sexual history. It is extremely rare in men. The causes in women often have to do with guilt or fear. Treatment includes talking through the feelings from the early life experiences and education regarding normal sexual pleasure. At times there is so much fearfulness of men or of passionate loss of control that self-stimulation to have an initial orgasmic release may be necessary (and curative). Sensate focusing can also be helpful. Dr. and Mrs. Wheat give a detailed description of this exercise in *Intended for Pleasure.*[7]

Secondary inorgasmia refers to cases in which a person has had sexual climax, but has now stopped. Unlike primary inorgasmia, a common cause of secondary dysfunction is organic pathology, particularly in men. There are a wide variety of physical conditions that may contribute in both sexes. Fatigue, the premenstrual syndrome, cardiovascular problems, diabetes, thyroid abnormalities, neuropathies, drug and alcohol abuse, and side effects of medications can all be implicated. Furthermore, the psychological response to illness can disrupt sexual function. For instance, anxiety about heart disease or depression about aging interfere with sexual responsivity. A good medical evaluation is a first priority.

Most incidences of secondary inorgasmia will turn out to be of psychological origin unrelated to physical disease. It is usually related to relational problems in the marriage. For men, this usually results in erectile failure rather than inorgasmia and will be discussed later. Women have trouble understanding how a man can want to have sex when there is tension between them. For a woman, sexual responsiveness is intricately interwoven with emotional closeness. Consequently, she may be willing to be available to her husband for his sexual release, but quite unable to become involved to the point of orgasm no matter how much he may try to stimulate her. This is not a matter of punishing him by not climaxing. The female psyche is just wired differently and feeling warm and intimate does not come from breast and clitoral stimulation. Lillian Rubin says that men see sex as a means to achieve closeness while women see closeness as a means to achieve sexual intimacy.[8] Obviously there is a problem here!

Inability to climax may also be related to guilt over an extramarital relationship. For some women with very scrupulous sexual morals, guilt may even be generated by romantic feelings or fantasies involving another man. These affairs, whether in reality or fantasy, may be submitted to the Lord for forgiveness and cleansing. If the romance has highlighted a boring marital relationship, work on enriching the marriage is necessary. At times, education in sexual technique may be essential.

Resentment and unforgiveness are important blocks to sexual responsiveness. Doubts about sexual adequacy with aging or after infidelity are powerful inhibitors. Depression almost always interferes with sexual function as does anxiety. Environmental stress and distractions (such as guests in the house or Sunday's sermon preparation) also have a detrimental effect.

As you can see, identifying the areas of tension or conflict and working toward resolution is often the treatment of choice rather than referral to a sex therapist. Overcoming the anxiety and expectation of failure that months or years of dysfunction create is a critical adjunct. The use of sensate focusing is successful for the vast majority of couples.

Erectile Failure

Inability to achieve or maintain an erection is a common sexual dysfunction in men. It is a natural aging phenomenon often beginning in the forties. There may be additional physical causes other than aging. These include those listed above for orgasmic dysfunction. Drugs for hypertension are particularly prone to cause secondary erectile problems and are commonly taken by middle-aged men. Sometimes a change of the antihypertensive agent or dosage adjustment will abolish the difficulty. Encourage your client to talk with his physician about this possibility.

Normal erectile function is also quite sensitive to a man's emotions. Anxiety over aging and the ability to perform is probably the most common single factor in the disability. Thus there is established a self-reinforcing cycle—failure to get an erection, anxiety over inability to perform, increased failure. A recent paper on treatment of erectile dysfunction shows that a significant percentage of cases have remission with reassurance alone.[9] A wife's attitude of encouragement and her willingness to give her husband more genital stimulation and romantic fantasy can also assist him in achieving and maintaining erections. Her critical putdowns about his inability to be a man even if made in humor may intensify his feelings of inadequacy. Ask about her response to his problem and correct it if it is negatively reinforcing.

Anger and conflict in the relationship, particularly if a man feels emasculated and controlled, will produce erectile dysfunction. This can be an important element in a man's infidelity. If he is castrated by his wife but adored by another woman, he will find his sexual interest and potency restored in the other relationship.

Guilt over infidelity can also cause erectile failure. This must be dealt with through confession and forgiveness.

At times, a wife's failure to properly care for her own body can contribute to her husband's sexual dysfunction. Of course that is true in the other direction. Good hygiene and staying "in shape" contribute to good sex.

Premature Ejaculation

The most common sexual dysfunction, premature ejaculation, is defined as not being able to delay ejaculation long enough to bring a sexual partner to orgasm in at least 50 percent of coital experiences. Needless to say this is a completely arbitrary definition. Perhaps a more practical one would be having ejaculation sooner than a couple desires. Like erectile failure, the incidence of premature ejaculation has increased with the emphasis on orgasm for women. It is made worse by performance anxiety.

The underlying cause may be a genetic predisposition to rapid sexual response. It may be conditioned by adolescent masturbatory practice in which a quick response was preferred to avoid detection.

There is a very effective treatment for premature ejaculation called the "squeeze technique." Ed and Gaye Wheat describe it in detail in *Intended for Pleasure*.[10] Basically it is a conditioning exercise in which the wife stimulates her husband's penis to erection and to the point that he feels ejaculation is imminent. At that point she squeezes the penis just below the glans firmly for several seconds. The process is repeated several times in each setting with the couple finally having intercourse to orgasm.

It has been found that the man's response time is gradually lengthened until he can last long enough to satisfy his wife sexually. It is also a good way for the couple to feel they are cooperating toward a more fulfilling sexual relationship. The negative feeling of failure and frustration can be replaced by hopefulness.

Dyspareunia

This term means pain in intercourse for a woman. There are many causes both physical and emotional. An adequate gynecological evaluation should be obtained initially. Some medical causes are malposition of the uterus, vaginal infection, inadequate vaginal lubrication, pelvic inflammation, ovarian cysts, and bladder infection. These may be treated with an excellent chance for recovery.

Emotional causes should be sought if the gynecological exam is normal. These are usually related to fear of intercourse leading to a tightening of the pelvic muscles around the vagina. This makes penetration painful. The fear may be related to early life sexual trauma, marital conflict, fear of pregnancy, or the expectation that intercourse will be painful. Some of the ideas about intercourse include the notion that penetration will be painful. Contributing to this is the concept of "sexual compatability" that includes the question of whether or not the vagina will be big enough to accommodate the erect penis. These myths can establish enough anxiety in a woman that she tightens up and the fear is realized.

An understanding of what happens can be enhanced by having the woman locate her pubococcygeus muscle by feeling it contract around the vagina entrance. She can then become aware of when it tightens involuntarily. Then, by gentle and gradual foreplay with adequate lubrication, she can begin to accept a finger, then two, and three without pain. Finally, with her in control of timing, as in the woman-above position, she can direct penetration at her level of comfort. Successful experience of enjoyable genital union will decondition her anxiety.

Homosexuality

Christian workers who are homosexual are caught in a painful dilemma. Those I have known have been very sensitive, committed believers who wanted to be in ministry. Their sexual preference disturbance created anxiety, guilt, and depression. Those I have seen came into therapy when their homosexual behavior was exposed either to their mates or to the church.

The cause of homosexuality has not been shown to be genetic or hormonally determined. The best evidence is that it is a developmental abnormality that has to do with early sexual identity patterns.[11] Often the male homosexual has either an absent father (emotionally or physically) or a fearfully rejecting father. The developing boy identifies with his mother and finds an attraction to men. Those I have had in therapy have recognized a desire to be held by a strong man that relates to their desire to identify with a man. One man said he was aware of fantasizing that he was being loved by his father. There is often a deep question of his own masculinity. In some homosexual men, the mother was a very controlling and threatening person who conditioned a dread of women. Leanne Payne's book *Broken Image* is very useful to the homosexual to begin to understand the roots of the disorder.

Treatment of homosexuality has been successful and the homosexual needs to have the hopefulness of change. In our day of "gay liberation," the popular idea that homosexuality is a genetic, biological "variant" that can't be changed leaves the Christian homosexual feeling helplessly programmed for a sinful lifestyle. For the sexual-object choice to be changed, the homosexual must be motivated toward change and must also feel acceptance of his personhood.

When the desire for change and an encouraging relationship are present, work on the conflicted feelings toward himself and his sexual identity is begun. Uncovering early life messages about maleness and femaleness and the parent–child interaction will help him identify the roots of his sexual orientation. Working toward spiritual maturity will assist in his making a choice away from homosexuality. He should be grounded in the scriptural teaching regarding homosexuality. One of the important ingredients is an adequate image of mature heterosexuality. A couple who can be loving parent role models will help him overcome negative early modeling.

A support group is also useful—where other Christian believers can call each other into accountability, encourage commitment, and help provide alternatives to a homosexual lifestyle. Dr. Bill Wilson, formerly at Duke University, has worked successfully with homosexuals. He recommends group work utilizing Scripture, prayer, and insight-oriented psychotherapy.[12]

Pedophilia

In church education, camping ministry, and music programs Christian workers may deal primarily with children. That is a dangerous position for the pedophiliac who is compulsively driven to have sexual contacts with a child. This may range from exposure or fondling of genitalia to engaging in more invasive acts, such as sodomy or intercourse.

Pedophilia represents a deep-seated abnormality in sexual identification and maturity. Normal adult heterosexuality is fearful, and there is often an arrested development from pre-adolescent or early adolescent stages. The pedophiliac seems driven to gain reassurance of his own sexual identification by seeing or touching a child's genitalia. That experience is sexually exciting and may culminate in masturbation or sexual play with the child.

Treatment calls for environmental changes to eliminate opportunity for abuse of children, dynamic psychotherapy to work through sexual maturation arrests, enhancement of the marital relationship if he is married (which is not uncommon), and a cognitive approach to changing fantasy patterns, replacing them with positive input regarding adequacy in God. It is also important for the pedophiliac to avoid pornographic material. This often encourages sexual abuse of children and definitely increases activity.

Masturbation

Since masturbation is practically universal in males and not uncommon in females, you will occasionally counsel Christian workers who are concerned about compulsive masturbation. They are usually guilt-ridden about the behavior and have tried to stop with varying success. Their failure to control the habit, especially if it is coupled with viewing pornographic material, may significantly interfere with their spiritual lives.

Masturbation is reinforced by physical and psychological factors. Physically, there is the powerful neurological stimulus response. The brain's most sensitive reward center releases neuronal discharges that are extremely pleasurable and habituating. In some experimental systems, animals prefer this stimulation to eating. Psychologically, masturbation releases tension and anxiety and can provide reassurance of one's sexual potency.

Dealing with masturbation as a problem involves three phases. One is spiritually relieving the guilt. The second is behaviorally deconditioning the neurological reward system; and the third is psychotherapeutically helping the person achieve a positive sense of sexual identity.

Often the guilt associated with masturbation is inappropriate. The act itself is not mentioned in Scripture as sinful. In fact, it is not mentioned at all. Sometimes simply informing a person of this will make a significant impact on the problem. By relieving false guilt, the person may be relieved of part of the tension that perpetrated the habit. True guilt may be related when the masturbatory fantasies are lustful and when the habit causes distance between spouses. Confession and repentance are important first steps in restoring a person spiritually. At times, the break in the marital sexual relationship is so severe that it needs to be restored. The open confession and discussion of the problem, which may have never been attempted, can enlist the help of the marriage partner.

To decondition the habit requires identifying the stimuli or circumstances that began the behavioral chain culminating in the masturbation. The earliest thoughts or actions must then be switched to an alternative pleasurable experience. Identifying other effective rewards is important. For example, if sexual release is an important drive, having sex with the spouse rather than masturbating may be an attractive alternative. Other rewards may also be instituted.

An important aspect of therapy is to investigate the psychosexual development of the person. Often masturbation began in adolescence as a reassurance of a person's sexual identity and/or an escape from tension. Helping the individual recognize his or her worth as a person and value as a man or woman can decrease the inner tension. Discover the early messages about sexuality and replace them with the truth about sex as a wholesome gift from God. It may also be helpful to investigate the patterns and attitudes of the spouse and guide the couple into a more satisfying sexual relationship.

Summary

Christian workers have normal sexual drives. They often need a place to deal with sexual issues. There are useful principles in helping them.

1. Talk openly and comfortably about sex.
2. Take a thorough sexual history.
3. Educate the minister and spouse regarding human sexuality.
4. Help the client bring a balanced psychological and spiritual approach to sexual perversions.

DRUG AND ALCOHOL ADDICTION

Dependency problems do occur among clergy and can destroy ministry. They are to be suspected in a clergyperson who is depressed, has begun to show erratic behavior, is often irritable and withdrawn, begins to miss work, has an increase in "sick" days, is not sleeping normally, or seems intoxicated at times. Any or all of these patterns should alert those involved to the possibility of abuse.

When addiction is suspected, the person should be confronted in a clear, forthright way. I say, "Your patterns of behavior strongly suggest a problem with alcohol or drugs.

What are you currently using?" Very likely there will be an initial denial that there is an addiction unless the person has already admitted a problem. He or she may say, "Well, I'm taking some medication for nerves (or pain, or sleep) but only what the doctor has prescribed," or "Oh, I have a drink occasionally, but I'm not an alcoholic." I then ask exactly how much they are taking of what drugs and what physicians prescribed them or how much alcohol is consumed. A spouse can often help.

If the clients continue to deny an addiction problem, I will ask them to explain the behavior patterns that have caused others to be concerned. If they are unable to do so, I might suggest hospitalization for evaluation of the problem. If a person has an addiction, there needs to be medical treatment available in case of withdrawal symptoms. If not, a period of observation and medical examination may help make a definitive diagnosis.

Once the presence of alcoholism or drug dependency is established, the individual should be referred to a qualified dependency center. I feel very strongly that until the person is detoxified in a safe setting and the addiction is successfully treated no other useful counseling will be accomplished. I have not found any program as effective as Alcoholics Anonymous. I refuse to counsel an alcohol- or drug-dependent person unless he or she is actively involved in A.A. When they are active in A.A., marriage counseling or psychotherapy may be started simultaneously.

It is important that some liaison be established between the minister and the church or other employer. There needs to be understanding and support for the minister during the treatment and recovery phase. Education of lay leaders can help them understand dependency as an illness and not simply as a "sin." The family as well should be given adequate information about the nature of addiction. Al-Anon has materials as well as support groups for families. You may be in a position to provide a bridge between the alcoholic and his or her world. Christians don't always overflow with love and supportive concern where they find out their leader is abusing drugs or alcohol. Rehabilitation can certainly be facilitated if they are empathic. A Christian counselor can assist them in working through their own anger and fear to a position of understanding. These principles also apply to a minister's spouse who has become drug or alcohol dependent.

Sometimes there are denominational facilities or officers who can provide assistance in treatment or relocation if necessary. Be sure you have your client's authorization to make those contacts.

Summary

Substance abuse is crippling for clergy. They are often susceptible to abuse because of their loneliness and isolation.

The addictive problem must be treated effectively before other areas of conflict can be successfully resolved.

PART THREE

THERAPEUTIC TECHNIQUES

CHAPTER SEVEN

BASIC PRINCIPLES OF COUNSELING

ONE OF MY TEACHERS of psychotherapy, Neil Krupp, said he had come to believe that therapists are born not made. By that he meant that there are innate qualities that enable certain people to become effective counselors.

Why then try to teach someone to do therapy? Can a person without the inborn qualities ever become an effective counselor? I'm not sure of the answers to those questions. I do know that without a basic sensitivity to feelings and compassion for those in emotional pain, being a counselor would be a miserable undertaking.

I'm also sure that the "born therapists" can improve their skills. In *How to Be a People Helper,* Dr. Gary Collins points out the importance of preparing oneself intellectually and emotionally to be a helper.[1] There are certain principles that make a difference in effectiveness.

Before our wedding, Melissa, eager to be a good wife, asked my mother for the recipes of my favorite dishes. After our wedding, still eager to please me, she began to prepare my favorite foods just the way my mother did. We soon discovered that something was lost in the translation. Her red dot chocolate cake just didn't taste as good as Mom's, and that is only *one* example.

Over the years, we discovered that Mother didn't include quite everything on the recipe card. Now I don't think my sweet mother deliberately set out to sabotage her new daughter-in-law. I'm not even going to try to psychologize about my mother's unconscious; you can if you like. I do believe that Mother did a lot of "seasoning to taste" that was hard, if not impossible, to measure precisely and write down on those index cards.

Faced with the task of describing how to counsel Christian workers has made me more than ever aware of the complexity of my profession. There are so many ingredients often added "to taste" that there can be no cook-book formula for how to prepare "cured clergy."

During these months of writing I have tried to be more consciously aware of what we do and how we do it. There are some skills that can probably be replicated—the knowledge of the problems ministers face, an understanding of the areas of resistance, an ability to offer acceptance, and so forth. There are many others that can't—such as when and how to use humor, the right time to cry, when to touch. As I looked at these factors, I became almost immobilized at times by the self-consciousness involved. Rather than moving naturally toward a hurting minister or spouse, I'd find myself questioning whether or not holding back would be better. Rather than sitting silently for a few minutes, I'd consider moving the process on. Rather than giving a slightly raised eyebrow or a slowly growing smile, I would wonder if that nonverbal signal was adequate for the message I wanted to send.

I'm glad to say that all the introspection and analysis didn't ruin my ministry while I was involved with writing. Allowing my instinctual responses to continue won out. Some of those responses I'll try to describe for your awareness, but not for you to mimic. (You may not have the eyebrows for it.)

One other discovery I want to share. That is that Melissa is a very good cook. She brings to the kitchen her own flair and creativity that is unique. She's never quite made red dot chocolate cake like Mom's, but her apple pie is unbeatable! You will bring your uniqueness into counseling and do things I could never do—so don't even try to be a copy.

KNOW YOURSELF

It seems only natural to begin with the issue of your uniqueness. You are (apart from God's work) the most important factor in the therapeutic process. That's why it is so critical for you to know who you are.

I like John's account of the last evening with Jesus. As John begins his description he gives such a beautiful picture of our Lord's personal effectiveness and servanthood. He says, "Jesus knew that the Father had put all things under his power, and that he had come from God and was returning to God, so he got up from the meal, took off his outer clothing, and wrapped a towel around his waist. After that, he poured water into a basin and began to wash his disciples' feet, drying them with the towel" (John 13:3–5). Jesus knew who he was. That knowledge seemed to equip him to humble himself and serve his friends. He had come from God and was going back to God. There is security in understanding your origin and destination. When fully comprehended, the knowledge that everything has come from God helps to protect us from arrogance and pride. Yet at the same time that knowledge can be the source of uncommon confidence.

I have been reviewing my textbooks on psychotherapy. It's interesting that two of the classics, by Freida Fromm-Reichmann and Hilde Bruch, both emphasize repeatedly the importance of self-awareness.

Dr. Fromm-Reichmann says, "Unless the psychiatrist is widely aware of his own interpersonal processes so that he can handle them for the benefit of the patient in their interpersonal therapeutic dealings with each other, no successful psychotherapy can eventuate." [2]

Dr. Bruch says in her initial description of the first meeting: "Both the therapist and patient bring their own personalities and past experiences to the therapeutic encounter, although the therapist, let us hope, has some greater awareness of the hidden factors and fewer anxieties about what lies ahead. Whatever the overt reason and manifest symptomatoloty that bring a patient into a psychiatrist's office, the therapist must be motivated by the wish to be of use to the patient and to understand him, and to give him the opportunity to express himself openly and freely." [3]

Understanding yourself is the foundation of being an effective counselor. This is especially true regarding your value as a person. You can be free to be truly involved with another only as you come to know that everything you have has come to you from God—that your life and uniqueness are gifts from Him, that your salvation is by grace, that you are loved enough that Jesus died for you, that you can do nothing to make Him love you less *or more.* You have to accept yourself, in this sense, love yourself, before you can love others or help them love themselves. Otherwise, your insecurities will drive you to use your patients to boost your own ego. Your needs will cause you to depend on your patients for gratification. Your unresolved conflicts will be transferred to your clients or projected onto them.

There are times in therapy when you may not understand a problem or have the answer to a question. It is essential that you are comfortable enough to say so. A client can tell when you're lying. Only a mature counselor who is secure in self can risk that honesty.

There will be instances in counseling when self-disclosure on your part can relieve a patient's feelings of inadequacy or fear of confession. Taking that risk is dependent on knowing the truth about yourself and that your sins have been taken care of permanently.

It's also important for you to be aware of your own current feelings and conflicts. When I recognize that I am depressed or anxious, I will work harder to attend to my patients. At times I have even mentioned to them that I am struggling with some problem in my own life, perhaps even asking for their prayers. However, a balance is essential. Too much disclosure can create anxiety and insecurity in the patient. If the personal conflicts are going to be so distracting that you are absent from the relationship, it is better to talk about it. Once this winter my father was seriously ill, and for about twenty-four hours I didn't know how he might respond to treatment. When I recognized the emotional effect the situation was having on me I chose to share with our group and ask for their prayers. They were very understanding and supportive. I was not incapacitated in the situation and was also able to reassure them fairly quickly that I would not have to leave.

Counter-transference feelings need to be identified within yourself and perhaps talked about with a colleague. Under most circumstances it would only be destructive toward the client to tell him or her your feelings. If you find yourself unable to work with a person, do the favor of referring him or her to someone else. You can say that you are unable to be the objective counselor that is needed and that you feel it is in the patient's best interest to see another therapist. Make it clear that it is your problem and not his or hers.

Similarly, learn your limitations. If there are certain kinds of problems you don't handle well, refer them. That is the beauty of being a part of the body of Christ. Not everyone can do it all, but someone can do what is necessary for the occasion. Let those who are gifted in a particular area exercise their gift.

If you feel you don't know yourself very well I would recommend a self-assessment like I described in the previous section. Make a list of the ideas you have about yourself in every area. See what specific messages you received to influence those conclusions. Who gave you those impressions and in what circumstances? Identify the truth and eliminate the lies. Replace the lies with truth about your real value. Accept the limitations but put them in proper perspective (e.g., it is true that I'm not very athletic, but that doesn't make me a less valuable person).

At one time all psychiatrists in training were required to have therapy for themselves. Although that is no longer a hard and fast rule, it is still a useful experience for most people. Experiencing counseling for yourself can help your understanding of yourself immensely. You will also identify with what your clients are going through. Whether or not you have formal therapy, as a Christian you are called to confess your sins to another believer, to allow others to help you bear your burdens, and to submit yourself to fellow Christians. This process will allow you to know yourself in a deeper, more honest way. Then you can take off your robes of self-righteousness or pride or defensiveness, gird yourself with a servant's towel, and wash the feet of fellow pilgrims.

ACCEPTANCE

Perhaps the most consistent comment we hear about the effectiveness of our counseling of ministers relates to the acceptance that was felt. Christian workers are frequently expected to live up to unrealistic standards. Either from within themselves or from the community, they hear a demand to be superhuman. Consequently, most have never felt it was safe to reveal their humanity. Instead, they live in fear that if people really knew them they'd reject them. To risk exposure in counseling and be met with acceptance rather than condemnation brings them new hope and healing.

In the atmosphere of acceptance it is possible to do the necessary work of teaching. Attempts to correct outside of a loving relationship only raise defensiveness. Tournier gives us a clear insight into the essential element of acceptance: "The practice of a Christian ministry constantly affords confirmation of this double truth, [that is the relationship between illness and sin] which is contradictory only to our rationalistic outlook. . . . as soon as there slips into our hearts the slightest spirit of condemnation in regard to one of our patients, we set up a barrier between him and us, and thereafter all our efforts and all our love will be powerless to help him." [4]

Many of our patients have reflected Carl's sentiments: "I came to the retreat feeling really on the defensive. I saw myself as a failure. I had let my wife down, God down, the church down, my parents down, and myself down. I knew I had sinned, but I wasn't going to admit that to anyone. I'd been Scripture-whipped by several self-righteous Pharisees and I wasn't going to hear anymore of that. I just wanted to run.

"Then, to my surprise, I felt loved and accepted in spite of my sin. My whole attitude changed from blaming everyone else and justifying me to wanting to really confess and be cleansed. I was surprised at the things I found out about myself when I wasn't so busy protecting my bruised ego.

"Another funny thing is that no one approved of what I had done. You said the same thing the Pharisees said—quoted the same Scriptures. I knew that was truth, and now I wanted to hear that truth confirmed. Before I had resisted it with all my might. Was that just the power of love?"

It is the power of love which is the spirit of Jesus.

How do you show acceptance? You may laugh when I say this, but you show acceptance by being accepting. If you know yourself to be common clay—a sinner saved by grace, how can you not show acceptance toward another one of God's creatures? If you find yourself feeling more judgmental than loving, see if there is a beam in your own eye.

Let me further answer the question by listing some specific behaviors that show acceptance.

1. Call people by name when you meet them and welcome them. Look friendly and make them feel at home. Shake hands firmly. Make eye contact.

2. Establish a positive link if there is one, e.g., "Your friend Henry Abbott called and expressed his concern about you, and I'm glad you were able to come in." (But don't break a confidence if "Henry" doesn't want to be identified.)

3. Let him know you respect his ministry endeavors, e.g., "I understand you're rector at Saint John's. That must be a pretty demanding parish."

4. Invite him to ask you any questions he might have about "therapy" or your program, e.g., "Before we get started you may want to ask some questions. I know most people wonder what's going to happen or may feel a little anxious about seeing a counselor."

5. Make it clear that you are more interested in hearing

his story from him than from others. "I've only heard a little about the problem you're having, and I'm really interested in hearing your perspective of the situation," or "Since our phone conversation I've been looking forward to meeting you and really getting to know you."

6. It may be important to define the contract. For instance, if you have been "hired" by the church or the bishop to evaluate this minister for them and to make recommendations about fitness to serve, that should be stated up front, e.g., "I have been asked by your trustees to write them a report giving my evaluation and recommendations. I wanted you to know that and that I will go over with you the substance of my report," or "Your bishop called and asked me to see you. He expressed his concern, but as far as I know he is not asking for any formal evaluation. I'd like to give him some feedback as we go along if it would seem helpful and if you agree," or "It's my impression that your mission director wants a report from me about whether or not I think you should return to the field. Is that your understanding as well?"

Since my particular ministry always entails therapy along with evaluation, I generally begin to form a therapeutic alliance by offering my services to the minister, e.g., "Even though I'll be making recommendations to your board, I'm primarily here to serve you. I'll talk everything over with you that I would say to them. While you're here, I certainly want us to work together on the things that concern you most."

7. In our group therapy sessions I let people know that we will not be invasive, but rather want them to feel it's safe to bring up the things that are of concern to them. I indicate that any subject is okay, and that we've discovered that most folks struggle with very similar problems in life— getting along with themselves, making a marriage work, avoiding killing their teenagers and two-year-olds, dealing with anger and sexuality, and trying to live with other Christians. I may mention that we're not stone throwers because we haven't yet found anyone sinless and therefore qualified to throw the first one.

All those things may not be what really gives the feeling of acceptance. It may be the architecture of our office building or the color of the carpets. It may be the warmth of our host couple who really make the first contact over a pot of steaming soup. I do know that we have a very deep respect for these people who are in Christian ministry. They have severe stress and need all the love we can give them. If you're going to work with them, I hope you'll bring that same positive regard.

LISTENING

Freida Fromm-Reichmann tells a story to emphasize the importance of listening. When she first arrived in the U.S. fleeing the Nazi persecution, she spoke very little English. Nonetheless, a friend insisted she have a counseling session with an important friend of his. Over her objections the appointment was made. She sat with the troubled man listening attentively for an hour trying to understand some of what he was saying, but really failing to do so intellectually. She did pick up his mood and nonverbal messages and was able to make appropriate nonverbal responses. Years later she received a letter from the man thanking her for seeing him. He said that their counseling session had changed his life.[5]

I wish I listened that well. As you know it is hard work to listen. It takes your undivided attention. It requires hearing between the lines. You must "hear" nonverbal messages as well as what is said. At times it will break your heart. But it is exciting and awesome to hear another person open the doors to the most secret and sacred areas of life. Dr. Gordon Moore, a Mayo consultant, used to say, "I feel guilty being privileged to such mystery and drama and romance and getting paid to listen."

One of the first ingredients to being a good listener is being curious. Each person you see is absolutely unique. Sure there are some similarities and shared patterns, but no two human beings are really alike. Enter each counseling relationship like you were opening a new novel with intriguing characters, fascinating subplots, and unexpected events. Too often people listen to confirm what they are expecting to hear rather than what is actually said. In counseling, it is tempting to show how intellectual we are by quickly figuring out the answers for the problems. Unfortunately, when we do that we put the person in a paint-by-number picture and set about hearing the information we need to fill in the blanks. Let me assure you that you'll miss out on lots of exciting color that way.

Here is a common experience. A pastor and his wife come to the retreat because of his problem with depression. On the surface, it sounds like a typical story of burnout. As their stories unfold, we begin to sense there is something else going on. His depression seems more and more like grief and related to their marriage. We finally discover that he thinks she was involved briefly with another man several years earlier. They have never confronted the issue, but he has built a web of circumstantial evidence that proves to him she was unfaithful. She has watched him become cold and withdraw his affections, but she has never understood why. She just thought he was distracted by his work and becoming burned out. He was so afraid to face the "facts" of her infidelity that he wouldn't bring it up. Listening to them carefully kept raising questions about the timing of events that didn't seem to fit with what they were reporting. His allusions to her friendships and something taking her away from him finally prompted the right questions.

In fact, she had felt romantically drawn to her boss, but never became sexually involved. As that was worked through, his "burnout" was cured.

Another important listening skill is hearing "between the lines." We have a stuffed toy owl who is a psychiatrist, Dr. Sigmund Owl. He makes several verbal responses when you pull a string on his back. One of his statements is, "There's something you're not telling me." [6]

Frequently you can hear in the tone of voice, or a hesitation in rhythm, or see in facial expression or body language that some feeling or thought is not being said. The person may say an event didn't cause any pain, yet get teary eyed for a split second. A minister may be sharing his appreciation for your efforts but be expressing tension and anger in his muscle tone and voice pitch. A question may seem to be a straightforward inquiry, but indicate an underlying personal concern that is really different. I am frequently asked how on earth

I can stand to listen to people's problems day after day. I believe that question is also asking, "Are you interested in my problems? Are you really willing to listen to me?" Learning to listen between the lines can give you clues to unexpressed areas of anxiety. You might take Dr. Sigmund Owl's line and say, "There's something you're not telling me."

You might make an observation about what you've seen or heard and ask what it may mean. For instance you might say, "When you were talking about your church just now you looked really sad (or angry or afraid). Tell me what you were feeling." At other times, you may simply make a mental note and be aware of possible feelings in that area. At times I will notice that a person reacted to a certain subject with restlessness. The second time I see the same response I reinforce my association about that mentally. If it occurs a third time, I'm likely to ask what is going on.

A third listening skill is to hear with empathy. Try to tune into the feelings the person must be having. Be sensitive about the range of human emotions and what you might be feeling under the circumstances. This is especially helpful counseling men who use denial and rationalization to handle their feelings. They may have their verbal communication so sterilized of feelings that nothing shows. Yet inside they may be really hurting. As you listen empathically you can suggest what they might have felt. This expression of genuine unfiltered feeling on your part will help them begin to identify their own buried emotion. It can also give them permission to have feelings.

A fourth ingredient is to be attentive. In marriage enrichment conferences on communication we frequently have a husband and wife rate each other on listening skills. The things they observe are: 1. making eye contact; 2. putting away distractions; 3. turning the whole body toward the speaker; 4. not interrupting; 5. showing interest in the subject; 6. giving a verbal response that indicates understanding. These are just as important in counseling as in marriage. Giving another person our undivided attention is a tremendous gift of love. Along with showing acceptance, listening to a person provides the opening for making interpretive remarks.

INTERPRETATION

Whatever counseling theory you use there will be new areas of understanding you want your client to achieve. The basic goal of psychotherapy is teaching, helping a person know self in a more complete and accurate way. Bringing those insights is done through "interpretation." This is a critical aspect of the therapeutic relationship.

For the Christian counselor, there are three areas of a person's life that must be evaluated—beliefs, emotions, and behavior. All three factors are important to achieve a balanced integration of one's whole being. What a person believes, how he feels, and how he acts must be brought into line with what the Creator of life intended.

Now it would seem that the task should be a simple matter of teaching everybody the biblical truths about humanity. When a person knows that the Bible teaches that there is a personal God who created mankind for fellowship, that sin interrupts that relationship, that Jesus broke the sin barrier by his death and resurrection, that a person can appropriate power over sin by trusting in Jesus, there should be no problems in living. Obviously, if it were that simple, Christians wouldn't have problems and Christian ministers would definitely be exempt.

What gets in the way of the maturity that represents the balanced integration of self? It is distortion of truth in a person's beliefs about self and the world, including God's order for life. These distortions occur primarily during childhood development but continue to be reinforced because of the faulty behavior patterns that exist.

For instance, if a boy was basically unwanted and treated with neglect or abuse he develops a repetitious pattern of responses to the environment. He may try lots of different ways to get attention and have his need for significance met. By the time he is school age, he has probably settled on a stereotypic system. He believes he is unloved and unlovable—a "bad" boy. He feels angry and hurt and perhaps guilty because he isn't good enough. He acts out his basic beliefs and feelings either through aggressive mischief (getting even with the hostile world and getting attention) or through withdrawal into himself (turning his anger toward self in depression). These basic patterns may be altered because of intervening relationships (like a loving teacher or a good friend), but the underlying distortions remain. Under stressful conditions the earlier systems tend to return. Marriage, raising children, conflicts in the ministry, financial pressures, and adult life-cycle changes are the kinds of events in a Christian worker's life that are likely to renew the old patterns.

Since Christian ministers know the Bible intellectually, a purely biblical approach isn't fully effective. Their old distortions of beliefs, feelings, and responses become barriers to accepting biblical truth. It is important then to explore developmental patterns. Interpretations of those early life events and how they produced distortions of God's truth will help a person exchange lies for truth. The three areas that interpretation of distortions should include are: current feelings and behaviors and how they relate to early life experiences, recent relational crises, and the relationship with the counselor.

Within these areas the faulty choices of behavior can be identified. They are probably well known to the client already, (e.g., withdrawal from conflict). You can also interpret the feelings influencing those choices (which may not be conscious, e.g., fear of rejection), and the beliefs underlying the feelings (e.g., I am unlovable and worthless). Coming to understand the genesis of the responses does not relieve the minister of taking responsibility for his everyday choices. Nor does it deny the moral aspect of those choices. Sin is still sin and needs to be confessed. But the damaged emotions and thinking can come under the healing power of the Holy Spirit.

From Paul's pen we hear a clear picture of the problem of repetitious, negative behavior. In Romans 7 he writes:

> We know that the law is spiritual; but I am unspiritual, sold as a slave to sin. I do not understand what I do. For what I want to do I do not do, but what I hate I do. And if I do what I do not want to do, I agree that the law is good. As it is, it is no longer I myself who do it, but it is sin living in me. I know that nothing good

lives in me, that is, in my sinful nature. For I have the desire to do what is good, but I cannot carry it out. For what I do is not the good I want to do; no, the evil I do not want to do—this I keep on doing. Now if I do what I do not want to do, it is no longer I who do it, but it is sin living in me that does it.

So I find this law at work: When I want to do good, evil is right there with me. For in my inner being I delight in God's law; but I see another law at work in the members of my body, waging war against the law of my mind and making me a prisoner of the law of sin at work within my members. What a wretched man I am! Who will rescue me from this body of death? Thanks be to God—through Jesus Christ our Lord! (vv. 14–25).

Scriptures also teach that the sins of the father (parents) are visited on the children to the third and fourth generation. The bad choices that parents make (morally wrong, i.e., against God's law) become the roots of the developing child's bad choice patterns. Even in the born-again believer (as Paul was) the "law of sin" remains at war with the reason. Old responses conditioned by a sinful environment and enhanced by Satan exert their influence for generations.

Not only is the content of interpretation important but the method makes a difference. As Dr. Fromm-Reichmann writes, "Any interpretation which the patient is able to unearth for himself is more impressive to him, hence more likely to produce an immediate and lasting curative effect, than any interpretation offered by the therapist." [7] As you begin to see patterns of thoughts, emotions, or behavior that represent distortion, you may begin to ask questions to help your client identify them. For example, you realize that the minister has a pattern of getting into power struggles with dominant women in his church and with his wife. You might ask him how he feels when faced with a powerful female and how that relates to his childhood experiences. That is far more effective than "making an interpretation" that he has unresolved anger toward his mother's control and is transferring those feelings into current relationships with mother-figures. Besides, that may not be true.

By asking interpretive questions that lead the client into exploring his distortions you can not only bring him to understand the pattern, but also teach him to become more aware of his choices and the factors which are determining them. He will begin to use the probing technique to investigate other responses that are detrimental. The process becomes self-reinforcing so that more and more of his behavior becomes conscious. Repressed memories and feelings are brought to awareness.

Dreams are a source of new insights or at least an area for work. As you know, people dream regularly every night as they go through the normal stages of sleep. Often people don't remember their dreams and may report that they "never dream." I suggest to clients that they will probably begin to remember their dreams more frequently during therapy and ask them to write them out. I have found dreams to be a significant help in understanding areas of conflict. As with other interpretative work, I ask questions about a dream's content. I do not accept the idea that there are specific dream symbols that always represent the same thing. I have found that individuals can usually make meaningful interpretations using their own unique symbolization.

A recurrent dream is perhaps more significant than others and should be asked about. A common type of recurrent dream is the fear of exposure dream. This may take the form of showing up for an exam totally unprepared. Another similar form is being suddenly naked in front of other people. Many pastors report dreaming that they stand up to preach and discover they don't have their sermon notes. These and other dreams may reveal underlying feelings of inadequacy, guilt, fear, or sexual conflict.

Finally, there may be times in therapy that the patient's feelings or behavior toward you may reflect distortions. Classical analysis focused primarily on this "transference neurosis." I don't generally focus on this and have a much more directive involvement with my patients. If they respond negatively toward me, it's probably related to something I (not their dad) did or didn't do. At times, however, even in our form of brief psychotherapy, some response to me will seem to come out of nowhere. When that happens I try to question what the patient was feeling and what may have prompted those feelings. Useful insights into the attitudes and relationship to a parent may be revealed.

"YOU" AS A THERAPEUTIC TOOL

Unless you practice an archaic form of Freudian analysis, you don't sit with your back to the patient recording his or her free associations. Even psychoanalysts usually sit facing their patients and are actually involved in the therapeutic process. The real relationship that develops and what you bring to it are highly significant aspects of therapy. I talked about the foundation of your self-knowledge. Of course your showing acceptance, listening, and interpreting are extensions of yourself. I'd like to discuss additional ways you as a Christian counselor exert your selfhood at the interpersonal interface.

A powerful expression of yourself is made through touch. Once an absolute taboo in counseling, physical contact is now seen as a positive means of communicating. I'm a touching person. My family is full of huggers, kissers, patters, pinchers, and back scratchers. I grew up feeling comfortable with body contact and have to remind myself at times that everybody doesn't share that background. I've come to develop more awareness of the difference in people's "comfort zones." At times, however, I disregard them and reach through to touch someone because physical expressions of affection are a need of human beings. I try to gauge my level of contact to the person's comfort level which often increases quickly as the client senses my absence of anxiety about touching.

I remember one young woman who physically withdrew and shuddered the first time I touched her shoulder. She talked about that later relating it to sexual conflicts. As we were saying good-bye at termination of counseling she initiated a full hug with apparent ease. I had respected her anxiety and allowed her to signal what touch was okay. That enabled her to move toward comfortable contact.

Touch tells people that you accept them. It helps them overcome feelings of being "untouchable." It breaks through the barriers they may have built around themselves and says, "I care about you enough to ignore the 'fragile-do not touch' sign and risk being rejected." At times you will be rejected as I was by the young woman I just talked about. When that occurs, see it as an indication of the level of fear and discomfort the other person has (which it is), not as personal rejection (which it isn't). There have been hundreds of men and women who have thanked me at some point in therapy for giving them a hug or a touch. They confessed that they often want affection but are afraid to initiate it even within their marriage. Your touch can begin to free a person from fear of contact.

Touch can take many forms. I like to simply reach out and touch someone on the arm or shoulder as we are talking casually in the hallway or kitchen. In group or in private sessions, I may touch a person in order to share in some meaningful emotional expression such as sadness or joy. If a person is really overcome with grief, I may even hold them around the shoulders or by the hand. Such touching can bring comfort and security when a feeling of being out of control is frightening. At times in prayer I will place my hands on a person's shoulder or head in the traditional form of giving a blessing. I believe there is a spiritual communion that occurs at those times that transcends the purely human event.

Before you go out and start being the phantom hugger, let me share some cautions. Avoid contact that has sexually seductive messages. You know yourself regarding your own lustful thoughts and you can sense seductive behavior in another person. If either is present or suspected, keep your contact to a minimum and only in the presence of others. If you do touch, don't let your hand linger in any subtly sexual way. Don't touch erotic areas like the back of the neck, the breasts, buttocks, or thighs. Don't entwine fingers in a romantic way. If the other person persists in such contact, you'd be wise to talk about it and to take steps to stop it. You may also want to listen to your spouse regarding your touching behavior. If your mate is uncomfortable or jealous, that's reason enough to adjust your style.

Another caution regarding touch is with adolescents of the opposite sex. Teenagers are becoming alive to sexual feelings and are easily aroused. They may misinterpret your touch— particularly if it progresses to a hug or a caress. An arm around the shoulders may be okay, but a full-bodied hug, too much.

Similarly, touch can be extremely threatening to a psychotic person. Individuals with severe shattering-of-their-ego boundaries, as in psychosis, may feel completely controlled or invasively assaulted by a simple touch. Take time to develop some relationship so that you can more accurately assess their feelings and ideas before taking that liberty.

The final touch: If you're uncomfortable with touch, don't do it. Your anxiety will be telegraphed and can be misinterpreted by your client.

You also bring yourself into therapy through verbal self-disclosure. I have found that the usual curiosity of clients regarding their counselor is greater among clergy (or other professionals). I think the discomfort with the "patient" role predictably motivates them to establish a sense of collegiality. I try to respect that need and let ministers know something of my background. I allow those identifying points of contact such as educational experience and call to ministry to be established. I am not fearful of losing respect or control of the therapeutic process. Most of our patients call me "Louis" rather than "Dr. McBurney" and consider themselves retreat "guests" rather than "patients." The familiarity has not been detrimental.

In the course of therapy, there are times when sharing your own life experiences can serve useful purposes. One is modeling self-disclosure. If your client is keeping up a professional mask, it may help for you to unmask a little. I might say, "You know, in my position, I really feel isolated at times— like there isn't any place for me to unburden. My pastor and best buddy, Doug, has really given me a place to unload. If I'm having a conflict with Melissa or one of the kids, I can just lay it on the line with him. Do you have anybody to unload on?"

Another beneficial use of self-disclosure is in teaching about self-awareness and self-esteem. Melissa went through a very painful but freeing battle over her self-concept several years ago. When group members seem to be confused about the process, she will share what she went through. That invariably opens individuals up to establishing their own worth in Christ rather than in some performance goal.

Self-disclosure of emotions gives a person permission to express feelings and models "straight talk" communications. It also helps identify feelings. When a person is well practiced at repressing or suppressing emotions, he or she may really not know what is happening on a feeling level. I may say, "That happened to me one time and I was really angry inside" or "I don't know what you may be feeling, but I'm hurting for you. You must feel put down and rejected."

We use self-disclosure to teach behavioral skills as well. Sharing our spiritual pilgrimage and our relational experiences can be used to reeducate a person away from ineffective communication patterns, unbiblical theological positions, or negative spiritual practices.

There are two cautions regarding self-disclosure: Avoid exhibitionism, where you spend the client's time (and money) focusing the spotlight on yourself, and don't use the therapy setting to work through your own conflicts. Either use is destructive to your client. I have had several patients who have told of negative experiences with previous counselors. One legitimate complaint is, "He spent all the time telling me about his problems. I started to send him a bill."

Another use of "yourself" in therapy is the injection of humor into the process. I think Jesus laughed a lot. In his book *The Humor of Christ,* Elton Trueblood points out Jesus' humor in a refreshing perception of our Lord. The positive effects of laughter have been shown repeatedly in all sorts of life stress. Being able to laugh at one's self is a distinctive sign of a healthy self-esteem. Psychotherapy can break a pattern of gloomy preoccupation with the seriousness of life and infuse laughter into its place.

I think I left this to last because I don't have the foggiest notion of how to teach someone to have or use a sense of humor. What's more, I have never seen a meaningful study of humor. Humor seems to be related to creativity. Both depend on the ability to abandon rigid logical thought patterns and engage in a free flight of ideas. In this associative mode, events and ideas are seen from a different angle and their humorous (incongruous or unexpected) aspect is apparent. Children look at life in this way. Perhaps that's one of the qualities Jesus had in mind when He said that we must become like little children to see His kingdom.

Some of the most healing times at Marble Retreat happen out of the counseling rooms—and without my presence. At some time during the two-week session, the group will sit around in the evening and swap funny preacher stories, favorite jokes, or even comical monologues. You can feel the lightening of their moods and quickening of their enthusiasm for life the next day. Since most are depressed when they come, they'll often say, "That's the first good laugh I've had in months. Boy, it felt good." It does feel good. The Book of Proverbs says, "A cheerful heart is good medicine, but a crushed spirit dries up the bones" (17:22).

Humor can be only a knife edge away from hostility, however, so one has to know his own motives and feelings. As a rule, I poke fun at myself rather than people in therapy, but I may encourage them to look on the light side of their own situation as well. I must admit though, occasionally, when someone is telling some serious event that has an apparent side-splitting, hilarious aspect, I lose it and break out with laughter. So far, I don't think I've done irreparable psychic damage. In fact, they usually begin to see the humor themselves and join in the laugh.

CHAPTER EIGHT

SPIRITUAL ASPECTS OF COUNSELING CHRISTIAN WORKERS

"HAPPY IS THE MAN who does not take the wicked for his guide" (Ps. 1:1, NEB). In my early years of counseling I felt comfortable just not being a wicked guide or ungodly counselor. Then I began to realize that I was stopping one step short of giving people what they desperately needed. They not only need a compassionate listener who can help them understand their developmental complexes or someone to give them symptomatic relief through medications, but they also need Jesus Christ living within. I began to ask about their spiritual beliefs and practices and share scriptural truth with them.

Paul Tournier says: "If I look honestly into my own heart,

and into the tragic situation of humanity, which my vocation as a doctor allows me to do day after day, I see that behind all 'personal problems' there lies, quite simply, sin.

"Man's moral drama so dominates the problem of man that if science is forbidden to have anything to do with it, science has no contact with life. It constructs systems which are satisfying to reason, but have nothing to say to the real anguish of man. They leave him to fight his inner battle alone, and he is always defeated." [1]

In *Whatever Became of Sin,* Dr. Karl Menninger writes: "Some behavior once regarded as sinful has certainly undergone reappraisal. It is no longer a sin to assert the earth is round. Tea and coffee drinking are generally allowed, now. Adultery is technically a crime but for many people it is certainly no sin. Lots of sins have disappeared; nevertheless, I believe there is a general sentiment that sin is still with us, by us, and in us—somewhere." [2]

The problem of sin. But what about the problem of sin in Christian workers? If they are in fact believers and followers of Jesus have they not been redeemed from sin? Perhaps they have never actually become Christians. Do they not know the Scriptures? Perhaps they don't believe in the authority of the Scriptures. Don't they try to live their lives according to the teachings of Jesus? They are called "Christians." Perhaps they don't actually see their vocation as having any connection with Jesus of Nazareth.

In dealing with Christian workers, you will discover a wide range of spiritual practices and religious beliefs. And you will find opportunity time and again to apply spiritual principles in calling people back to God. That is godly counsel.

CONFESSION AND REPENTANCE

Elizabeth O'Connor, in *Search for Silence,* reminds us that confession is for the sinner, not to inform the omniscient Creator.[3] Confession and repentance occur whenever man is confronted by a Holy God. We see ourselves as we really are and fall to our knees. The Bible is filled with stories of men being overwhelmed by fear and awe when coming into the presence of God.

So we seem to avoid coming into the presence of God. Many clergy come before God only to conduct the religious rituals of the church. They have forsaken meditation, for it brings them face to face with themselves. Paul Tournier points out that more unconscious material, particularly our sins, is brought to awareness through meditation and confession than through years of psychoanalysis. And confession leads to the cleansing of sin. And cleansing of sin leads to wholeness and joy and life.[4]

One of the most frequent roles you will play as a counselor to clergy is confessor. They have no confessional. They seek out no priest to hear their sin. They forget to confess to one another, as James teaches. You become their priest. You can hear their confession. You must hear their confession. They can't carry their sin.

Again quoting Tournier: "If we have a theory of medicine which denies sin, so that we encourage the patient to blind himself to his sin and to use his illness as an excuse for it, we are preventing him finding liberation. For liberation comes only when we are humble enough to see ourselves as we really are." [5] By encouraging your clients to come to awareness of sin and to confess, you will be helping them to become aware of themselves as they really are—the purpose of psychotherapy.

An advantage to working with Christian workers is that they have a knowledge of the need for confession and repentance. Often they only need an accepting authority figure to give them permission to deal with their problems in spiritual terms.

REGENERATION THROUGH CHRIST

The gospel is still good news, and those in ministry at times need to be reminded of God's grace. Most cry out like David, in Psalm 51, "Restore to me the joy of your salvation." It's important for ministers to know it's all right to talk about their spiritual drought. They often feel deserted by God. Their prayers seem empty and they have often given up Scripture reading altogether.

Some, in fact, haven't really trusted Christ as their Savior and Lord. We had one minister recently from a liberal theological background who had once had a "conversion experience." Afterwards, he was ministering to others, studying the Bible and enjoying the happiest few years of his life. Then he began to move away from his fundamental stance and became entirely "freed from the myths of the Bible" in seminary. He learned that Jesus was the universal Christ figure and that we all have the Christ figuratively within us. He had been enlightened to realize that there was no personal God, but some impersonal creative cosmic force. The Bible, he learned, was a collection of Hebrew myths filled with contradictions. All of this knowledge had made him miserable. He ended in despair. He needed the Good News—that Jesus was God incarnate who came to restore mankind to Himself. He hasn't yet overcome his intellectual barriers to regeneration, but I'm hopeful that the message of 1 Corinthians 1:18–24 will again call him to faith.

Dr. Bill Wilson has scientifically investigated the benefits of regeneration. In those he studied he found changes toward happiness and a new perception of the world. They showed behavioral changes that improved their interpersonal relationships. Those with intellectual barriers might profit from Dr. Wilson's report.[6]

THE WORK OF THE HOLY SPIRIT

I don't understand all of the workings of the Holy Spirit. I know that I've seen men come to remarkable changes in response to prayer. Melissa and I have both experienced times in therapy when we had certain wisdom and insights into a problem that had never occurred to us until that moment as we prayed. I have, on rare occasions, felt impressed to recommend a certain Scripture to an individual not even fully aware of the text, but finding that it had a special meaning to that person.

I can't rationally explain those kinds of events, but I am glad they occur. The Spirit was given as one who would guide us into all wisdom. I believe that He does.

The Scripture teaches that "You did not receive a spirit that makes you a slave again to fear, but you received the

Spirit who makes you sons" (Rom. 8:1–15). That is news of healing for those who have been crippled by anxiety or depression.

What bitter, angry person would not like to have the fruit of the Spirit; love, joy, peace, patience, kindness, goodness, fidelity, gentleness, and self-control. Those life qualities are available as we choose to allow God's Spirit to guide our lives.

FORGIVENESS OF OTHERS

We have seen the life-changing release that the practice of forgiveness brings to individuals. This is one of the most fundamental spiritual truths and yet one that is often ignored even in the lives of clergy. We find many ministers who are jealously guarding some hoard of bitterness and unforgiveness. Sometimes this dates to their childhood hurts by a parent. Sometimes it relates to a brother or sister who got a greater inheritance. Frequently it is held toward a spouse for the accumulated hurts of marriage.

The emotional energy wasted on unforgiveness is amazing. There is little wonder that so many unforgiving people are depressed. They have little strength left for life after rehearsing their hurts day in and day out.

Unforgiveness also cripples a person's spiritual life. Ministers who are unforgiving do not approach God. There is a sense of uncleanness and disobedience that interferes with the relationship. Jesus said that we cannot even experience God's forgiveness until we forgive others. Our forgiving others restores us not only to them, but to God.

Lewis Smedes describes forgiveness as performing "spiritual surgery" within our soul, cutting away the wrong that was done so that we can be healed.[7] It is an act of the will, deciding what to do with a hurtful memory. I discussed previously the emotional, spiritual, and physical aspects of forgiveness (Section II).

PRAYER

Like confession, prayer is not designed to inform God of our needs or thoughts. Prayer is for the person who prays. It acknowledges before God who we are and that we know who He is. A dynamic of dependency and gratitude is engaged and we come into the presence of God. Ray Stedman says that "true prayer is an awareness of our helpless need and an acknowledgment of divine adequacy." As with all acts of faith, prayer brings us into direct, personal, vital touch with God.[8]

There is a great danger for the "professional Christian" to lose this vital touch with God. Have you ever noticed that ministers are our "professional pray-ers"? No matter where they are, if there is a prayer to be said, they are invited to say it. It is so easy for such praying to become more of a performance for the people gathered than communication with God. It is also easy for ministers to be so busy with public praying and other religious tasks that they neglect their own personal, private prayer lives. This has been the case for nearly all of the ministers we have counseled.

If we believe that it is primarily in prayer that we demonstrate our childlike dependency on a heavenly Father, then abandoning prayer denies that relationship. We either say that we are not His dependent children or that we don't believe that God is adequate to provide us our needs. A third alternative is that we don't believe there is a God who really cares about us one way or the other. For many ministers who don't pray there has been an attitudinal progression through all three of these positions. Clergy often become so busy in ministry that they begin to do the work in their own power and begin to forget their childlike need for God. When they confront problems they can't handle alone and feel their prayers for miracles go unheard, they begin to doubt that God really acts in people's lives. Then, as they reach a point of despair, they don't think God cares anyway. In moving away from God, they lose touch with how God answers prayer. Rather than seeing God work in prayer by changing them, they begin to want prayer to be a way of changing God—or the world around them.

In evaluating a minister's prayer life it is useful to see how he felt about his earthly father. Chances are, his emotional attitude toward God will reflect that closely. If his dad was a caring father who was available to him, he is less likely to have abandoned faith in prayer. If his dad was a critical, disapproving man he may be afraid to come to God for fear of His judgment. Correcting these distortions can open the way for a renewal of personal prayer.

Restoring a Christian worker to a private life of prayer and meditation can be one of the keys to his recovery.

I pray for my patients before, during, and after they are actually in therapy. I believe that makes me more sensitive to their hurts and more open to God's leadership for my work with them. I also pray with them on some occasions. I don't pray as a routine way of opening a counseling session—perhaps I should. My desire has been not to make prayer a ritualistic form, as ministers themselves may have done. If prayer has become trite and meaningless for them, I don't want our relationship to start out with an additional negative impression.

THE USE OF SCRIPTURES

I think you know by now that we use Scriptures in many ways in therapy. Certainly we use them to bring hope to the hopeless. Those we see in counseling are often pessimistic and doubtful that any healing can occur. Words of hope are encouraging even if their doubts have eroded their faith. Scriptures of reassurance will begin to renew that faith and restore their hope.

We use Scriptures that describe God's love. Those in despair feel unloved and unlovable. They don't sense God's presence or love. To be reminded that "nothing can separate us from the love of God that is in Christ Jesus, neither sword nor famine, nor principalities nor powers, nor things present, nor things to come, nor height, nor depth, nor any other creature" begins to refocus their trust in an immovable God who cares (Rom. 8:35–39, my paraphrase).

There are many Scriptures that deal with human emotional wholeness. "Do not conform any longer to this world, but be transformed by the renewing of your mind" (Rom. 12:2). Frequently those we counsel have become "conformed to the despair of this world" and need to renew their minds—accepting who they are in Christ.

"Do not be anxious about anything, but in everything, by

prayer and petition, with thanksgiving, present your requests to God. And the peace of God, which transcends all understanding, will guard your hearts and your minds in Christ Jesus" (Phil. 4:6–7). What a promise.

Jesus' Sermon on the Mount is filled with positive behavioral and attitudinal truths (Matt. 5–7). Paul's description of love gives us guidelines for all human relationships (1 Cor. 13). John's epistles are loaded with powerful images for a meaningful life.

We use Scriptures for praise and for thanksgiving and for comfort and for exhortation. With ministers we frequently use Scripture to bring their priorities into balance, for He said, "Take my yoke upon you and learn from me. . . . For my yoke is easy and my burden is light" (Matt 11:29–30). They need to hear those words and ask whose yoke they've been wearing.

Those in ministry have often forsaken reading Scripture except to prepare a sermon or Bible study. They don't read the Word for their own spiritual nurture and often they aren't ministered to by anyone else. Giving them permission and encouragement to establish a devotional time for themselves is something only you can do.

You may feel hesitant to use these spiritual weapons when counseling a religious professional. Remember, they are human like you and me. They have the same sin nature and perhaps even greater spiritual need because they've been giving out continually with little being given to them. They desperately need someone to pastor them emotionally and spiritually. Be a pastor *pastorum*.

How beautiful on the mountain are the feet of them who bring the gospel of peace.

AFTERWORD

I REALIZED after completing the manuscript that I have frequently referred to "Marble Retreat" without describing the program. I hope this short history will help integrate the observations I have included.

Marble Retreat is a counseling center in Marble, Colorado (near Aspen), operated exclusively for clergy and their spouses. It was started in 1974. Since occupying our lodge building in 1977, we have scheduled sixteen or seventeen two-week therapy sessions each year. The program is based on a brief, intensive psychotherapeutic approach. We work with a maximum of four couples in each session. There are three hours of group therapy each day with Melissa and me as cotherapists. Each person also has four hours of individual therapy. The guests live together in the lodge in a secluded area of the Crystal River valley. They eat their meals family style with our host couple, Bob and Sandy Sewell. There is time for recreation, meditation, and working on individual and marital conflicts.

In the first ten years, we counseled 246 couples, 37 singles, and 13 family units (52 individuals), for a total of 551 people.

Their ministry positions have been: 144 pastors, 101 foreign missionaries, 15 parachurch ministers, 9 home missionaries, 8 music ministers, 8 other church staff personnel, and 20 in other types of ministry (denominational offices, teachers, journalists, and counselors).

Geographically, they represented thirty-eight states and missionaries serving in thirty different countries.

All major denominations have been represented except Roman Catholicism (which has facilities specifically for their clergy).

Approximately 50 percent came because of a marital crisis. Thirty percent had a vocational conflict, such as burnout or forced termination. Twenty percent had an intrapersonal problem alone, such as depression or sexual dysfunction. There has often been a combination of symptoms and conflict areas.

We have been pleased with the results of this brief, intensive therapy approach. Our follow-up has indicated lasting benefits for approximately 75 percent of our guests. We feel that limiting the groups to clergy has a distinctly positive influence. There is rapid identification within the group and facilitation of self-disclosure. Their common concerns enhance the mutual supportiveness.

Further information on Marble Retreat is available. Address requests to: 139 Bannockburn, Marble, CO 81623 or telephone (303) 963–2499.

AVOIDING THE SCARLET LETTER *

WE'RE ALL SHOCKED when we hear a respected fellow minister has been exposed as an adulterer. We think to ourselves, *Boy, what an idiot! I'll never do a thing like that,* and we mean every word of it. We're as convinced of it as any commitment we've ever made.

Almost every minister I've counseled who found himself entangled in sexual infidelity had that same confidence. I can remember only two men who consciously set out for sexual conquest. One seriously questioned his masculinity and sought to prove himself through repeated sexual encounters. The other was sociopathic and used others impulsively for his own pleasure or profit in many ways, including sexually.

What derailed all the others, who were so sure it could never happen to them? Although they were neither deeply disturbed in their sexual identity nor sociopathic, they did neglect some important principles and crucial warning signs. By becoming more aware of these, we can avoid falling into an adulterous affair and earning our scarlet letter.

Recognizing Our Vulnerability

Men in ministry are especially vulnerable to sexual temptation because they work in what is often a female subculture, the church. Simply their presence on the job exposes them to potential romantic or sexual relationships.

In addition, our world is rapidly removing the restraints to sexual involvement. Men and women are even encouraged to "find themselves" through sexual encounters. Perhaps some women in your church flirt with that very idea. Or with you.

Another reason for increased vulnerability is the similarity between spirituality and sexuality. In both, we lower personal barriers,

---

* This article by the author first appeared in *Leadership* (Summer 1985).

encourage intimacy, become open and vulnerable, and experience profoundly moving emotions. Some individuals compare their deepest spiritual moments to sexual climax. Both provide an intense response, a loss of ego boundaries, a sense of oneness with those who share the experience.

Our personality also makes us more vulnerable. As sensitive, caring, giving persons, we resemble a warm living room for the lonely and dependent. Thousands of people, single and married alike, seek closeness. Most married women name as their primary marital problem their husband's insensitivity to their emotional needs. It makes them desperate for a companion who will talk with them and listen.

Enter the minister, the model husband. As long as they don't consult our wives, women may see us as ideal—strong and capable, yet gentle, warm, and loving. The church even encourages us to be that sensitive person to everyone in need, which includes many lonely women, whose activity in the church masks hunger for attention and affection. Both our personal warmth and our professional calling put us in jeopardy.

From my experience, I'd identify yet another danger—the angry seductress. Some women cherish a deep, inner hatred for men and a compulsion to gain control over them. Frequently they were rejected or abused by their fathers. Often they learned in childhood and adolescence that sensuality is their most effective weapon. Consciously or unconsciously, they form a pattern of conquests while they appear to be helpless women who need a strong man to care for them.

What man of the cloth is not eager to help damsels in distress? Yet many pastors who have ridden to the rescue find themselves seduced, exposed, and expelled in short order. The "helpless damsel" sometimes even garners the love and compassion of the church. She plots her next assault while the unsuspecting minister is still trying to remove the tar and feathers. One such woman had been the hapless "victim" of sexual advances by the last three pastors in her church. All had left in disgrace, their ministries nullified.

A minister is a particularly enticing target for this kind of woman. With a man of God, she can act out her hostility toward men in general, authority figures, symbolic fathers of society, and even God the Father all at once. It gives a gratifying sense of power. She again proves the male to be weak and inadequate.

It's also critical that we know our own particular vulnerability. Only I am aware of my individual sexual thoughts and drives. I may have frustrations with marital sex or doubts about my potency. I may find certain female physical characteristics particularly tempting. Midlife transition may raise questions about what I've been missing or how long I can continue to function successfully. Any of these issues may contribute to my vulnerability to an affair.

Maintaining Our Safety

Given our vocational vulnerability, how do we protect ourselves?

Primarily (if we are married), we must maintain our marriages—have a continuous romantic affair with our first love, put some of our creativity into rekindling those fires of passion. Most of those who get into trouble have allowed marriage to become dull, unsatisfying, even unfriendly.

Tell the truth: Do you look forward to being home with your wife? Does she make you feel you're the most wonderful man in the world? Do you light up her life in a special way? Does she light up yours? Do you find yourself distracted from work at times by fantasies of your lover at home? Maybe we need to court our best girlfriend.

Without a doubt, being in love with our mates provides the best defense against a sexual affair. If we're not there now, it may take months of inventive, energetic courting to relight that fire, but it can be done as we build on the foundation of our commitment—not on our present feelings.

The second defense: reassessing our attitudes about falling in love. A common path to sexual sin is the notion that feelings are not only all-important but also totally uncontrollable; they just happen to you. A story I hear frequently from the adulterous minister is "I had no intention of becoming involved with her, but suddenly we realized we were deeply in love." He makes it appear he was strolling along innocently one sunny day and was suddenly caught in a thunderstorm. Once it struck, he was soaked to the skin and powerless to dry himself. In fact, it felt so good he didn't *want* to dry off. He was glad he'd forgotten his umbrella.

Now, I confess, I like women. I find females exciting, fun, intriguing, nice to the senses, and often more comfortable companions than men. I suspect many of you could make the same confession. Feeling as I do, I could conceivably fall in love with a different woman every other day if I allowed my feelings free rein. But I don't. I keep a tight rein on my feelings.

One further caution: A commonly held notion claims you can be genuinely in love with two people simultaneously. That rationalization tries to give me permission to fall in love with another woman without admitting unfaithfulness to my wife. Don't believe it! Jesus' words about your heart being where your treasure is apply to romantic relationships as well as the kingdom. When we begin to invest emotional energy, we store up treasure in the object of our attention. Our hearts will follow. Treasure cannot be invested equally in two people. We must not kid ourselves. We do have control over where we put our treasure. When we find ourselves contemplating doing that special something for the other woman, we must redirect that energy into our marriage relationship.

A third defense: Avoid every appearance of evil, and every opportunity. I've learned to exercise care about being alone with a woman. Long periods alone not only raise suspicion but can leave us vulnerable to false accusations or intense temptation. Every time my college roommate went out on a date, he would ask me to pray that he'd "have temptation to withstand." Naturally he sought only to "develop his spiritual strength!" That's not a recommended technique for building ministerial defenses.

One pastor told me an attractive young woman began attending his church. She was a new Christian, but he soon discovered her sordid past. She had many problems and started asking his advice. Then she requested counseling. Because of her job, she could only come in the evening after the church secretary was gone. At first he said no, but she was so persistent, in such need, and seemed so sweet, he finally gave in. Dropping his guard proved his undoing.

Alone with him in his office, she closed the door and pulled the curtains. Before he knew what was happening, she was sitting on his lap, unbuttoning her blouse, exposing her bra-less breasts. She threw her arms around his neck and confessed her burning desire for him.

Now, while you fantasize about that situation, let me quickly tell you that what followed was no dream. It was a nightmare. He did succumb, but declared they couldn't let it happen again. She threatened to tell all if he didn't continue to see her. Then she began to tell all anyway—to his wife, to other church members, and finally to one of the elders. The church board ultimately confronted him and asked him to resign. His wife almost left him, but fortunately she recognized the pathology of the seductive woman and forgave her foolish husband. They had a lot of rebuilding to do, and his guilt nearly destroyed him.

We simply must avoid all appearance of evil. No matter how safe and innocent the situation may seem, it can sour in the twinkling of an eye or the popping of a button.

Blatant seduction, however, is unusual. More often we need to guard against a far more subtle pattern. The most common story of infidelity involves an attractive, committed church member who seeks counsel for marital problems. She is neither seductive nor sociopathic, but rather a thoughtful, wholesome, sensitive woman whom the minister had not particularly noticed as a stunning beauty. She is lonely and neglected by her husband, who doesn't communicate. The pastor does listen, and she appreciates him for it. She begins to show her gratitude in many ways, particularly with her praise. That feels good, and the pastor begins to enjoy the attention and affirmation. He gradually realizes what a truly insightful person she is.

This is the critical crossroads in the relationship: It can remain professional or slide into a romantic affair. It's a point of decision. We either set limits on time with her, guard against her romantic fantasies (and our own), work on involving her husband in counseling (perhaps referring them both to another professional), and avoid comparing her with our wives; or we may make a costly mistake.

A decidedly dangerous, yet completely conscious behavior often begins at this point. It may seem justified as an innocent, even helpful, thing to do. We might convince ourselves we are only identifying with our client and modeling openness, but it is a fatal choice. That drastic mistake is to share with her our own inner hurts and the areas of our own marital disappointment. I know of no other single event that so dramatically shifts the direction of a relationship. Then I am no longer a helpful, concerned counselor; I have become a lonely man who needs her love. It's as destructive and decisive as reaching for a zipper.

All the barriers come down, and counselor and client begin to focus on each other's needs. Intense energy flows into the relationship. The two feel they were meant for each other—this love is so perfect it must be ordained by God (a frequent rationalization). Such feelings become so overwhelming that sexual involvement is a natural by-product. What began as an innocent professional relationship burns out of control. They are possessed.

External Danger Signs

Anywhere along this flower-strewn path to destruction we can back off and escape if we recognize the danger and understand the disastrous consequences. A quarterback approaching the line of scrimmage assesses the defensive alignment. When he senses a blitz, he may change the play to protect himself from being sacked. We also need to recognize the warning signs that indicate a blitz of the heart, and quickly call an audible. Here are a few of the indications I watch for in the other woman.

Growing dependence. She may express this in many ways. The most common is increasing requests for my time. Ostensibly legitimate crises arise that demand my attention. She may also want me to make decisions for her or to give my approval for what she does.

Affirmation and praise. We're all vulnerable to being complimented. It feels especially good if we're not getting much praise at home. One pastor told me his difficult choice to either go home to criticism or be with the other woman who understood and admired him.

Complaints about loneliness. She may begin to confess that her loneliness seems even worse now that she knows what meaningful companionship is like. Now she escapes the hurt and pain with me. I am the only one who has ever done that for her. What a hook!

Giving gifts. No matter how trivial the gifts may seem, they can be a serious indication of her increasing emotional investment. She is thinking about me and how to make me happy. A sense of obligation on my part may soon develop.

Physical contact. This usually begins in innocent ways—brief nudging of bodies in a crowded room or a light touch of her hand on the arm, but it can escalate to a hug of gratitude or a "holy kiss" that communicates more than sisterly affection. A common occurrence is a woman saying, "You've helped me so much, Pastor. Can I just give you a hug to show my appreciation?"

This doesn't apply to physical contact with every female in my life. Many innocent hugs show warmth and caring on a purely platonic level. You know the difference as well as I. I'm very careful about touching some women, either because of signals from them or feelings of attraction within myself. Yet there are many others whom I can quite safely embrace.

Other seductive behavior. I notice how a woman dresses, whether she wears perfume, makes subtle suggestions or jokes about my irresistibility as a man, sends messages about her availability when her husband is away, or increasingly talks about sexuality in the counseling sessions. She may begin to report dreams about us together in romantic situations.

I have learned to spot these red flags for my own safety.

Internal Danger Signs

These same signs, as well as others, may also lurk within me. Using the quarterback illustration, it's as though I realize my running backs occupy the wrong position for the play I've called. I may need to call time out to get the team rearranged so I don't make a costly mistake.

Here are some inner signals I monitor:

Thinking about her. At first I may explain this as my professional interest in her problems, but the focus slowly shifts from her problems to her person. This is not necessarily sexual. More likely it involves her personality traits and behavior patterns. Pleasant feelings build around the positive new relationship. It's only natural to enjoy them and begin to reflect on the experience.

Comparing her to my wife. The other woman always looks better than a wife. She is new, different, and usually seen at her best. She is well groomed, exudes positive vibes, and isn't demanding. She laughs at my jokes; she thinks I'm fascinating. Suddenly a wife's faults begin to look bigger. I eventually tell my wife she should be more like Mrs. Jones in some way or another.

Finding excuses to be with her. This will probably be in group situations at first. Usually many opportunities occur to see her in the church context. It's amazing what a truly significant part of the ministry the youth fellowship clean-up committee can suddenly become.

Beginning to have sexual fantasies about her. These may occur while working in the office or while looking at her during a worship service. They are likely to progress to masturbatory images or even intrude upon marital lovemaking.

Scheming ways to be alone. Arranging to be at group events is one thing, but inventing ways to be alone is quite another. Invariably this calls for some degree of deception. It starts by lying to one's wife and secretary. The lying multiplies, and manufacturing alibis becomes frequent. There follows an increasing irritability toward your wife's demands for attention or her expressions of suspicion. Isn't it interesting that I could resent my wife's legitimate claim to my affection? It is as though she has become an intruder into my private life.

Wives are in fact one of our most important protective screens. They are often much more sensitive to other females threatening their territory. We may be oblivious to some of the early nonverbal signs, or they may just be flattering enough that we don't want them to stop. If we learn to listen to our wives, they may save us from becoming too involved in a potentially destructive relationship.

Wanting to share my marital problems with the client. "My wife hasn't been sensitive to my needs, either. She isn't a good partner sexually. She doesn't understand me as a person or show me the respect I deserve." The more I complain about my mate, the more unhappy I will feel about my marriage, and the more appealing the other woman appears. To complicate matters, that other woman probably does care about me and must struggle to keep her nurturing instincts separated from her romantic attraction. It is a losing situation.

Settle for an "F"

The problem of adultery is as difficult as the dangers are real. Why else would so many seriously committed ministers fall into it? The vulnerability of our position on the one hand and the powerful effect of feelings on the other set us up.

Only by staying alert to the possibility of trouble, keeping our marriage vital and growing, and watching for the danger signs can we be sure to survive. We can do it. We do have a choice.

For once in our lives, let's not strive for an "A"—at least not the scarlet variety. Let's settle for a true-blue "F"—for faithful.

APPENDIX 2

RESOURCES FOR MINISTERS

Denominational

Most denominations have a national office that provides assistance for ministers who need counseling. Many also have regional offices for the state, diocese, synod, conference, association, presbytery, or area. We have found that individual clergy are frequently unaware of these resources or need encouragement to overcome their fear of exposure.

Nondenominational

Barnabas Ministries
P.O. Box 37179
Omaha, NE 68137
402–895–5107
Director: Dale Fremodt

Individual counseling, support groups, and clergy growth conferences.

Bon Secours Spiritual Center
1525 Marriottsville Road
Marriottsville, MD 21104
301–442–1320

Retreat center available for workshops, conferences, and individual retreats.

Center for Career Development and Ministry
70 Cahse Street
Newton Center, MA 02159
617–969–7750
Director: Harold Moore

Career counseling resources for clergy and other ministry vocations.

Center for Continuing Education
Virginia Theological Seminary
Alexandria, VA 22302
703–370–6600, ext. 70

Six-week renewal/growth group experience for clergy.

Chalet I
90 Trail West Village
Buena Vista, CO 81211
303–395–6423
Director: Hazel Goddard

Mountain chalet for small number of clients. Offers individual, marriage, and family therapy on daily basis.

Fairhaven Ministries
Rt. 2, Box 1022
Roan Mt., TN 37687
615–542–5332
Director: Charles Shepson

Mountain retreat with lodge and individual cabins for rest and relaxation with counseling available for the minister or for couples.

Interaction
P.O. Box 2177
West Brattleboro, VT 05301
802–254–2844
Director: Dave Pollock

Ministry to missionary families, developing resource network for TCK's (third-culture kids).

Laity Lodge
P.O. Box 670
Kerrville, TX 78028
512–896–205
Director: Howard Houvde

Extensive variety of conferences, workshops, and individual contemplative retreats for clergy and laypersons.

Link Care Center
1734 West Shaw Avenue
Fresno, CA 93711
209–439–5920
Director: Brent Linquist, Ph.D.

Residential and outpatient assessment and treatment for missionaries, pastors, other clergy and their families.

Marble Retreat
139 Bannockburn
Marble, CO 81623
303–963–2499
Director: Louis McBurney, M.D.

Two-week sessions for clergy and spouses providing intensive small group and individual psychotherapy.

The Midwest Career Development Service (two locations)
2501 North Star Road, Suite 200
Columbus, OH 43221
614–486–0469

1840 Westchester Boulevard
Westchester, IL 60153
312–343–6268
Executive director: Rev. Frank C. Williams

Career assessment and counseling for clergy and their spouses.

Remuda Ranch Ministries
P.O. Box 2655
Wickenburg, AZ 85358
602–684–5986
Director: Marv Thompson

Marriage counseling, marriage enrichment.

Ring Lake Ranch
Box 806
DuBois, WY 82513
307–455–2663

Retreats for personal growth and renewal for clergy, laypersons, and families.

SonScape Re-Creation Ministries
P.O. Box 777
Carbondale, CO 81623
303–963–2499
Directors: Bob and Sandy Sewell

Recreation, camping, and conference programs for clergy and their families for personal spiritual, physical, and emotional renewal.

Support Ministries International
3826 Buell Street, #3
Oakland, CA 94619
415–530–3470
Director: Teresa Dunham, Ph.D.

Assists missionaries in renewal and retraining during furlough.

The Alban Institute
4125 Nebraska Avenue, NW
Washington, D. C. 20016
202–244–7320
800–457–2674 for literature
Director: Loren Mead

Study center involved in all aspects of clergy life. Provides consulting service, conflict negotiation, literature, and seminars.

The Buford Foundation
P.O. Box 9090
Tyler, TX 75711
214–561–4411
Director: Fred Smith, Jr.

Supportive networking for clergy and various ministries to ministers.

The Center for Ministry
7804 Capwell Drive
Oakland, CA 94621
415–635–4246
Director: John R. Landgraft, Ph.D.

Individual, couple, and group programs for career development in ministry.

Uphold Ministries
8787 East Mountain View Road, #1055
Scottsdale, AZ 85258
602–998–3307
Director: Ed Pittman

Short-term individual and marital counseling for clergy.

Villacita Pastoral Counseling
17576 County Rd. 501
Bayfield, CO 81122
303–884–2901
Director: Jerry Brown, Ph.D.

Crisis counseling, marriage and family therapy, and career assessment for clergy. Personal and professional growth seminars.

NOTES

Chapter 1. Problems and Pressures of the Ministry

1. Baptist General Convention of Texas. Research Project on Psychological Needs of Ministers. *Annual Report* 1971.

2. David and Vera Mace, *What's Happening to Clergy Marriages?* (Nashville: Abingdon, 1980), 32.

3. Episcopal Church of America, unpublished data regarding attrition from parish ministry, 1980s.

4. J. Clifford Tharp, Jr., *A Study of the Forced Termination of Southern Baptist Ministers* (Nashville: Southern Baptist Convention Sunday School Board Research Service Department, 1984).

5. Ministers conferences I participated in from 1980 through 1985 sponsored by: Episcopal Diocese of Wyoming; Rocky Mt. Synod of the Lutheran Church of America; Illinois Baptist Convention; Northwest Texas Conference of the United Methodist Church; Birmingham Ministerial Association; Baptist Convention of North Carolina; and others.

6. John Cionca, "To Fight or Not to Fight," *Leadership* 6 (Spring 1985):86.

7. Fred Smith, "Inerrant Love," an unpublished poem used by permission of the author.

8. Edward G. Bratcher, *The Walk-on-Water Syndrome* (Waco, Tex.: Word Books, 1984), 26–28.

9. Gerald Caplan et al., "Mastery of Stress, Psychological Aspects," *American Journal of Psychiatry* 138 (April 1981):413–19. Caplan's other two factors are knowing the time limits of the stress and not going through the stressful situation alone.

10. Mace, *What's Happening to Clergy Marriages*, 33.

11. Bratcher, *The Walk-on-Water Syndrome*, 22–46.

12. Gerald J. Jud et al., *Ex-Pastors* (Philadelphia: Pilgrim Press, 1970), 96.

13. Carlyle Marney, *Priests to Each Other* (Valley Forge, Pa.: Judson Press, 1974).

Chapter 2. Role-Specific Pressures

1. Fred Smith, "Dissecting Sense from Nonsense," *Leadership* 1 (Winter 1980):101.
2. John Claypool, *Tracks of a Fellow Struggler* (Waco, Tex.: Word Books, 1974).
3. Daniel Levinson et al., "The Psychosocial Development of Men in Early Adulthood and the Mid-Life Transition," *Life History Research in Psychopathology*, vol. 3, (Minneapolis: University of Minnesota Press, 1974).

Chapter 3. Resistance to Counseling

1. M. Scott Peck, *The Road Less Traveled* (New York: Simon and Schuster, 1978), 98–99.
2. Lillian Rubin, *Intimate Strangers* (New York: Harper and Row, 1984), 55–59.
3. M. Scott Peck, *The People of the Lie* (New York: Simon and Schuster, 1983), foreword.

Chapter 4. Marital Maladjustment

1. Daniel Levinson et al., *The Seasons of a Man's Life* (New York: Alfred Knopf, 1978), chap. 3.
2. Sherod Miller et al., *Straight Talk* (New York: New American Library, 1982).
3. A. Kenneth Thomas, "Conflict and Conflict Management," *The Handbook of Industrial and Organizational Psychology*, vol. 2 (Chicago: Rand McNally, 1975), Thomas–Kilmann Conflict Mode Instrument.
4. Richard Foster, *Money, Sex, and Power* (San Francisco: Harper and Row, 1985), 139.
5. Ed and Gaye Wheat, *Intended for Pleasure* (Old Tappan, N.J.: Revell, 1977), 111–14.
6. Mace, *What's Happening to Clergy Marriages?* 36 (see chap. 1, n. 2).
7. John Howell, *Equality and Submission in Marriage* (Nashville: Broadman, 1983).

8. Foster, *Money, Sex, and Power,* 205–7.

9. Peck, *The Road Less Traveled,* 81–84 (see chap. 3, n. 1).

10. Levinson, "The Psychosocial Development of Men" (see chap. 2, n. 3).

11. Erik H. Erikson, *Childhood and Society* (New York: W.W. Norton, 1950), 263–69.

12. Rubin, *Intimate Strangers,* 65–97.

13. Levinson, *The Seasons of a Man's Life,* 197.

14. For further reading on the adult life cycle, see George Valliant and Charles McArthur, "Natural History of Male Psychological Health. I. The Adult Life Cycle from Eighteen to Fifty," *Seminars in Psychiatry* 4 (November 1972):415; and Roger Gould, "The Phases of Adult Life: A Study in Developmental Psychology," *American Journal of Psychiatry* 129 (November 1972):527.

15. Jud et al., *Ex-Pastors,* 46–47.

16. Daniel Levinson et al., "Individual and Marital Stages of Development," *American Journal of Psychiatry* 132 (June 1975).

17. Peck, *The Road Less Traveled,* 81–182 (see chap. 3, n. 1).

18. Floyd and Harriett Thatcher, *Long-Term Marriage* (Waco, Tex.: Word Books, 1980).

19. Louis McBurney, "Treatment for Infidelity Fallout," *Leadership* 7 (Spring 1986).

20. Lawrence C. Pakula, "Children and Divorce," *Medical Aspects of Human Sexuality* (July 1983), 24–34.

21. Judith Wallerstein, "Children of Divorce: Long-term Outcome," *Medical Aspects of Human Sexuality* (April 1985), 60–67.

22. Lisa Swanson and Mary Kay Biaggio, "Therapeutic Perspectives on Father-daughter Incest," *The American Journal of Psychiatry* 142 (June 1985):667.

23. David and Vera Mace, *How to Have a Happy Marriage* (Nashville: Abingdon, 1979).

Chapter 5. Depressive Illness

1. Board of Mental Health and Behavioral Medicine, Institute of Medicine, "Research on Mental Illness and Addictive Disorders: Progress and Prospects," *The American Journal of Psychiatry* 142 (July 1985):11.

2. Ibid.

3. Herbert Freudenberger and Geraldine Richelson, *Burnout:*

The High Cost of High Achievement (New York: Bantam, 1981).

4. "Clergy Burnout: A Survival Kit for Church Professionals," Ministers Life Resources, 3100 W. Lake St., Minneapolis, Minn. 55416.

5. "Burnout," *Theology News and Notes* 31 (March 1984).

6. William P. Wilson, "Christian Psychotherapy," Department of Psychiatry, Duke University Medical Center, Durham, North Carolina.

7. Sheldon Vanauken, *A Severe Mercy* (San Francisco: Harper and Row, 1977), 181–82.

8. Board of Mental Health, "Research on Mental Illness," 11.

9. Jerome A. Motto et al., "Development of a Clinical Instrument to Estimate Suicide Risk," *The American Journal of Psychiatry* 142 (June 1985).

10. Aaron T. Beck et al., "Hopelessness and Eventual Suicide: A Ten-Year Prospective Study of Patients Hospitalized with Suicidal Intentions," *The American Journal of Psychiatry* (May 1985).

Chapter 6. Dysfunctional Personality

1. Thomas Harris, *I'm OK, You're OK* (New York: Harper and Row, 1969).

2. Carlyle Marney, Interpreter's House Brochure, Lake Junaluska, North Carolina, 1972.

3. James Joliff, *Too Much of a Good Thing* (Waco, Tex.: Self-Control Systems, 1980).

4. Lewis Smedes, *Forgive and Forget* (San Francisco: Harper and Row, 1984), 123–51.

5. Wheat, *Intended for Pleasure,* chap. 5 (see chap. 4, n. 5).

6. Ann Landers, "What 100,000 Women Told Ann Landers," *Family Circle,* 11 June 1985.

7. Wheat, *Intended for Pleasure,* chap. 7 (see chap. 4, n. 5).

8. Rubin, *Intimate Strangers,* 101 (see chap. 3, n. 2).

9. R. T. Segraves et al., "Spontaneous Remission in Erectile Dysfunction: A Partial Replication," *Behavioral Research Therapeutics* 23 (1985):203.

10. Wheat, *Intended for Pleasure,* 93–99 (see chap. 4, n. 5).

11. William P. Wilson, *What You Should Know About Homosexuality* (Grand Rapids: Zondervan, 1978).

12. William P. Wilson, "Christian and Homosexual: A Contradiction," *Journal of Psychology and Christianity* 4 (1978).

Chapter 7. Basic Principles of Counseling

1. Gary Collins, *How to Be a People Helper* (Santa Ana, Calif.: Vision House, 1976), 41–52.
2. Freida Fromm-Reichmann, *Principles of Intensive Psychotherapy* (Chicago: University of Chicago Press, 1950), 3.
3. Hilde Bruch, *Learning Psychotherapy* (Cambridge: Harvard University Press, 1974), 2.
4. Paul Tournier, *The Healing of Persons* (New York: Harper and Row, 1965), 227.
5. Anecdote from a lecture by Dr. Shervert Frazier, Professor of Psychiatry, Baylor College of Medicine, Houston, 1963.
6. Dr. Sigmund Owl, Commonwealth Toy, Inc.
7. Fromm-Reichmann, *Principles of Intensive Psychotherapy,* 128.

Chapter 8. Spiritual Aspects of Counseling Christian Workers

1. Tournier, *The Healing of Persons,* 225–26 (see chap. 7, n. 4).
2. Karl Menninger, *Whatever Became of Sin?* (New York: Hawthorn Books, 1973), 17.
3. Elizabeth O'Connor, *Search for Silence* (Waco, Tex.: Word Books, 1972), 29.
4. Tournier, *The Healing of Persons,* 225–59 (see chap. 7, n. 4).
5. Ibid., 227.
6. William P. Wilson, "Mental Health Benefits of Religious Salvation," *Diseases of the Nervous System* 33 (June 1972):382–86.
7. Smedes, *Forgive and Forget,* 27 (see chap. 6, n. 4).
8. Ray Stedman, *Jesus Teaches on Prayer* (Waco, Tex.: Word Books, 1975), 7.

BIBLIOGRAPHY

Baker, Don, and Emory Nester. *Depression.* Portland: Multnomah Press, 1983. Another personal story of experiencing depression, this is a very clear account of this illness. It describes the symptoms, explains the multifaceted causes, and most importantly gives hope for recovery.

Bratcher, Edward G. *The Walk-on-Water Syndrome.* Waco, Tex.: Word Books, 1984. One of the most thorough books on problems in ministry. The insights are accurate and clearly delineated. I think this is a must for anyone in ministry or working with clergy.

Claypool, John. *Tracks of a Fellow Struggler.* Waco, Tex.: Word Books, 1974. This is one of the best books I know of regarding grief and faith. It is a poignant account of Claypool's own struggle with the loss of a child.

Crabb, Lawrence J., Jr. *Effective Counseling.* Grand Rapids, Mich.: Zondervan, 1977. Dr. Crabb does an excellent job contrasting various psychological approaches to biblical counseling both in theoretical foundation and practical application.

Joliff, James. *Too Much of a Good Thing.* Waco, Tex.: Self-Control Systems, 1980. This work comes with a booklet and an audiocassette dealing with perfectionism. We have used it extensively and with gratifying success.

Mace, David, and Vera Mace. *What's Happening to Clergy Marriages?* Nashville: Abingdon, 1980. The Maces pioneered marriage counseling and bring their rich background to the subject of marriage and ministry. They present data from interviews with several hundred ministers and their spouses.

McIlhaney, Joe S. *1250 Health Care Questions Women Ask.* Grand Rapids, Mich.: Baker Books, 1985. Dr. McIlhaney brings his depth of experience as a gynecologist and his wisdom as a mature Christian to provide broad coverage to basic questions of health including sexuality. I think every counselor, pastor, and church could benefit from having this book in their libraries.

Miller, Sherod, et al. *Straight Talk: A New Way to Get Closer to Others by Saying What You Really Mean.* New York: New American Library, 1982. This book has developed out of the work at the Couples' Communication Workshops. It is based on solid principles of communication styles and has been extremely helpful to us. We make it required reading. The early chapters are a little hard to get through but worth the effort.

Payne, Leanne. *The Broken Image.* Westchester, Pa.: Crossway, 1981. This book brings understanding and hope for change to homosexuals. The author has had significant experiences of healing with individuals she has counseled from a spiritual and psychological approach.

Peck, M. Scott. *The Road Less Traveled.* New York: Simon and Schuster, 1978. Dr. Peck gives us a clear, no-nonsense description of love, growth, spiritual maturity, grace, and psychotherapy. After writing this book, Dr. Peck became a Christian and has made a firm confession of Jesus' Lordship.

Penner, Clifford and Joyce. *The Gift of Sex.* Waco, Tex.: Word Books, 1981. A professional, sensitive guide to the physical and spiritual dimensions of the sexual relationship. Designed for any couple, newlywed or long-term married, who want to enhance their marital relationship and are looking for a biblical view of sex. Cassette tape series also available.

Schmidt, Jerry A. *Do You Hear What You're Thinking?* Wheaton, Ill.: Victor Books, 1983. Dr. Schmidt is a Christian psychologist and uses a cognitive therapy approach to help the readers reprogram their thinking about themselves. It is quite helpful for those struggling with low self-concept.

Smith, Fred. *You and Your Network.* Waco, Tex.: Word Books, 1984. One of the most frequent factors we find in lives of ministers is their isolation. They don't form supportive networks. Fred Smith's easy-to-read book has practical insights into establishing friendships. Fred's most recent book, *Learning to Lead* (Leadership Library series), is useful for developing management skills.

Swihart, Judson T. *How Do You Say, "I Love You"?* Downers Grove, Ill.: Inter-Varsity Press, 1979. This easy-to-read book has very practical insights into communicating love in marriage.

Tournier, Paul. *The Healing of Persons.* New York: Harper and Row, 1965. *Understanding Each Other. Guilt and Grace.* New York: Harper and Row, 1983. *The Meaning of Persons.* New York: Harper and Row, 1982. Tournier is, in my opinion, a remarkable Christian counselor. He has shared with us deep understanding of the human soul. I highly recommend his books.

Wheat, Ed, and Gaye Wheat. *Intended for Pleasure.* Old Tappan, N.J.: Revell, 1977. This very straightforward book presents a healthy, Christian, scriptural viewpoint of human sexuality. The Wheats have also produced a cassette tape series on the subject. Either can be used in counseling or in sex education series.

INDEX

Louis McBurney

Louis McBurney received his M.D. from Baylor Medical College and his psychiatric training at the Mayo Clinic. He is certified by the American Board of Psychiatry and Neurology and is a member of the American Psychiatric Association, the American Medical Association, and the Christian Association for Psychological Studies. He is author of *Every Pastor Needs a Pastor, Families Under Stress,* and contributed to *God Called Ministry* and *Clergy Couples in Crisis.* He has also written numerous articles on ministry pressures.

Dr. McBurney and his wife, Melissa, counsel clergy at Marble Retreat in the Colorado Rockies. They have three children: Bruce, Andrea, and Brent.